FROM PURGE TO COEXISTENCE

FROM PURGE TO COEXISTENCE

ESSAYS ON STALIN'S & KHRUSHCHEV'S RUSSIA

by
David J. Dallin

Henry Regnery Company
Chicago

Copyright © 1964 by Henry Regnery Company, Chicago, Illinois
Manufactured in the United States of America
LIBRARY OF CONGRESS CATALOG CARD NUMBER: 64-20524

FOUNDATION FOR FOREIGN AFFAIRS SERIES

NUMBER 1:
Globe and Hemisphere: Latin America's Place in the Post-war Foreign Relations of the United States, by J. Fred Rippy

NUMBER 2:
Massive Retaliation: The Policy and Its Critics, by Paul Peeters

NUMBER 3:
Peaceful Co-Existence: An Analysis of Soviet Foreign Policy, by Wladyslaw W. Kulski

NUMBER 4:
Germany's Eastern Frontiers: The Problem of the Oder-Neisse Line, by Zoltan Michael Szaz, with a foreword by Harold Zink

NUMBER 5:
Strategic Intelligence and the Shape of Tomorrow, by William M. McGovern

NUMBER 6:
The German Opposition to Hitler: An Appraisal, by Hans Rothfels, translated by Lawrence Wilson

NUMBER 7:
Berlin and the Future of Eastern Europe, edited by David S. Collier and Kurt Glaser

NUMBER 8:
From Purge to Coexistence, by David J. Dallin

PREFACE

It is a privilege, albeit a melancholy one, for me to introduce these last pages from the pen of David Dallin. Like so many whose work lies in the field of recent Russian and Soviet history and politics, I owe him a debt of gratitude for the illumination I have derived from the work to which he devoted his life. Death has recently taken a heavy toll among the older Russian Social Democrats in exile—Dallin's death was followed by that of Rafail Abramovitch, and shortly after that by the death of Lydia Dan. The life of the political exile is at best hard, bitter, and lonely, and his death too often passes unnoticed beyond his small circle of friends and colleagues. It is fitting that this book, a tribute to a man of integrity, honesty, and consistency to his ideals as a Socialist—for such a man was David Dallin—should be published for a wide circle of readers.

David J. Dallin was born in Rogachev in Russia on May 24, 1889, and died in New York, an American citizen, on February 21, 1962. He studied at the universities of St. Petersburg, Berlin, and Heidelberg, and was awarded his degree of Doctor of Philosophy and Political Science by the latter in 1913. He had started his activities as a Social Democrat in 1907, but it was only after the fall of the Russian monarchy in March, 1917, that he was able to return to Russia. Until 1921, he remained active as one of the leading Social Democrats (Mensheviks) inside Russia, having been elected a member of the Menshevik Central Committee soon after his return to Russia.

These were hard years of virtually underground work for the Russian Mensheviks, who rejected any policy of armed opposition to the Bolsheviks. But they persisted in arguing the case of socialism, as they understood it, against the ever-growing tyranny of Lenin's bolshevism within the increasingly narrow limits which Bolshevik persecution and obstruction imposed on them. All this activity required determination and a good deal of courage—many other Mensheviks capitulated, finding it easier to persuade themselves that the Bolsheviks were, after all, on the right side. Not so Dallin, who remained true to his principles.

By spring, 1921, the Menshevik struggle had become hopeless; partly as a result of their own precarious position, the Bolsheviks, whose power now hung by a thread, threatened virtually to crush once and for all their Menshevik opponents, whose cirticism had repeatedly been proved right by events. However, some Bolshevik leaders, including Lenin, were not yet prepared to exterminate Social Democrat critics, and so many Menshevik leaders were allowed to go into exile—a course preferable, in Lenin's eyes, to having them alive and vocal inside Russia.

In Berlin in 1923, Dallin joined the editorial board of the *Socialist Courier*, founded by Martov. He remained an active contribution until 1948, when disagreements with his fellow exiles on issues of emigré policy led to his retirement from political activity. As a Menshevik leader he was perhaps never in the first rank. But in consistency, sound sense, sober and trenchant analysis of the Russian political scene, and his devotion to justice and the principles of humanity, he surpassed many whose names were better-known as political leaders.

Dallin's memorial is his published work. The admirable bibliography of his writings, which will be found in the pages that follow, lists fifteen books and over 650 articles, published between 1911 and 1962. It was the happy thought of the editors of these posthumous papers to include a few of his articles which are now difficult to obtain and are not available in English. For much of Dallin's literary activity was not merely ephemeral journalism but was based on deep, soundly reasoned analysis. It is however, on his books, published after he had settled in the United States in 1940, that Dallin's more recent reputation has been built. I should particularly like to mention two of them, *The Real Soviet Russia* (1944) and *Forced Labor in Soviet Russia* (1947), written jointly with Boris Nicolaevsky.

Today it is not difficult to be well-informed on the life and institutions of the Soviet Union. There is a vast literature of scholarly and reliable work in many languages, and many universities and institutes sponsor research and provide academic instruction on all aspects of the U.S.S.R. The situation was very different in 1947, let alone 1944, as far as the majority of the public was concerned. The universities had hardly made a start on the study of the Soviet Union, and where they had, their work was too often colored, consciously or unconsciously, by ignorance, radical prejudice, and Communist propaganda, to be of any scholarly value. The somewhat naive hopes engendered on both sides of the Atlantic that wartime cooperation between the democratic countries and the U.S.S.R. would be succeeded by peacetime cooperation, and the admiration and acclaim which the achievements of the Soviet Army deservedly won in the Second World War, did not predispose public opinion to accept any criticism of Stalin's tyrannous rule. General ignorance on Soviet conditions, carefully fostered by the Soviet authorities as an integral part of their policy, and intensive Communist propaganda had hardly been dispelled. For example, the detailed and usually completely accurate reporting on the Soviet scene (much of it by Dallin), which was to be found in the pages of the *Socialist Courier*, was scarcely known outside a narrow circle. It was the main achievement of the two books I have mentioned to dissipate some of this fog. They helped to lay the foundation and to establish the standards from which others drew their inspiration. It is fitting to recall that one of the outstanding younger scholars in the Soviet field in the United States today is David Dallin's son, Professor Alexander Dallin.

The Soviet authorities, with the assistance of many sincere, misguided, and intellectually unperceptive public men in the West, have branded Dallin's work and that of the many who followed him as "cold war." Political labels are ephemeral, and always misleading. Future historians of our times will take a different view. They will perhaps recognise in the work on Soviet reality, to which Dallin and a few others made so effective a pioneer contribution, one of the most important blows for freedom struck in our generation.

The strength of the Communist threat to freedom lies in its ability to conquer the minds of men. Secrecy, misinformation, dissemination of falsehood, and discrediting of attempts to expose that falsehood are all an integral part of the technique of Communist conquest. This technique is already becoming a thing of the past, if only because the truth is gradually and partially being allowed to emerge. If the time ever comes when real cooperation between the U.S.S.R. and the West is possible, it will only be because internal changes have taken place inside the U.S.S.R., making the main obstacle to cooperation—the Communist denial of the liberty and dignity of the individual—a thing of the past. If this obstacle is ever eliminated, it will in large measure be because of the breaking down of the walls of silence and the countering of lying propaganda by such men as David Dallin.

History knows no victors and no vanquished. Events do not turn out as foreseen by those who take part in them, and the "vanquished" of one generation may still live to see their ideas vindicated, even if without acknowledgement, in the actions of the "victors." Perhaps it will be so with the Mensheviks, even if some, like Dallin, after a long life of exile, do not live to see it. So many of those early Russian revolutionaries capitulated to the victorious Bolsheviks and fell under the wheels of Stalin's juggernaut along with many of the "victors" themselves. Who can say whether the greater victory does not belong to those who lived in exile and exposed the sham socialism of Lenin and Stalin?

Leonard Schapiro

London School of Economics and Political Science.

September, 1963.

CONTENTS

	Preface	i
Part One:	TRIALS AND ERRORS	
	The Pyatakov—Radek Trial	3
	Introduction	3
I	Prelude to a New Trial	14
II	Stalin's Role in the Charges	22
	The Charge of Wrecking	23
	The Charge of Bacteriological Warfare	30
	The Charge of Collaboration with Nazism and Fascism	33
	The Charge of Terrorism	39
III	The Defendants	46
	Yuri Pyatakov	47
	Karl Radek	49
	Nikolai Muralov	51
	Leonid Serebryakov	51
	Grigori Sokolnikov	52
	Mikhail Boguslavsky	53
	Yakov Drobnis	54
IV	The Investigation	55
	The Appeal to Loyalty	55
	Threats to the Family	57

		Witnesses..............................	58
		Witnesses of a Special Kind..............	58
		Obligatory Torture......................	62
	V	NKVD Agents Abroad in Search of Materials for the Indictment...........	64
	VI	The Trial in Novosibirsk................	72
	VII	The Confessions........................	78
	VIII	The Military Tribunal...................	86
		The Testimony of the Chief Defendants...	88
		The Testimony of Heads of the Coal Industry and Railways................	100
		The Testimony of Heads of the Chemical Industry...........................	108
	IX	After the Trial.........................	111

Austria: Where Stalin Failed 117

Part Two: TRENDS AND PORTENTS

The Coming Era 147

	I	After the Revolution.....................	147
	II	How It Will Happen.....................	148
	III	Russia, Europe, and America.............	152
	IV	The Meat-grinder of the Revolution......	154
	V	The Victorius Triad.....................	157

The Soviet Revolution: Shattered Hopes...161

	I	The Fateful Years.......................	161
	II	Solemn Vows and Reality................	162
	III	Stalin and After........................	172

Social Change and Soviet Foreign Policy...175

	I	The Eastward Path of Social Revolution..	175
	II	The Star over the Kremlin or over Peking?.............................	178
	III	The Semi-Intellectuals...................	179
	IV	The New Middle Class in Russia.........	185

A Revolution Transformed.................189
Methods of Soviet Diplomacy..............195
Soviet Russia as a World Power...........213
Competition and Conflict.................225

Bibliography of David J. Dallin's Writings..........241
Index...273

Part One:
TRIALS AND ERRORS

THE PYATAKOV RADEK TRIAL*
INTRODUCTION

One of the most extraordinary phenomena in recent history is the series of purges that afflicted the Communist Party in the Soviet Union over a period of two decades, during the '20's and '30's. During these purges 1,500,000 to 2,000,000 people were expelled from the Party, and the number of those refused admission was also great. A party that at the beginning of the '20's numbered about 500,000 members subsequently expelled or refused admission to numbers that vastly exceeded its former total membership.

What underlay this purging operation was Lenin's classic idea that the Party had to remain an instrument in the hands of the chosen few, and that this instrument, like all instruments, constantly had to be kept in fighting trim—repaired, honed, and polished. A logical inference from this conception is of course the right of the leader to institute purges.

The first general purge in the Party took place in 1921. Within a period of a few months nearly thirty per cent of the members were expelled or thought it wise to leave. This first application of a purge differed from later ones in

* The Pyatakov-Radek study was sponsored by the International Commission Against Concentration Camp Practices (of Paris and Brussels).

that almost none of those "purged" were arrested or made to suffer any other loss, most of them simply remaining at their former posts.

The second of the great purges took place in 1928. In the interval between 1921 and 1928 two smaller, partial purges took place, in 1924 and 1926. In May, 1924 there was an outburst of inner-Party dissension marked by gains made in favor of Trotsky among students and some government employees, and the consequent purges struck Party cells in the government and in educational institutions. In 1926 a purge was carried out in various rural Party organizations.

Thus the number of those expelled and of those who left the Party voluntarily was roughly as follows: in 1922, 45,000; in 1923, about 40,000; in 1924, 23,000; in 1925, 32,100; in 1926, 35,000; in 1927, 44,000; and in 1928—before the great purge—40,000. Accordingly, the number of those who were expelled or who left the Party in the interval between the two purges, i.e., 1922–1928, was approximately 260,000. Meanwhile the Party had grown: from 500,000 to 1,304,000.

The end of the '20's was marked by bitter conflict between various Party factions. The "leftists" advocated a great program of communism. The "rightists" advocated private enterprise for the peasantry for the immediate future; they were also prepared for economic concessions. From this fight Stalin, who had been in the "center," emerged victorious. The great purge of 1929, which had been designed to consolidate captured positions, was the natural consequence of Stalin's victory. More than 160,000 Party members were expelled. The rural organizations were especially hard hit; fifteen per cent of their members were driven from the Party.

Stalin's unrestricted dictatorship began about 1930. If there was a shadow of dissension among the leaders at that time it was kept secret within the Party's Central Committee and the Politburo; it was limited mainly to the issue of whether leading members of the Communist Party could be persecuted and executed in the same way as other citizens of the Soviet Union. Lenin had strongly advised against such fratricidal acts.

Introduction 5

In 1932, however, when a group of surviving "right oppositionists" dared to formulate, secretly, a sharply worded anti-Stalinist "platform," Stalin, when he learned of it, demanded the death penalty for at least some of them. The Politburo rejected this demand, and the culprits were instead sent to prison and into exile. Stalin never forgot this defeat; and he waited for an appropriate moment to resume his offensive against any surviving opponents within the Party.

The new purge, begun in 1933, continued for several years. Nearly 200,000 members were eliminated from the Party in the first year. It was expected that the purge would be concluded by 1935; the announcement of a forthcoming restoration of normal Party life was actually made. This, however, did not happen.

December 1, 1934, was the date that marked the start of an unprecedented avalanche of terrorism. On that day Sergei Kirov, member of the Politburo and a rising star in the Communist Party, was killed in Leningrad by a young Communist, Leonid Nikolaev. This act was immediately inflated into a great political event. In the evening of the same day, December 1, a decree was issued providing that:

I. Investigative agencies are directed to speed up the cases of those accused of the preparation or execution of acts of terror.

II. Judicial organs are directed not to hold up the execution of death sentences pertaining to crimes of this category in order to consider the possibility of pardon, because the Presidium of the Central Executive Committee U.S.S.R. does not consider as possible the receiving of petitions of this sort.

III. The organs of the Commissariat of Internal Affairs are directed to execute the death sentences against criminals of the above-mentioned category immediately after the passage of sentences.[1]

Pardons and appeals were thus no longer permitted.
The members of the Presidium of the Central Executive

[1] The secret report by Nikita Khrushchev (February 24, 1956) at the 20th Party Congress.

Committee, elected by the Congress of Soviets, in whose name the decree was promulgated, were not consulted; on Stalin's instructions the decree was signed by the Secretary of the Presidium. Two days later it was reported to the Politburo, whose timid and frightened members did not dare to oppose it.

Attributing the assassination of Kirov to "white" emigrés, the NKVD executed 104 "terrorists" selected at random, and deported to concentration camps many thousands of innocents arrested in the provinces. After a secret trial Nikolaev and thirteen others were executed on December 30, 1934.

On January 22, 1935, twelve leading NKVD officials in Leningrad were tried on the charge that, "having received information about the preparations for the attempt on S. M. Kirov . . . they failed to take the necessary measures to prevent the assassination." The sentences imposed were extremely mild. Two years later, however, the most important of these twelve defendants were executed.

The charge that Stalin must have played an active role in the assassination of Kirov was first made by Leon Trotsky, who claimed that the NKVD undoubtedly knew of Nikolaev's plans and reported them to Stalin well in advance.[2] The truth of this charge was confirmed later by two NKVD defectors, Walter G. Krivitsky and Alexander Orlov, and, in 1956, Khrushchev gave some details of the plot in his secret report at the 20th Party Congress.[3]

The official though false version of Kirov's assassination, given by Stalin, was as follows:

> The investigation established that in 1933 and 1934 an underground counter-revolutionary terrorist group had been formed in Leningrad consisting of former members of the Zinoviev opposition and headed by a so-called "Leningrad Center." The purpose of this group was to murder leaders of the Communist Party. S. M. Kirov was chosen as the

---

[2] *Byulleten' Oppozitsii (Bolshevikov–Lenintsev)* (Bulletin of the Opposition (Bolsheviks–Leninists), Paris, No. 42, (February, 1935), p. 11.

[3] Khrushchev's secret report of February 24, 1956, and even more at the 22nd Party Congress of October 1961. (*Ed.*)

Introduction 7

first victim. The testimony of the members of this counter-revolutionary group showed that they were connected with representatives of foreign capitalist states and were receiving funds from them. . . .

Soon afterwards the existence of an underground counter-revolutionary organization called the "Moscow Center" was discovered. The preliminary investigation and the trial revealed the villainous part played by Zinoviev, Kamenev, Yevdokimov and other leaders of this organization in cultivating the terrorist mentality among their followers, and in plotting the murder of members of the Party Central Committee and of the Soviet government.[4]

On the basis of this version, accepted by the members of the Politburo and propagated by the Soviet press, a trial behind closed doors was staged against the Zinoviev-Kamenev group in January, 1935. The defendants were accused of having organized an underground counter-revolutionary group in Moscow and Leningrad. The Military Collegium of the Supreme Court in its sentence stated that the defendants knew "about terrorist trends in the Leningrad group and themselves inflamed those trends." Four of the defendants were sentenced to prison terms of ten years, five to eight years, seven to six years, and three to five years.[5]

There was another purge in 1935, and in the summer of 1936 there began the greatest and the most terrible of all Party purges.

On May 13, 1935, the Central Committee ordered a general screening of Party ranks ("renewal of membership cards"); this was tantamount to a general purge of the Communist Party. The purge operation lasted for almost three years, until 1938, and in the army and navy for another year, until 1939; it resulted in thousands of arrests,

[4] *History of the Communist Party of the Soviet Union (Bolsheviks) Short Course* (Moscow: Foreign Languages Publishing House, 1939), p. 326.

[5] *Obvinitel'nye materialy po delu podpol'noi kontrrevolyutsionnoi gruppy zinovievtsev* (Accusation Materials in the Case of the Underground Counter-Revolutionary Group of Zinovievites), (Moscow: Partizdat TsK VKP (b), 1935), p. 42.

trials and executions, of Party members as well as of non–Communists.

The fearful holocaust started with the appointment by the Politburo of a special "Commission" to watch over the NKVD in general as well as over the carrying out of the purge in particular. The most active member of the "Commission" was Nikolai Yezhov, whose meteoric career as Stalin's watchdog over the NKVD now started. The NKVD was to be rigidly restricted to the status of a tool in the hands of the Leader.

In the course of the purge, Party members were invited to "reveal" and "expose" their comrades; a flood of denunciations, often from persons seeking to save their own necks, inundated the Party committees as well as the NKVD. The domestic spy network, which had been growing since the early years of the Soviet regime, assumed unprecedented proportions: thousands of so–called *seksots* (*sekretnyi sotrudnik*, i.e., secret collaborator) were recruited and planted in the Soviet government and economy.

In September, 1936 Stalin decided to part with his henchman Genrikh Yagoda, who had spent sixteen years in the secret police, and to replace him with Yezhov. Yagoda was given another post, but he was soon arrested, tried, and executed. A few months later (February–March 1937), a plenary session of the Central Committee endorsed Stalin's course of unlimited terrorism. Yezhov became its living symbol, and his twenty–six months in office went down in history as the era of "Yezhovshchina."

Yezhov's first act was to purge the NKVD itself. About two hundred officers were dismissed and replaced by Yezhov's obedient subordinates; a great many officials were arrested and treated with extreme severity.

A partial list of Yezhov's victims includes almost all the eighty members of the Soviet Council of War created in 1934; the majority of the members of Stalin's own Central Committee and his Central Control Commission; most of the Council of the Executive Committee of the Soviets, of the Council of People's Commissars, of the Council of Labor and Defense, of the leaders of the Communist Interna-

Introduction

tional; all chiefs and deputy chiefs of the OGPU; a host of ambassadors and other diplomats; the heads of all the regional and autonomous republics of the Soviet Union; 35,000 members of the officers' corps; almost the entire staff of *Pravda* and *Izvestia*; a great number of writers, musicians, and theater directors; and finally a majority of the leaders of the Young Communist League, the cream of the generation from whom the greatest loyalty to Stalin was expected.[6]

The general aim of the arrests, interrogations and trials was to extract "confessions" from those arrested. To the primitive minds of the new legal personnel, including the heads of the police and Stalin himself, a confession was irrefutable proof of guilt. Accordingly, everyone arrested had to be made to plead guilty; for those arrested it was usually better to confess than to deny their guilt. Fictitious confessions and "legends of self–incrimination" became standard.

The tasks of the "purged" NKVD, and especially of the corps of interrogating officials, were greatly increased; their working hours were unlimited. The execution of "sentenced" prisoners was one of their responsibilities. Many NKVD men broke down themselves; some went out of their minds.

Krivitsky gave us some graphic testimony to this bizarre situation:

> In the office of every prosecuting investigator the most important article of furniture is his couch. For the character of his work is such that it often keeps him going at consecutive stretches of twenty to forty hours. He is himself almost as much a captive as the prisoner. His duties know no limits. They may extend from grilling prisoners to shooting them.
>
> For it is one of the peculiarities of the Soviet judicial process that despite the tremendous numbers of executions, there are no regular executioners. Sometimes the men who go down cellar to carry out the death decrees of the collegium of the OGPU are

---

[6] W. G. Krivitsky, *In Stalin's Secret Service* (New York: Harper and Brothers, 1939), p. 177.

officers and sentries of the building. Sometimes they are the investigators and prosecutors themselves. For an analogy to this, one must try to imagine a New York District Attorney obtaining a first degree murder conviction and then rushing up to Sing Sing to throw the switch in the death chamber.[7]

Khrushchev later admitted that in the years of the purge

> ... the only proof of guilt used, against all norms of current legal science, was the "confession" of the accused himself; and, as subsequent investigation proved, "confessions" were secured through physical pressures against the accused.[8]

Confessions were extracted by threats, by torture, and by promises, rarely kept, of lenience or freedom. On the other hand, attempts by accused persons to retract previously made confessions were obstructed by all possible means. Torturing of prisoners, forbidden by Soviet law, was not only introduced in 1937 by a special instruction, but was even made obligatory.[9]

Prisons became overcrowded; concentration camps filled up with hundreds of thousands of newcomers. Estimates of the numbers of arrested and deported went into the millions. Actual trials were held only in rare cases, and, when held, were staged for propaganda purposes. Sentences were pronounced *in camera*, the defendants being given only a short statement concerning the term of imprisonment. Death sentences were submitted to Stalin for approval.[10]

Several of the show trials of these years were held in provincial cities, but the most important were the five great "Moscow trials," held between August, 1936 and March, 1938, which ended in the physical destruction of most of the surviving Old Bolsheviks and Soviet leaders of the initial post–Lenin era. The standard accusations were

---

[7] *Ibid.*, p. 145

[8] Khrushchev's secret report of February 24, 1956.

[9] *Ibid.*

[10] *Ibid.*

espionage for a foreign power, "diversion" and sabotage, conspiracy against the Soviet regime, and attempts on the lives of Soviet leaders. The prosecutor in the Moscow trials was Andrei Vyshinsky, a former Menshevik, servile toward Stalin and hated by everybody, including Communists. Well aware of the falsity of the accusations, he demanded the death sentence in every case.

The chiefs of the NKVD didn't dignify Vyshinsky with their confidence and treated him with the same humiliating condescension with which Stalin's influential bureaucrats treat non–party men. And even then, when they were instructing Vyshinsky how cautious he should be with the weak points of their judicial forgeries, they never openly used the word "falsification," but instead employed hypocritical phraseology for their explanations.

Vyshinsky had grounds to hate his haughty bosses. He knew that *he* would have to cover up at the trial their clumsily concocted forgeries and outdo himself in eloquence in order to lend at least some plausibility to their idiotic fabrications. He also knew that if their falsifications came out during the court proceedings, the inquisitors would make *him* responsible for the fiasco of the trial and maybe even accuse him of "sabotage."[11]

On August 19–24, 1936, in Moscow a new Zinoviev-Kamenev trial was staged. It was the first phase in this series of trials. The first trial (in January, 1935) had been held behind closed doors, but the new trial was widely publicized. Zinoviev, Kamenev, Grigori Yevdokimov and thirteen others were again the defendants; they were charged with the organization of a "Terrorist Center," preparation of the assassination of Sergei Kirov and a number of other terrorist acts. All confessed; all were sentenced to death and executed.

Orlov tells us:

Exactly six days after Stalin had executed Zinoviev, Kamenev and all other defendants of the first trial, he

[11] Alexander Orlov, *The Secret History of Stalin's Crimes* (New York: Random House, 1953), p. 328.

ordered Yagoda and Yezhov to select five thousand of the more active members of the former opposition, who were being kept in concentration camps and exile, and have them executed in secret.[12]

In the flood of suicides that accompanied the purge, a number of prominent Soviet leaders and writers took their lives, probably to avoid trial, prison, and execution. Among them was Mikhail Tomsky, an "Old Bolshevik," an associate of Lenin's and head of the Soviet trade unions; he committed suicide during the Zinoviev–Kamenev trial.

In January, 1937 there took place the trial of the "Anti–Soviet Trotskyite Center," in which the defendants were Yuri (Georgi) Pyatakov, Karl Radek, Grigori Sokolnikov and fourteen others accused of treason, espionage, diversion, wrecking activities and preparation of terrorist acts. All the defendants confessed. Thirteen were sentenced to death; three were given ten years', and one eight years' imprisonment.

The case of eight leaders of the Red Army[13]—Marshal Mikhail Tukhachevsky, Generals I. E. Yakir, I. P. Uborevich, and five others—was tried in June, 1937. The trial was conducted behind closed doors before a Special Session of the Supreme Court. The defendants were charged with treason, the wrecking of the Red Army, and espionage in favor of a foreign power. They "sought to prepare for a defeat of the Red Army, in case of a military attack on the Soviet Union, and to help restore in the U.S.S.R. the role of landlords and capitalists."[14] All the defendants allegedly confessed. All were sentenced to death and executed. Of the judges at this trial (Marshal V. K. Blyukher, Ya. I. Alksnis and six others) all but two (Marshal Semion Budenny and General Boris M. Shaposhnikov) were subsequently executed.

On December 16, 1937, the Yenukidze–Karakhan group

---

[12] *Ibid.*, p. 170.

[13] One of the prospective defendants, General Yan Gamarnik, Deputy People's Commissar of Defense and Chief of the Main Political Administration of the Red Army, committed suicide on May 31, 1937.

[14] *Pravda*, June 11, 1937.

Introduction 13

was tried in a closed session of the Military Collegium of the Supreme Court. They were found guilty of treason, terrorism and espionage. All eight defendants were sentenced to death and executed.

In March, 1938, the leaders of the "Right" opposition were put on trial; despite the fact that the Trotskyites had already been tried and sentenced earlier, the new proceedings were called, for purely propaganda reasons, the trial of the "Bloc of Rightists and Trotskyites." The most important among the twenty-one defendants were Nikolai Bukharin, Alexei Rykov, Nikolai Krestinsky, Christian Rakovsky, and Genrikh Yagoda. The defendants were charged with treason, espionage, diversion, wrecking, and terrorist activities. All confessed, and all but three were sentenced to death. Of the remaining three, one was sentenced to twenty-five years, one to twenty years, and one to fifteen years in prison.

By the middle of 1938 most of the "first Party secretaries" of the Soviet provinces and most of the Central Committee members had been executed.

The organs of state machinery suffered badly from the purges; had they continued for another year, unprecedented chaos would have engulfed the country. An end had to be put to the wave of terror; the pressure had to be eased. In July, 1938, Lavrenti Beria was appointed deputy to Yezhov; in December of the same year he took over the NKVD. Yezhov, removed to another post, soon disappeared; he was probably executed.

Lavrenti Beria, like Stalin a Georgian, and an official of the secret police since 1921, rose in the early 1930's to become secretary of the Georgian Communist Party. While still in this post he published a history of the Bolshevik movement in the Caucasus; the book, which contained many inaccuracies, was in its tone extremely servile to Stalin. When Stalin decided to get rid of Yezhov, he turned to his admirer, the experienced secret police chief, Beria, and appointed him head of the NKVD.

By the beginning of 1939 the great purges had come to an end. Arrests grew fewer. It seemed a new era had begun.

I PRELUDE TO A NEW TRIAL

The first of the Moscow show trials, that of the Zinoviev–Kamenev group, was only the first stage in a wholesale purge which was to develop with accelerating speed and was not to end until a number of other trials, public and secret, had taken place and thousands of other former oppositionists had been liquidated.

The scope of the trials that followed was broader than that of the Zinoviev–Kamenev trial. The latter had in the main stressed only the "terrorism" of the Trotskyites, their alleged attempts and preparation of attempts on the lives of the leaders. In the subsequent trials it was necessary to expose, in addition, (1) the alleged ties of the opposition with, and its services to Nazi and Japanese intelligence, and (2) "wrecking" as one of the most important of the activities of the opposition.

The purge operations were controlled by Stalin and carried out by Genrikh Yagoda and Nikolai Yezhov. Yagoda, head of the NKVD, had acquired considerable experience in the former trials as to the techniques of confessions, "amalgams," interrogations, and frame-ups. Yezhov was actually chief of a special commission appointed by the Central Committee a year before to carry out the great purge and supervise the NKVD in this respect; the commission was one of those sinister and powerful little bodies—the "quintets," "sextets," and "septets"—that Stalin used to create in order to keep the Politburo from interfering with his designs.[15]

In the process of preparing for the Zinoviev–Kamenev trial, even before the public sessions started, Yagoda and Yezhov laid the basis for a new trial. Before the Zinoviev–Kamenev group was destroyed, they had to forge a new link in the chain of purges, just as the defendants in the second trial were to forge a link to the third (Bukharin–Rykov) trial. The task of forging the link to the second trial was assigned to Reingold, Zinoviev, and Kamenev.

[15] The secret report by Nikita Khrushchev (February 24, 1956) at the 20th Party Congress.

I Prelude to a New Trial

Having confessed to Yezhov their own "crimes," they confirmed that certain other opposition leaders had been conspirators—namely, the "rightists" Bukharin, Tomsky, and Rykov; the "leftists" Pyatakov, Radek, and Serebryakov; and Sokolnikov, who did not belong to any faction.

In open court, on August 19, 1936, Reingold was the first of the defendant–witnesses to make charges against the "leftists" as well as the "rightists," in particular Sokolnikov, Bukharin, Rykov, and Tomsky. The following day Zinoviev said:

> " . . . certain underground groups of the Right as well as of the so–called 'Left' trend, sought contact with me and Kamenev. Approaches were made by the remnants of the 'Workers' Opposition': by Shlyapnikov and Medvedev. Approaches came from the groups of the so–called 'Leftists': that is, Lominadze, Shatskin, Sten and others. Approaches also came from the so–called 'individuals,' to whose numbers belonged Smilga, and to a certain extent, Sokolnikov."[16]

At the same session, Kamenev repeated the official version.

> "Knowing that we might be discovered, we designated a small group to continue our terroristic activities. For this purpose we designated Sokolnikov. It seemed to us that on the side of the Trotskyites this role could be successfully performed by Serebryakov and Radek. . . . They [Tomsky and Bukharin] sympathized with us. When I asked Tomsky about Rykov's frame of mind, he replied 'Rykov thinks the same as I do.' "[17]

How well the stage had been prepared in advance is seen from the fact that no sooner had word of the new accusations been made known than "workers' meetings" were held to demand investigation and punishment of the second set of the accused. At a meeting of five thousand

---

[16] *Report of Court Proceedings. The Case of the Trotskyite-Zinovievite Terrorist Centre, Heard Before the Military Collegium of the Supreme Court of the USSR, Moscow, August 19-24, 1936* (Moscow: People's Commissariat of Justice of the USSR, 1936), pp. 71-72.

[17] *Ibid.*, pp. 67-68.

workers at the Dynamo Plant in Moscow, on August 21, 1936, the speakers expressed indignation against the leaders of the opposition: "The workers demand that the whole criminal knot be disentangled to its end." *Pravda* (August 22, 1936) ran the report of this meeting on its front page under the heading, "Investigate the Ties Between the Tomsky–Bukharin–Rykov and Pyatakov–Radek Groups and the Trotskyite–Zinovievite Gang." The following day the workers of the Hammer and Sickle Plant adopted a resolution demanding "investigation of the ties between Bukharin, Rykov, Radek, Pyatakov and the terrorists."

Khrushchev appeared in Moscow as a speaker before a meeting of the so–called "aktiv" (the lower strata of the party leadership). His speech was summarized in the resolution adopted by the meeting demanding " . . .execution of the despicable bands of murderers. . . . Investigation of the ties between Tomsky, Rykov, Bukharin, Radek,Pyatakov,Uglanov and others with the Trotskyite–Zinovievite Counter–Revolutionary Center (*Pravda*, August 23, 1936).

The basis having been laid for a new trial, Vyshinsky announced to the court:

> " . . . I consider it necessary to inform the Court that yesterday I gave orders to institute an investigation of these statements of the accused in regard to Tomsky, Rykov, Bukharin, Uglanov, Radek and Pyatakov, and that in accordance with the results of this investigation the office of the State Attorney will institute legal proceedings in this matter. In regard to Serebryakov and Sokolnikov, the investigating authorities are already in possession of material convicting these persons of counter–revolutionary crimes, and, in view of this, criminal proceedings are being instituted against Sokolnikov and Serebryakov."[18]

Some of the new culprits were arrested immediately, and an investigation of the others was initiated. The newly accused men, aware of the danger threatening them, began to proclaim their loyalty to Stalin by attacking Zinoviev,

[18] *Ibid.*, pp. 115–116.

I Prelude to a New Trial

Kamenev, and their co-defendants in a not very dignified way. Pyatakov, Preobrazhensky, Rakovsky, and a number of other former Communist leaders made deep obeisance. "Fiery leftists" ten years ago, their youthful enthusiasm for political fighting had now evaporated. Advanced in years, they wanted only amnesty from the leader in the Kremlin, and to be able to live in comparative peace. They were willing to go to great lengths, even to betray their friends and comrades, if at this price they could buy what they now valued above everything else,—life.

"Unmercifully destroy the despicable murderers, assassins and traitors," wrote (or was forced to write) Pyatakov. "They must be destroyed, destroyed like carrion.... By my complacency I have made it easier for these bandits to do their dirty jobs. It is fortunate that the NKVD organs have exposed this gang. It is fortunate that it could be destroyed."[19] "For the highest measure of treason and baseness—the highest measure of punishment," wrote Yevgeni Preobrazhensky in *Pravda* (August 24, 1936).

Karl Radek, whose last regular column appeared in *Izvestia* on August 10, 1936 (on which date Stalin apparently made his decision about a second trial and Radek's role in it), was permitted, however, to attack the defendants of the first trial in one more article on August 21: "Their chieftain," he wrote, "the fascist chief bandit, Trotsky, thanks to the kindness of the Soviet government, managed to save his skin.... The fascist chief bandit Trotsky cherishes false hopes that he will be able to throw dust in anybody's eyes.... People who rose in arms against the life of the beloved leaders of the proletariat must pay with their heads for their enormous guilt. Trotsky, the main organizer of this gang and its deeds, has already been placed by history in the pillory. He will not escape the verdict of the world proletariat." His article ended with the words, "There should be no mercy—they must be shot."[20]

The fight in the Politburo between the Stalinists and their tame opponents entered a new phase. Feeling that his

[19] *Pravda*, August 21, 1936.
[20] *Izvestia*, August 21, 1936, p. 3.

majority was not sufficient to plunge the Party into the holocaust of the trials, Stalin submitted the case of the new accused to a session that was attended by a number of the members of the Central Committee, and that took place about a week after the execution of the defendants in the Zinoviev–Kamenev trial, early in September, 1936.[21] Yezhov, actual head of the Politburo's Commission of Security, was the main speaker at this session. He accused the Bukharin faction of having entered into a conspiracy with the Trotskyites and having become agents of the Gestapo. He proposed a resolution recommending the expulsion of Bukharin and Rykov from the Communist Party and their indictment on criminal charges. (Tomsky had committed suicide on August 22, 1936.) In his retort, which took three hours, Bukharin accused Stalin and Yezhov of conspiring against the Communist Party and appealed to his comrades to return to "Lenin's traditions." When Bukharin had finished, Stalin's lieutenants—Molotov, Kalinin, Kaganovich, Voroshilov, Mikoyan, Zhdanov, Shkiryatov, and Andreev—took the floor to attack the rightist opposition. When Yezhov's resolution was put to a vote, however, it was rejected by a two–thirds majority. The collective leadership was not willing to initiate the great purge. By indicating their opposition to it, the majority of its members were signing their own death warrants.

Stalin made a characteristically sly and diplomatic move. He declared his wholehearted acceptance of the decision of the Central Committee and promised to carry it out. He complimented the members of the Central Committee on their criticism and self–criticism, worthy of real Bolsheviks. Those who knew Stalin realized, of course, that he had not given in, and that his anger was only increased by the "liberal" decision.

Following the dramatic developments in the Central Committee, the Chief Prosecutor announced, on September 9:

The Prosecution of the Union of Soviet Socialist

---

[21] Our account on this session follows that given by Alexandre Ouralov in *Staline Au Pouvoir*, pp. 34–41. (Paris: Les Iles d'Or (Diffusion Plon), n.d.). While some details of Ouralov's story might be disputed, his account is on the whole trustworthy.

I Prelude to a New Trial

Republics has now completed the investigation instituted in regard to the indications made by some of the accused at the trial of the Trotskyite–Zinovievite Terrorist Center in Moscow on 19–20 August of this year about a certain complicity of N. I. Bukharin and A. I. Rykov in their counter–revolutionary activities.

The investigation did not establish judicial bases for legal proceedings against N. I. Bukharin and A. I. Rykov. The case is therefore considered closed.[22]

The wording was carefully chosen by the Prosecutor with an eye on Stalin. No "judicial bases" for prosecution of the rightist leaders meant that there might well be political reasons and that the door was being kept open for a revival of the charges.

Bukharin was ostensibly permitted to resume the direction of *Izvestia*, and his name continued to appear as Chief Editor until January 16, 1937.

With the rightist opposition rehabilitated, there remained the other former leftist leaders who had been mentioned as friends and agents of Trotsky and Trotskyism. Stalin had no intention of closing the case against them; on the contrary, they were to constitute the body of defendants at a new trial. But since the charge against them could not read "the creation of a rightist–leftist bloc," only a "Trotskyite conspiracy" could be substituted. This is why a short while after the first trial ended, Stalin staged, and not very adroitly, a second Trotskyite trial, in which Pyatakov, Radek, Sokolnikov, Serebryakov, and thirteen others were accused of having organized a second "Parallel or Reserve Trotskyite Center," whose purpose, it was alleged, had been to take over the functions of the first, Zinovievite, Center in case the latter should be liquidated. This version of the existence of two leading Trotskyite groups, one active and the other to remain passive for a number of years, is contrary to political good sense as well as to all the traditions of the Russian underground. But under the given conditions nothing better could be offered the Russian and non–Russian public.

[22] *Pravda*, September 10, 1936.

Meanwhile the fight between Yagoda, chief of the NKVD, and Yezhov, of the Central Committee, entered a new phase. The decision of the highest party bodies to drop the case against the rightists—a rebuke to Yezhov—automatically improved the standing of Yagoda. To the Soviet people Yagoda personified the brutal and ruthless police. He had been the most merciless purger, jailer, slave-driver, and executioner in Russia or abroad. But in the Stalin milieu, both before and after Yezhov's defeat, Yagoda was accused of leniency, lack of zeal in the fight against the "enemies of the people," and even of sympathy with the "rightists." At this juncture the fight between the Soviet state machine, of which the NKVD was a component part, and the Communist Party, of which Yezhov was a representative, appeared in a strange light: of the two, it was the NKVD that appeared as the more humane agency!

Pushing toward his great new purge, Stalin supported Yezhov against Yagoda. On September 25, two weeks after the rehabilitation of the Bukharin group, Stalin (and Andrei Zhdanov) sent a telegram from Sochi to the members of the Politburo in Moscow:

> We deem it absolutely necessary and urgent that Comrade Yezhov be nominated to the post of People's Commissar of Internal Affairs. Yagoda has definitely proved himself to be incapable of unmasking the Trotskyite–Zinovievite bloc. The OGPU is four years behind in this matter. This is noted by all Party workers and by the majority of the representatives of the NKVD.[23]

The very next day a decree of the Central Executive Committee removed Yagoda from the NKVD post he had held for fifteen years. He was appointed to the unimportant post of People's Commissar of Communications.

Yezhov's elevation to power as People's Commissar of Internal Affairs was hardly due to his personality. A slight, thin man, with no abilities, he was remarkable only for his devotion to Stalin; even in that era of universal adula-

---

[23] Khrushchev's secret report of February 24, 1956.

I Prelude to a New Trial

tion and adoration, Stalin could hardly have found a more blindly obedient servant prepared to go to such criminal lengths on orders from "the Leader." A photograph widely distributed at the time shows Stalin sitting in a chair looking down with a fatherly air at Yezhov, kneeling beside him.

Yezhov's record was that of a mediocre "Party worker." Born in Leningrad in 1892, he joined the Bolsheviks in 1917, took part in the Civil War, and after a short period in the War Commissariat became a Party official in 1922. His first assignments were in the Party *apparat* in Central Asia. From 1927 on, he was on the large staff of the Central Committee in Moscow. For a short time during the de-kulakization drive, he served as Assistant People's Commissar of Agriculture, but he returned to the party's Central Committee to work in the Bureau of Appointments. At the 17th Party Congress in 1934 he was elected to the Central Committee as well as to the Central Control Commission. His election to the Orgburo and to the chairmanship of the Central Control Commission in 1934 marked his advance to the ranks of the leadership. In 1935 he also became a member of the Executive Committee of the Comintern. Finally, as a member of the unpublicized Security Commission of the Politburo, established in 1935 to carry out the purge, he ranked higher than Yagoda and watched over the NKVD.

To the Soviet people, however, Yezhov was still an obscure personality when he succeeded Yagoda. The ominous nature of the appointment was not immediately obvious, but it revealed itself in the following months.[24]

In preparing for the grandiose operation that Stalin had in view, Yezhov's first task was a sweeping purge of the

---

[24] A few over-eager correspondents in Moscow hastened to announce that the appointment of Yezhov meant the end of the era of terror. One of these was Harold Denny, of the *New York Times*, who, in his cable of September 27, 1936, said Yezhov was "honest, conscientious, of humane qualities, and 'a man who knows how to smile.' " Yagoda's dismissal, he indicated, signified the end of the terror era; Yagoda represented "the old OGPU psychology," but now "there is no longer a need for such powers."

NKVD itself. Yagoda's close collaborators were removed; some were jailed, some executed. A new staff of police leaders was necessary if the cleansing operation was to succeed. Walter Krivitsky estimated the number of these new "boys" taken over from the Party machine into the NKVD at two hundred.[25] A few months later Yagoda himself was charged with having served in the tsar's police, spying for Germany, and other crimes. He was tried, along with the "rightists," sentenced to death, and executed in March, 1938.

II STALIN'S ROLE IN THE CHARGES

Stalin's role in the purge trials was a much more important and dominant one than was once assumed. Only in the light of what has become known about him in the years since the trials have we come to understand that he was not only the initiator and the guiding spirit of the trials, but the actual manager of the operations. The two other actors in the great purge, Yezhov and Vyshinsky, were merely tools, with no personalities and no ideas of their own.

That the Pyatakov–Radek trial was Stalin's affair, in the conduct of which he was personally responsible for every important detail, appears plain.

The delicate task of selecting the defendants, some of whom would have to "expose" their co–defendants, while others would have to come from among officers of the secret police, was performed by Stalin.

The plot—the "legend"—was certainly conceived by Stalin. The criminal deeds the defendants were accused of were typical products of Stalin's mind.

Stalin prescribed the methods of interrogation. The questions put to the defendants—the answers to which were expected to fit into the legend—and the charges against the leading defendants were all couched in terms plainly devised by Stalin.

[25] W. G. Krivitsky, *In Stalin's Secret Service* (New York: Harper & Brothers, 1939), p. 146.

II Stalin's Role in the Charges

From the "stalinisms" contained in the indictment it is clear that its preparation was a joint effort of Stalin and Vyshinsky. While it was written by Vyshinsky, to anyone familiar with Stalin's writings it appears obvious that it had been submitted to him before it was presented to the court and that he made abundant changes, as he customarily did in official documents.

The sentences were pronounced on Stalin's instructions and carried out on his orders.

Thus, Stalin was the initiator, interrogator, prosecutor, judge, and executioner.

The Charge of Wrecking

One of Stalin's favorite maneuvers was to accuse his political adversaries of intentional and systematic wrecking. It should be pointed out that Stalin's military–political experience dated from the Civil War, which was his main source of understanding of both war and political warfare.

"Wrecking" is a method of fighting a civil war. Demolition of railways and destruction of industrial plants and food stores are a natural and logical part of civil warfare. When passions run high and hatred is the dominant emotion, wrecking tactics rather than grand strategy play the decisive role. That thousands of human beings might be killed or maimed in the operations is seen as an unavoidable necessity in a civil war. Such was Stalin's experience, conviction, and strategy, and he applied them widely in his wars both at home and abroad.

Industrial and railway accidents in Russia were mounting in the '20's and '30's as Soviet industry was rehabilitated and new plants were added to the old. The leading positions in industry were occupied by young, often inexperienced, engineers and workers, while the old corps of industrial captains was being removed. In many instances the fact that there was no one really interested in or responsible for the normal working of an industrial plant was the cause of carelessness and accidents. In other cases, speed–up was responsible for disasters and casualties. "Fulfillment of the plan" at any price meant (and still means) disregard of the well-being of the workers and neglect in providing safety measures. "Economy" often meant diverting all available funds to production, leaving nothing for measures to protect the workers.

Accidents during this period were so frequent that the government did not permit them to be reported in the press. Railway disasters, fires, explosions were kept secret. Under the pretext that the Soviet press, unlike the so-called "boulevard" press of the capitalist countries, must serve higher purposes than the satisfying of the low instincts of the mob, Soviet newspapers often omitted items of more general interest. But the accidents could not remain a secret from the local population, since thousands of persons were either directly involved in these accidents or were relatives of victims. Despite all attempts at secrecy, indignation was widespread.

In the great Shakhta trial of 1928, forty-nine engineers were accused of precisely the same crimes as those that appeared nine years later in the indictment against Pyatakov-Radek, namely, deliberate disorganization and wrecking of the coal industry, flooding of mines, and, in general, sabotage with the object of turning the workers against the Soviet regime. "About two years ago," declared Stalin in June, 1931, " ... the old technical intelligentsia was infected with the disease of wrecking. ... Wreckers exist and will continue to exist as long as we have classes and as long as capitalist encirclement exists."[26] Two years after the Shakhta trial, a similar trial of the so-called Industrial Party took place, in which another group of intellectuals was accused of wrecking and spying.

In January, 1933 Stalin again thundered public threats against wreckers and saboteurs, including those "professors [who] go to such lengths in their passion for wrecking as to inject plague and anthrax germs into the cattle on the collective farms and state farms, help to spread meningitis among horses," etc. He accused them of organizing "mass theft and plundering of state property, cooperative property and collective farm property. Theft and plundering in the

[26] J. V. Stalin, *Works*, XIII, 71, 75.

II Stalin's Role in the Charges

factories and plants, theft and plundering of railway freight, theft and plundering in warehouses and trading enterprises—particularly theft and plundering in the state farms and collective farms—such is the main form of the 'work' of these 'have–beens.' "[27]

The same idea on a larger scale was now to be exploited in the fight against the Communist opposition. The accidents mentioned in the Pyatakov–Radek trial were real; the mismanagement cited by the prosecution was a fact; the human losses had indeed been high. It was only the connection of these facts with the Communist opposition that was a fraud. The list of accidents mentioned in the Pyatakov–Radek trial is so long that it itself explains why Stalin had need of the wrecking fabrication. (We must remember that almost all these accidents occurred in one province of Siberia, but they were indicative of the situation over the whole of the Soviet Union.) The following is a list of the accidents charged against the defendants in the Pyatakov–Radek trial:

Accidents in the Coal and Chemical Industry

Kemerovo Mines:
  Severny Khodok District, explosion, December, 1935; two workers killed.
  Tsentral'naya Pit, explosion, September 23, 1936; ten workers killed, fourteen seriously injured.
  Prokop'evsk, explosions, 1933 to October, 1936; five killed, twenty–one seriously injured.
Kemerovo Combined Chemical Works, serious breakdowns, 1935–36; "a number of workers seriously injured."
Gorlovka Nitrogen Plant Construction, breakdowns, March 22 and April 5, 1936; six workers injured.
Gorlovka Nitrogen Fertilizer Works, three explosions, April 7, 1934, November 14, 1934, and November 11, 1935; five workers killed.
Voskresensk Combined Chemical Works, breakdowns, April–May, 1934 and August 1, 1936; seventeen workers killed, fifteen injured.

[27] *Ibid.*, p. 212.

Linde Installation, explosion, November, 1934; two
workers killed.
Kemerovo District Electric Power Station, explosion,
February, 1936.

In addition the defendants and the prosecutor enumerated forty-two other wreckings, breakdowns, and "acts of diversion," with no details as to casualties; among them:

Railway Accidents

South–Urals and Perm–Urals Railroads:
Shumikha Station, troop train, October 27, 1935; twenty-nine Red Army men killed, twenty-nine injured.
Yakhino–Ust–Katav section, December, 1935; casualties among train guards.
Yedinover–Berdyaush section, February 7, 1936; casualties among train guards.
Rosa–Vargashi section, January and May 13, 1936; two killed, one injured.
Chistaya–Chumlyak station, train wreck, February 27, 1936.
Logovushka station, train wreck, 1936.
Chumlyak station, train wreck, January 18, 1936.
Sverdlovsk Passenger Station—Sverdlovsk Sorting Station (the accident occurred between these two stations), April 26, 1936; one killed, five seriously injured, some slightly injured.
Sagre–Iset, train wreck, June, 1935.
Monzino station, train wreck, September 30, 1935.

In addition, Ivan Knyazev, a high-ranking Soviet railway official, testified, "In 1934 there were altogether about 1,500 train wrecks and accidents."

Cross-examination was as follows:

Vyshinsky: Is it true that in 1935, forty-six persons were killed and fifty-one were injured in train disasters which you organized? Do you confirm these figures?

Knyazev: That is correct.

Vyshinsky: And in 1936, seventeen persons were killed and 103 injured?

II Stalin's Role in the Charges

Knyazev: Yes.[28]

And, the witness continued, the enemy (meaning the Communist opposition) had tried to cause the greatest number of casualties in these accidents, for in order to "arouse the population" against the Soviet government, victims were needed, the more the better. This vulgar and unrealistic picture of political warfare was made to come out of the mouths of the defendants; their "confessions" abound in statements like these:

> Knyazev: ... Livshitz [the former Trotskyite] said that we must now pass from general methods of undermining activity to train wrecks involving loss of human life. I thereupon asked Livshitz whether we Trotskyites could really be against the working class, against the population in general. Livshitz said that it was a question of a very fierce struggle against Stalin, that we must cause the Party leadership to become completely discredited in the eyes of the people, and, by a number of separate blows against the population, cause embitterment against Stalin, against the government, and create the impression among the population that the government was to blame for all of this. . . .[29]

> Pyatakov: The sharpest thing was acts of diversion. It was impossible to commit acts of diversion without sacrificing human life.[30]

> Norkin: It was said that the responsibility would fall not on those who performed the diversive acts but on the leaders of the Party and the government.[31]

> The President: Did you not inquire why loss of life should necessarily be involved?

> Turok: I did not inquire because I was told the same thing in greater detail by Maryasin, who gave

---

[28] *Report of Court Proceedings in the Case of the Anti-Soviet Trotskyite Center. Heard Before the Military Collegium of the Supreme Court of the USSR, Mcscow, January 23-30, 1937* (Moscow: People's Commissariat of Justice of the USSR, 1937), pp. 371, 372, 378-381. (Hereafter called *Proceedings*).
[29] *Ibid.*, p. 364.
[30] *Ibid.*, p. 51.
[31] *Ibid.*, p. 52.

as a reason that it was necessary in order to arouse resentment against the government.[32]

Stalin's faith in the strategy of wrecking again became evident a few years later, during the war, when he himself applied these methods against the Germans. In his first wartime speech (July 3, 1941) he appealed to the Soviet people and to the Soviet armed forces retreating before the Germans to leave behind them "scorched earth," and destroy communications, industrial plants, and stores of goods. Soviet guerrillas working behind the German lines were sometimes instructed not only to wreck industrial units and railways and destroy stores, but to act with cruelty toward the Russian population and then attribute their inhumane acts to the Germans.

A student (in 1942) at one of the three "schools of diversion" in Byelorussia has described the kind of instructions given concerning "the work behind the enemy's front" in the German-occupied areas of the Soviet Union:

> We were taught that we have to see to it that the enemy should not get support from the population of Byelorussia. . . . If our activities among the population did not yield results, stronger methods were permitted. For this purpose we were to select a village where the population was the least inclined to cause trouble for the Germans, and at a nearby point open fire against a German detachment, blow up trains, etc.; the result would be reprisals by German punitive companies.
>
> These instructions caused confusion among us. It should be kept in mind that we were working in our home regions. . . . One of us asked: "Comrade instructor, by mining the nearby region we will kill many innocent old men, women, and children!" The instructor looked at the questioner coolly and keenly: "We must realize, comrades, that victims don't count, if the interests of our fatherland are at stake."[33]

[32] *Ibid.*, p. 394.
[33] A. Prorvich, *Sovetskaya Diversionno-Shpionskaya Sluzhba v gody Vtoroi Mirovoi Voiny* (Soviet Diversion-Espionage Work in the Years of the Second World War) (unpublished manuscript), pp. 13–14.

II Stalin's Role in the Charges   29

Another study had the following to say on this subject:

> It is conceivable—as has at times been alleged—that it was the deliberate policy of the Soviet partisan command to provoke the Germans into taking reprisals against the population. The more brutal the actions of the Germans, the more hatred they would generate, and the more willing the population would become to support the partisans.[34]

And another:

> Another hypothesis, which cannot be supported by clear-cut evidence, has been advanced most frequently by Soviet refugees who lived in partisan-threatened areas: the inevitable result of partisan attacks on German personnel was ruthless German retaliation—not so much against partisans, on whom they generally could not lay their hands, as against innocent civilians. The result of this process was a chain reaction in which the interests of the Germans and those of the bulk of the indigenous population drew further and further apart. German eradication of entire communities in retribution for partisan raids could only rally neighboring residents to the partisans' side.[35]

The theory of wrecking used as part of a political scheme against the Communist opposition was childish, primitive, absurd. Neither Vyshinsky, the defendants, nor the Soviet press were ever able to explain what use the opposition could make of these accidents and catastrophes. Wrecking activities that might have made sense during a civil war were illogical in peacetime. An explosion in a coal mine

---

[34] A refugee informant who, as a chief of police for the Germans, observed Rodionov (head of a guerrilla unit) in action, affirmed that "his unit was cruel with the civilian population, something that provoked resentment, brought about greater German retribution, and in turn led people to join the partisans." (Alexander Dallin and Ralph S. Mavrogordato, "Rodionov: A Case-Study in Wartime Redefection," *American Slavic and East European Review*, February, 1959.

[35] Air Research and Development Command, Human Resources Research Institute, Maxwell Air Force Base, Alabama, *Partisan Psychological Warfare and Popular Attitudes Under the German Occupation*, January, 1954, sec. II, p. 18.

could cause only infinitesimal harm to the Soviet economy; a railway accident might stop traffic for a few hours or at most a few days in a certain locality in some corner of Russia; a slow-down in construction in a given plant could halt the pace of Soviet industrialization to only a small degree. Stalin's use of the wrecking pattern reveals his personality, his shrewdness, the level of his ideas, and his primitive strategy.

The Charge of Bacteriological Warfare

The idea of bacteriological warfare had apparently struck Stalin's imagination at a rather early date; he saw it as a political weapon of great propagandistic force; his intense interest in the subject increased as his influence and power grew. To condemn the use of bacteriological warfare on the one hand, while at the same time preparing for it and accusing the enemy of using it on the other, was a typical Stalinist political tactic.

We have already seen how in 1933 Stalin had accused Russian professors of the absurd crime of helping "to spread meningitis among horses," etc., by injecting "plague and anthrax germs into the cattle on the collective and state farms. . . ." When Yagoda was standing trial in 1938, Vyshinsky accused him of having concocted and used poisons. This story, though intentionally left unclarified, was not entirely false: Yagoda had prepared and used poisons, but had done so, of course, on Stalin's orders.

On the basis of his experiences in Soviet Military Intelligence Headquarters in 1943, Igor Gouzenko wrote, two years before the outbreak of the Korean war:

> . . . in another war the enemies of Russia will have to be prepared for the 'epidemic' weapon as well as the atomic bomb. . . . If the spreading of cholera in the Near East would affect England badly, whether Russia was at war or at peace with England, I have no hesitation in saying *full use of the germs would be made* [emphasis supplied]. The only thing that would worry

II Stalin's Role in the Charges

the Kremlin would be fear that its action might be discovered.[36]

In December, 1949 a sensational though dubious trial against Japanese war criminals was held in Khabarovsk. Preparation for a bacteriological war was among the accusations; Emperor Hirohito was accused of personally ordering the use of this inhumane method of warfare:

> On orders of Hirohito and on instructions of the War Minister and the General Staff of Japan, special bacteriological formations of the Japanese army were organized where deadly plague germs, cholera, typhus, malignant anthrax (Siberian anthrax), and other dangerous epidemic germs were cultivated in enormous quantities, missiles and devices for spreading germs were produced, and special army formations were trained for mass contamination of populations, reservoirs, dwellings, crops, and cattle.
>
> The Japanese aggressors not only prepared but frequently used the bacteriological weapon in carrying out their aggressive plans: in 1939 against the Mongolian People's Republic and in the U.S.S.R. in the region of the Khalkhyn–Gol River; in 1940–42 against China in the Ninbo region and others, where bacteriological diversion of the Japanese army spread epidemics of pestilence and typhus.[37]

Stalin tried to make use of "bacteriology" during the Korean war, when epidemics, the inevitable concomitant of a war under the conditions of the Far East, broke out. He considered it clever strategy to hold the Americans responsible for them. This episode in the history of Stalin's "bacteriological war" fable is well remembered. In 1950 the Moscow Academy of Sciences published a book entitled "The Bacteriological War—A Criminal Instrument of Imperialist Aggression." In it the history of preparations for bacteriological wars starts with the first experiments during World War I. Germany, Japan, and, of course,

---

[36] Igor Gouzenko, *The Iron Curtain* (New York: Dutton & Co., 1948), pp. 103–104.

[37] *Large Soviet Encyclopedia*, 2nd ed., IV, 84.

the United States are charged with having engaged in such preparations, but not the Soviet Union.

This somewhat protracted review has been necessary in order to describe and explain Stalin's obsession with the idea of bacteriological warfare as a political weapon. Against this background there can be no doubt as to the source of some of the monstrous charges made at the Pyatakov–Radek trial. The indictment mentioned preparations by the defendants for bacteriological warfare against Soviet troops. In court, Vyshinsky interrogated Ivan Knyazev:

> Knyazev: . . . in October, when my conversation with Mr. X [S. Hiroshima, railway expert at the Japanese Embassy in Moscow] took place, he strongly stressed the necessity that "we not only set the task of merely causing fires, but if necessary of even contaminating the cars which are assigned for the transport of military detachments."
> Vyshinsky: Contaminating with what?
> Knyazev: Bacteria. . . .
> Vyshinsky: But sanitary treatment was mentioned here.
> Knyazev: That's just what I am saying, before the troops are embarked. The cars are made ready twenty-four hours ahead of time, at specific points where they are washed with hot water and then dried, and in the course of this sanitary treatment. . . .
> Vyshinsky: That is to say, they are cleaned?
> Knyazev: Yes.
> Vyshinsky: And what must you do?
> Knyazev: Infect them.
> Vyshinsky: And then fill those cars with people, infect the people, so that they will get sick and die?
> Knyazev: Yes.
> Vyshinsky: He [Mr. X] proposed this to you?
> Knyazev: Yes.
> Vyshinsky: He promised to provide the bacteria at the proper time?

II Stalin's Role in the Charges

Knyazev: Yes.[38]

Demanding the death sentence for Knyazev, Vyshinsky stressed anew the importance of the bacteriological warfare issue in his summation, the text of which must have been edited by Stalin personally:

> ... Knyazev confirmed that the Japanese intelligence service emphatically stressed the necessity of organizing diversive acts by employing bacteria on the outbreak of war for the purpose of infecting troop trains, and also army provision bases and sanitary centres, with highly virulent bacilli.[39]

The Charge of Collaboration with Nazism and Fascism

Collaboration with Germany and Japan was among the most serious charges leveled against the defendants in the Pyatakov–Radek trial. As a matter of fact, this crime, so damaging in Russian eyes, had not been sufficiently stressed in the first trial. Stalin no doubt decided to compromise the Communist opposition by producing evidence that it had cooperated with Nazi Germany and militarist Japan. Trotsky, in fact, maintained that Stalin's chief aim in staging the new trial was to prove the opposition's ties with Germany and Japan. In any event, the "outrageous" deeds of the opposition that were to be "proved and confirmed" in the second trial were:

(1) Agreements between Trotsky and the German and Japanese governments, and contacts between the oppositionist leaders in Russia and German and Japanese representatives inside the country—all on the level of an alliance between them against the Soviet government. According to the indictment:

> ... L. D. Trotsky and his accomplices in the Parallel Center entered into negotiations with agents of foreign states with the object of overthrowing the Soviet government with the aid of armed intervention.[40]

[38] *Proceedings*, pp. 384–385.
[39] *Ibid.*, p. 504.
[40] *Ibid.*, p. 6.

In a "letter" to Radek, Trotsky was alleged to have written:

> It would be absurd to think that we can come to power without securing the favorable attitude of the most important capitalist governments, particularly of the most aggressive ones, such as the present governments of Germany and Japan. It is absolutely necessary to have contacts and an understanding with these governments right now. . . .

The indictment continued:

> The investigation has established that *L. D. Trotsky* entered into negotiations with one of the leaders of the German National–Socialist Party with a view to waging a joint struggle against the Soviet Union.[41]

Pyatakov likewise testified:

> . . . He [Trotsky] then told me that he had conducted rather lengthy negotiations with the Vice-Chairman of the German National–Socialist Party—Hess. . . . Trotsky put it to me as though an agreement existed, one which, it is true, still had to be given definite shape by certain other persons. . . . [42]

(2) Promises of important territorial concessions to Germany and Japan, in particular the turning over of the Ukraine to Germany and the Maritime Province in the Far East to Japan.

This was confirmed in court by the leaders of the alleged Trotskyite–Zinovievite bloc, Pyatakov, Radek, and Sokolnikov. The latter, for example, testified:

> In this agreement [with the Nazis] they [the territorial concessions] were stated as follows: that Japan, in the event of her taking part in the war, would receive territorial concessions in the Far East in the Amur Region and the Maritime Province; as regards Germany, it was contemplated to "satisfy the national interests of the Ukraine." Beneath this transparent veil was understood the establishment of German control over the Ukraine coupled with the secession of the latter from the U.S.S.R.[43]

[41] *Ibid.*, p. 7.
[42] *Ibid.*, p. 64.
[43] *Ibid.*, p. 153.

(3) The supplying of funds by Germany and Japan to the Trotskyite organization in Russia and abroad.

Pyatakov testified that with the help of Trotsky's son, Lev Sedov, an ingenious financial operation had been agreed upon between two well-known German firms (which had no doubt been operating as a cover for German intelligence) and himself, as the head of Soviet economic agencies: he (Pyatakov) would pay excessive prices for the goods of the German companies, the difference to go to Trotsky. Japanese intelligence officials, for their part, gave certain sums directly to members of the "bloc" in Russia.

Defendant Yosif Turok replied to a pertinent question as follows:

>Vyshinsky: . . . did you receive money?
>Turok: Yes, I did.
>Vyshinsky: From the Japanese intelligence service?
>Turok: Yes.
>Vyshinsky: When did you receive money?
>Turok: January 1935—35,000 rubles.
>Vyshinsky: What did you do with it?
>Turok: I kept 20,000 rubles for my own organization and gave 15,000 to Knyazev's organization.
>Vyshinsky: To whom did you hand it over?
>Turok: To Knyazev in person, in May, 1935.
>Vyshinsky: Accused Knyazev, is this correct?
>Knyazev: Yes, I received it.[44]

(4) A projected "adjustment" of the social system of the Soviet Union to that of Germany and Japan. This, according to the prosecutor, meant a return to capitalism.

Trotsky's instructions, which were accepted and obeyed, contained the general advice to "retreat" to capitalism as a consequence of collaboration with Germany and Japan: "Retreat to capitalism. How far and to what degree, it is difficult to say now—this can be made concrete only after we come into power."[45]

[44] *Ibid.*, p. 347.
[45] *Ibid.*, p. 6.

The commitments also included one "to permit German industrialists, in the form of concessions (or some other forms), to exploit enterprises in the U.S.S.R. which are essential as complements to German economy (iron ore, manganese, oil, gold, timber, etc., were meant)." Moreover, in case of war the Soviet Union would, if the opposition won out, have to supply Germany and Japan with goods necessary for their war on the Western powers:

> We shall have to yield the oil of Sakhalin to Japan and to guarantee to supply her with oil in case of war with America. We shall also have to permit her to exploit gold fields. We shall have to agree to Germany's demand not to oppose her seizure of the Danube countries and the Balkans, and not to hinder Japan in her seizure of China.[46]

(5) Supplying secret information to agents of Germany and Japan—espionage in favor of foreign powers.

To understand the origins of these charges against the opposition we must recall the main lines of Soviet policy in regard to Germany and Japan, and especially toward Germany, in the 1930's.

During the entire Soviet period, but particularly in the Stalin era, two mutually contradictory courses of policy toward Germany prevailed. On the one hand Germany was seen as a mighty capitalist nation, a target of the Communist offensive, a great new stage in the world revolution; on the other, capitalist and Nazi Germany was seen as a possible ally against the capitalist West. Soviet political and financial support of German communism were manifestations of the first tendency—an orientation toward a social revolution in Germany; the Rapallo treaty, the contacts between the military forces of the two countries, and the secret production in Russia of arms for Germany illustrate the second trend—toward an alliance with a non–Communist Germany against the West.

The Soviet government and its press naturally reacted violently to Nazi political attacks on Soviet Russia and

[46] *Ibid.*, p. 8.

II Stalin's Role in the Charges   37

communism. In Russian schools and universities, nazism and fascism were the targets of extensive propaganda. The prospect of an alliance with Germány, even a Nazi Germany, was, however, never discarded. Many people still entertain serious misconceptions about the Soviet policy during the period 1935–38. It has often been represented as a radical break with the Soviet past, with the fifteen years of obsession about the role of the "third power," with the policy of collaboration with Germany and antagonism toward the Western powers. Actually, the Kremlin policy of those years continued without the slightest break the old principles, though dressed in a different style.

Kaganovich, with Stalin's consent, of course, stated on January 17, 1934: "If the German government wishes to establish relations with us similar to those that prevailed before the Fascist regime, our government is ready to reciprocate."

On January 28, 1935, when "collective security" was at its height and at the very moment when the Soviet government was preparing the treaty of alliance with France, Molotov told the Seventh Congress of Soviets: "For our part we can say that we have never wished for anything other than the continuance of good relations with Germany...." Even on the eve of the Soviet–French anti-Nazi pact of 1935 Stalin continued to repeat, in meetings of the Politburo, "and with the Germans we have to reach an agreement."

Another year went by, a year filled with reports of German rearmament. On January 10, 1936, Molotov appeared before a session of the Central Executive Committee and submitted his regular report, in which, among other things, he said: "I'll say frankly, the Soviet Government would like to establish better relations with Germany than those existing at present.... But realization of this policy rests not [only] with us but also with the government of Germany...."

Some two months later, on March 19, 1936, Molotov, in an interview with the editor of *Le Temps*, said:

> The main trend among our people, the trend that determines the policy of the Soviet government, considers an improvement in relations between Germany and the Soviet Union possible.... The participation of Germany in the League of Nations would be in the interest of peace and would be favorably regarded by us.

"Even of Hitler Germany?" asked the editor. "Yes," replied Molotov, "even of Hitler Germany."

Along with these open and public offers of conciliation there was much sounding out by the quieter means of diplomacy, only muffled reports of which reached the avid newspaper correspondents and the equally avid diplomats of other powers.

While the Moscow trials were going on, the Soviet government explored the possibility of an agreement with Berlin. It was two or three years, however, before Stalin's efforts were crowned with success. The long–awaited pact was signed in Moscow on August 23, 1939. During all the years from 1933 to 1939 Stalin must have wondered what such an agreement with Germany against the Western powers would mean in practice: what steps would the Soviet government have to take to aid Germany in her opposition to the West or in a German war against the West? The only possible answers were: collaboration in world affairs; agreement about "spheres of interest" in Europe and the Far East; extensive trade; territorial concessions made necessary by the circumstances. The two "variants" that Radek "read" from Trotsky's fictitious letters (a war situation, or no war) would decide the scope of Stalin's compromise. Everything depended on how badly Germany and Japan needed Soviet friendship.

Thus, in the trials of 1936–38 Stalin accused his political opponents of plans and policies in regard to Germany and Japan that he himself was preparing.

In 1939, cooperation with Germany (the "realistic" policy, as Radek termed it in court) became a fact. Supplies of goods, especially food and oil, to warring Germany materialized at the outset of the war, and most of the Balkans were conceded to be a German "sphere."

II Stalin's Role in the Charges

Even the complicated procedure of financing an underground by means of trade and "kickbacks" was derived from Stalin's methods in the Comintern. According to Vyshinsky, as mentioned above, two German firms, Demag and Borsig, were to charge high prices and transmit the overcharges to the Trotskyites. As a matter of fact, in Germany as well as elsewhere, so–called "mixed companies"—Soviet–German and, later, Soviet–Japanese—were organized as agencies for the sale of Soviet goods. A percentage of the proceeds was paid as "brokerage fees" to certain persons or private groups who actually were intermediaries between the local legal or illegal Communist Party and the Soviet Trade Organization. This was a large–scale Soviet plan to finance friendly Communist parties abroad; it still exists and in certain countries works satisfactorily.

Once it was "established" that the defendants—diplomats and trade agents—had been in touch with representatives of a foreign power, it was only a step to the accusation of espionage in favor of that power. Elsewhere, contacts with a citizen of a foreign country are deemed to be a private and harmless occurrence, and the visit of a citizen to a consul of a foreign country is likewise an innocent matter. To the Stalinist mind, however, every contact of this kind is "collaboration," and collaboration means supplying information, and supplying information is espionage.

The Charge of Terrorism

The charge of practicing "individual terror" (that is, attempts on the lives of Soviet leaders), one of the main charges against the defendants in the Pyatakov–Radek trial, had a two–fold meaning.

In the history of the revolutionary movement in Russia, as it is taught throughout the Soviet school system, the transition from the "Populist" (Narodnik) underground trends of "Land and Freedom" (*Zemlya i Volya*) to the "People's Will" (*Narodnaya Volya*) in the late 1870's is an important landmark. The "Land and Freedom" group expected a great popular uprising against the old autocracy, and therefore devoted its substantial intellectual forces mainly to "propaganda" among the Russian peasants. The movement, however, proved unsuccessful, and a group of the leading "Populists" organized the "People's Will," which held to the belief that the overthrow of the Russian autocracy must be achieved by means of "individual terror," that is, assassination of the leaders of the government. The assassination of Tsar Alexander II in 1881 was the most notorious, though not the only, terroristic act of *Narodnaya Volya*.

Transition from "mass movements" to tactics of "individual terror" implied disappointment in popular movements. "Terrorism," wrote Lenin, "was a result, as well as a symptom and concomitant, of distrust in an uprising and of the lack of prerequisites for an uprising."[47]

Stalin not only shared these views of Lenin but himself emphasized them in one of his books.

> The Narodniks first endeavored to rouse the peasants for a struggle against the tsarist government.... But they found no backing among the peasantry.... The majority of them were arrested by the police. Thereupon the Narodniks decided to continue the struggle against the tsarist autocracy single-handed, without the people, and this led to even more serious mistakes.
>
> A secret Narodnik society known as "Narodnaya Volya" ("People's Will") began to plot the assassination of the tsar. On March 1, 1881, members of the "Narodnaya Volya" succeeded in killing Tsar Alexander II with a bomb. But the people did not benefit from this in any way.[48]

The above passage was written about the time that the great Moscow trials were taking place. The ideas contained in it were incorporated in the indictments. The charge that the Communist opposition, which had previously set its hopes on the labor movement, had now turned to guns and

[47] V. I. Lenin, *Sochineniya* (Works), 3rd ed., IX, 26.
[48] *History of the Communist Party of the Soviet Union (Bolsheviks) Short Course* (Moscow: Foreign Languages Publishing House, 1939), p. 10.

II Stalin's Role in the Charges

bombs was to be proof of its loss of faith in popular support, especially from the Russian workers. The defendants had to spell out this version of the accusation: the assassination of Kirov, alleged to have been carried out by the oppositionist groups as their first act of terrorism, was comparable to the assassination of Tsar Alexander II fifty-three years before by the Populists.

The opposition no longer counted on the support of the Russian people—this was what Stalin intended to prove by the trials. A statement to that effect was drawn from nearly every one of the defendants. Pyatakov, for instance, described his (fictitious) conversation with Lev Sedov in Berlin:

> ... Sedov went on to outline the nature of the new methods of struggle: there could be no question of developing a mass struggle in any form, of organizing a mass movement; if we adopted any kind of mass work, we would come to grief immediately; Trotsky was firmly in favor of the forcible overthrow of the Stalin leadership by methods of terrorism and wrecking.[49]

Norkin testified:

> As for internal forces, we had reckoned on the masses, at first to a greater extent. Subsequently the masses disappeared, and we began to reckon on elements who had an interest in a change of policy— that is to say, on kulak and capitalist elements.[50]

Vyshinsky interrogated Sokolnikov on the same issue:

> Vyshinsky: Specifically on what forces within the country did you calculate? On the working class?
> Sokolnikov: No.
> Vyshinsky: On the collective farm peasantry?
> Sokolnikov: Of course not.
> Vyshinsky: On whom then?

[49] *Proceedings*, p. 23.
[50] *Ibid.*, p. 290.

Sokolnikov: To speak quite frankly, I must say that we reckoned on being able to rely on the elements of the peasant bourgeoisie. . . .
Vyshinsky: On the kulaks, on the few remnants of the kulaks?
Sokolnikov: That is so. . . .[51]

Shestov testified: "We had no support whatever among the workers and peasants. . . . "; and the witness Vladimir Loginov said: " . . . it was impossible to rely on the workers and proletarian masses within the country. . . . "[52]

The accusation of terrorism had another motive. The list of Soviet personalities "chosen" by the terrorists for assassination—inclusion in the list was a mark of honor in the prosecution's eyes—was as follows: first, of course, Stalin; then Molotov, Kaganovich, Voroshilov, Ordzhonikidze, and Zhdanov; then top leaders from Kiev, Postyshev and Kossior;[53] the then secretary of the West–Siberian Committee of the Communist Party, Robert Eikhe, later alternate candidate to the Politburo; and two NKVD men, Yezhov and Beria. Yezhov, who, as we have seen, was little known before, was receiving an early honor by being included in the list; the inclusion of Beria was significant because, while still an obscure personality in the Caucasus, he was already rising in Stalin's eyes as a future aide and disciple.

Strange things must have happened to Molotov during this period. For a time his name disappeared from the list of "victims"; this was a terrible omen. In the Zinoviev–Kamenev trial the list of victims included the other leaders but not Prime Minister Molotov. This fact was widely discussed at the time.[53] The prosecutor, Vyshinsky, had omitted Molotov from the list of "our wonderful Bolsheviks, the tireless and gifted builders of our state," in his speech of accusation. In his bloodthirsty article (*Izvestia*, August 21, 1936) condemning "the enemies of the people," Radek

---

[51] *Ibid.*, p. 155.
[52] *Ibid.*, pp. 162, 180.
[53] See, for instance, *Byulleten' Oppozitsii*, no. 54–55 (March, 1937), p. 37; Alexander Orlov, *The Secret History of Stalin's Crime*, (New York: Random House, 1953), p. 69.

II Stalin's Role in the Charges

likewise omitted (or was instructed to omit) Molotov as a target of terrorism. He listed only Stalin, Kirov, Voroshilov, Ordzhonikidze, and Kaganovich. Later that year, after his reconciliation with Stalin, Molotov was restored to the list of prospective victims. He was even rewarded for his mortal anxiety by an exceptionally involved story of "attempts" on his life during his trip to the east.[54] He could breathe again.

All over the country, according to the accusation, the "Parallel Center" had set up "terrorist groups" with the main objective of organizing attempts upon the lives of Soviet leaders. The defendants in the Pyatakov–Radek trial testified that "terror groups" were at work in twenty places, in some of which there were several units. The groups named at the trial were those in Moscow, Leningrad, Kiev, Rostov/Don, Sochi, Novosibirsk, Ural, Tula, Odessa, Dnepropetrovsk, Kuzbass, Omsk, Tomsk, Prokop'evsk, Anzherka, Kemerovo, the West Siberian center, the Ukrainian center, the Transcaucasian center, and the Siberian center.

The "leaders" of these underground groups were invariably prominent Communists, more often than not first secretaries of local party organizations; many were members of the Central Committee. In rank they were equivalent to governors of states in the United States or prefects of departments in France. All of them, along with the members of the "terror committees," were arrested and purged.

... The investigative materials of that time show [states Khrushchev] that in almost all *krais, oblasts* [provinces] and republics there supposedly existed "rightist Trotskyite, espionage–terror and diversionary–sabotage organizations and centers" and that the heads of such organizations as a rule—for no known reason—were first secretaries of *oblast* or republic Communist Party committees or central committees.

Many thousands of honest and innocent Communists have died as a result of this monstrous falsification of

---

[54] *See* page 108.

such "cases," as a result of the fact that all kinds of slanderous "confessions" were accepted, and as a result of the practice of forcing accusations against oneself and others. In the same manner were fabricated the "cases" against eminent party and state workers— Kossior, Chubar, Postyshev, Kosarev and others.[55]

The absurdity of the charges is also seen from the fact that despite their numbers, their connections in the highest circles of the Communist Party, and the easy access they had to every leader, the "terrorists" were charged at the Pyatakov–Radek trial with only two specific acts of "individual terror," strangely unsuccessful attempts, namely, the attempts on the lives of Molotov and Ordzhonikidze. It would seem logical, too, that if these two leaders were to be killed, the killing should be carried out by terrorist groups in Moscow, where the intended victims lived. Instead, the Trotskyite "conspirators" assigned their men in the far–off Kuznetsk Basin to perform this task by means of automobile "accidents" while the victims were visiting in the area.

Automobile Accidents

The automobile "accident" method of terror is revealing of the authorship of the "terror" fabrication. A number of well–known personalities, Russian and non–Russian, opponents of Stalin, had died in the Soviet Union in automobile and other "accidents." The French bulletin *Est et Ouest* (Paris, March 16–31, 1957, p. 24) calls attention to some of these accidents and makes the conclusion unavoidable that the automobile accident was one of Stalin's favorite methods of doing away with his political opponents. In his secret report to the 20th Congress, Khrushchev revealed some facts connected with the assassination of Kirov in December, 1934, among them the fact that Kirov's bodyguard, a member of the NKVD, was killed, the day after Kirov's death, in an automobile accident on his way to an interrogation about the death of his chief.

It is an unusually suspicious circumstance that when the Chekist [member of the secret police] assigned to

[55] Khrushchev's secret report of February 24, 1956.

II Stalin's Role in the Charges

protect Kirov was being brought for an interrogation, on December 2, 1934, he was killed in a car "accident" in which no other occupants of the car were harmed.

After the murder of Kirov, top functionaries of the Leningrad NKVD were given very light sentences, but in 1937 they were shot. We can assume that they were shot in order to cover the traces of the organizers of Kirov's killing.[56]

Stalin's role in the Kirov affair, although not clear in detail, has been established beyond any doubt.

Est et Ouest recalls the case of Mikhail Lashevich, an Old Bolshevik, who was killed in an automobile accident in Siberia in 1928. Lashevich had been a political friend of Zinoviev and a passionate opponent of Stalin. According to *Est et Ouest*, "Lashevich's friendship with Zinoviev provoked Stalin's enmity; he was exiled to Siberia and died in a fatal 'automobile accident.' "

In 1946 the Iranian Communist leader, Pishevari, was reported to have been killed in an automobile accident in Soviet Central Asia. Pishevari had been assigned to lead the Communist uprising in northern Iran after the Soviet troops were forced to withdraw. The program obviously called for the transformation of Iranian Azerbaidjan into a "people's republic," a satellite of Moscow. For a short time Pishevari headed the new government in Tabriz. When, however, Washington and London assumed a belligerent attitude, Stalin decided to withdraw, and the new "republic" was easily recovered by loyal Iranian forces. Pishevari and a few other leaders escaped to Soviet Azerbaidjan along with about 10,000 of their men. Subsequently all except the leaders were resettled around Kirovabad. The life there was hard, and when the refugees started to protest, Pishevari and two others set out for Kirovabad to quiet them. An "accident" occurred on the way in which Pishevari was killed instantly and one of his companions suffered a broken arm; the driver and the others in the party were unhurt. Well-informed Iranian leaders are certain that Pishevari was killed because he

[56] *Ibid.*

was talking too much about mistakes that had been made during the revolt.

In the light of this background of "automobile accidents" the alleged attempt on the life of Molotov comes into proper focus. That plot was the child of the same brain that had applied the "automobile accident" method more than once before.

III THE DEFENDANTS

With the Bukharin group eliminated from the list of the accused, the aim of the new trial was to destroy the last remnants of the Trotskyites. The chief defendants, therefore were: Pyatakov, Radek, Leonid Serebryakov, and Nikolai Muralov, all of whom had taken part in the strife of the 1920's.

The group of leaders around Trotsky in the mid-1920's [Natalia Sedov, Trotsky's widow, related to the author] met regularly in our apartment in the Kremlin once and sometimes twice a week. Usually there were present Pyatakov, Radek, Rakovsky, Serebryakov, Smirnov, Preobrazhensky, Smilga. Toward the end of this period, in 1926–27, after the reconciliation, Zinoviev and Kamenev also used to appear. The opposition was legal at the time; in the beginning we had no reason to hide. Later, when Stalin organized the tapping of our wires, we ceased to discuss our affairs by 'phone, and personal visits became more frequent. When Party conferences were taking place and our friends from the provinces were among the delegates, we met in other houses, put at our disposal by our members or friends.

The six, seven, or eight men mentioned above were, each in his own way, interesting and well-known. Pyatakov enjoyed general esteem for his seriousness, quietness, and devotion; Preobrazhensky had the theoretical brain; Smirnov inspired respect by his honesty and firmness; Rakovsky was Trotsky's personal friend. On the other hand, personal relations between Trotsky and the Zinoviev–Kamenev duo,

III The Defendants

even after the rapprochement, never became close. Once they urged Trotsky to go out to the industrial plants and try to arouse the workers against Stalin; Trotsky was very dubious about this because he felt the masses were tired. He himself viewed Zinoviev and Kamenev as men of feeble character; he often used to recall Lenin's remark about Zinoviev that he could "serve as a barometer of approaching danger."

Yuri Pyatakov

Pyatakov's service to the Communist Party can be judged by the fact that he was one of the six leaders mentioned by Lenin in his testament as comprising the best collective leadership in the future. (In addition to Pyatakov, the list contained the names of Trotsky, Stalin, Zinoviev, Kamenev, and Bukharin, in that order.)

Pyatakov, born in 1890, was the son of a well-to-do general manager of a sugar refinery near Kiev who, when he died, left an estate of more than three million rubles. From the age of fourteen Pyatakov belonged to revolutionary student groups. In 1905 he was expelled from high school for revolutionary activities. The following year he joined the anarchists, and first belonged to a clandestine body of "expropriators." In 1907 he joined an anarchist-terrorist group which planned an attempt on the life of the Governor–General of Kiev, Vladimir Sukhomlinov.

Pyatakov entered the University of St. Petersburg and soon embraced Marxism in the most orthodox, Bolshevik form; he tended always to assume the most extreme ideological and political position in his party. After several arrests and deportation, he escaped in 1914 from Siberia to Japan; he went from there to Switzerland, where he met Lenin. With Lenin and Bukharin, Pyatakov published the "theoretical" magazine *Kommunist*; differences, however, arose between the more flexible Lenin and the diehards Pyatakov and Bukharin. In 1916 Pyatakov moved from Switzerland to Scandinavia, where he lived until the outbreak of the revolution in 1917.

Returning to Kiev in the early days of the revolution, Pyatakov became a member of the local Bolshevik committee. In September, 1917 he was elected chairman of the Kiev Soviet, and in October of that year chairman of the "Revolutionary Committee." In 1918, he disagreed with Lenin, opposed the signing of the Brest–Litovsk treaty, returned to the Ukraine, and joined Bolshevik military units. During the Civil War his activities were devoted to the Red Army, but in 1921, when the war ended, he was assigned to a post in industry and was soon appointed deputy chairman of the Supreme Council of National Economy.

In 1922 Pyatakov served as president of a special tribunal to try the leaders of the Socialist–Revolutionary Party. The trial attracted worldwide attention, and a group of Western lawyers and political leaders, most of them Socialists, came to Russia to defend the twenty-two men and women in the dock; despite their efforts, the tribunal sentenced twelve defendants to death. The sentences, however, were not carried out. Fifteen years later, when Pyatakov was fighting for his own life, he must certainly have recalled his role in the Socialist–Revolutionary trial.

In 1923 Pyatakov, now a high-ranking member of the Party as well as of the state machine, joined Trotsky and his associates while continuing his services to Soviet economic institutions, which were absorbing more and more of his interest. His heart and soul were with the industrialization projects. "I cannot imagine," he told his friends, "how I can stand aside if our industrialization plans are to be carried out." By 1925–26 he was becoming somewhat tired of opposition and high-level political activity. Though he remained a member of Trotsky's group and continued his personal contacts with it, he was moving away from the fight against Stalin and Stalin's regime.[57] He continued as a member of the party's Central Committee after 1930, and as Vice Commissar of Heavy Industry he wielded more power and exerted greater influence than his superior, Grigori Ordzhonikidze, the People's Commissar.

[57] "If a revolution breaks out tonight [Trotsky used to joke about his friend Pyatakov], tomorrow morning Yuri Leonidovich will take his briefcase and go to his office."

III The Defendants

In the 1930's, as one of the creators of the second Five-Year Plan, and as one who had turned his back on Trotsky years before and was completely devoted to his job, Pyatakov was in no sense an oppositionist, a fact that Stalin was well aware of. But to add weight to the new trial and establish the pattern of a "Parallel Center" of the Trotskyites, Stalin had to sacrifice one or two of his most able lieutenants. In addition, Stalin never forgot a single person who had ever opposed him. For both these reasons, Pyatakov, a prominent former Trotskyite, was to be destroyed.

Karl Radek

Radek, better known abroad than any of his co-defendants, was a brilliant journalist, a man of knowledge and wit. Born in 1885 in Lwow (the Austrian part of Poland), he became an ardent Polish patriot in his youth; his dream was to see the three parts of Poland—the Russian, the German, and the Austrian—reintegrated into one nation. Since this could be brought about only by opposing the will of the three governments, Radek developed into a nationalist revolutionary. Revolutionary nationalism brought him into the fold of revolutionary socialism. He was expelled from high school for his revolutionary activities, went to Krakow, and at an early age began to write for the Socialist press; he joined the left-wing of the Polish Socialists. In 1904–05 Radek spent some time in Switzerland, where he met Lenin and Zinoviev; later, in Warsaw, he met the older leaders of leftist Polish socialism, Rosa Luxemburg, Adolf Warski, and Jan Tyszka. After several arrests in Russia, Radek was deported to Austria in 1907, but by 1908 he was in Germany, where he began to work for leftist Socialist papers in Bremen and Leipzig. Always with the extreme wing, Radek, along with several Socialist leaders, tried, in 1914, after the outbreak of the war, to organize the German extreme left. The effort did not succeed, although members of the group comprised the embryo of the future Spartakus Bund. In Switzerland again, Radek collaborated with Lenin and took part in the Zimmerwald and Kiental conferences, the first attempts to organize what later became the Communist International.

Radek made the famous trip through Germany with Lenin in April, 1917. During the Kerensky period he was in Stockholm, serving as Lenin's representative abroad, and came to Petrograd after the November revolution. Lenin soon sent him back to Sweden to start negotiations with the German government; he accompanied Trotsky to Brest–Litovsk for the peace negotiations. From that time on his main interest was foreign affairs. In 1919 he spent ten months in a German prison, maintaining from behind bars connections with the German Foreign Office, and German political personalities. He was recognized as an outstanding representative of Soviet communism. In 1920–21 he was a member of the Central Committee, but not of the Politburo.

Radek became secretary of the new Communist International in March, 1920; in 1922 he took part in the conference of the "Three Internationals" in Berlin—the last effort to unite the Socialist and Communist groups. In 1924 he joined Trotsky. He was not re-elected to the Executive Committee of the Comintern, nor was he elected to the Central Committee of the Soviet Communist party. Stalin hated him for two reasons—because he was a Trotskyite, and because he was the originator of a multitude of bitter jokes pointed at the "Great Leader." For all his ability and knowledge, Radek did not enjoy universal esteem and confidence either in the Party or among the Trotskyites. Clever, but over–cynical, he was considered unstable and unreliable; he was a controversial figure; this was the reason he never attained a more enduring position in Lenin's entourage.

At the time of the break between Stalin and Zinoviev [wrote Trotsky] Radek tried to lead the leftist opposition into a bloc with Stalin.... But inside the opposition he was always tossing between the right and the left. In 1929 Radek capitulated [to Stalin] not with any hidden aims. oh no!—he capitulated unreservedly, definitely, burning all bridges behind him, to become a most outstanding mouthpiece of the bureaucracy.[58]

From 1930 on, Radek served Stalin loyally in the field of foreign affairs; his articles and statements were studied in the foreign offices of all capitals. In 1930 he demonstrated, in a despicable way, his new loyalty to Stalin by denouncing Yakov Blyumkin, the Trotskyite, to the GPU. (It was Blyumkin who had carried Trotsky's message from Turkey to Russia, for which he was executed.)

Nikolai Muralov

Muralov, born in 1877 near Taganrog, came from a peasant family with leftist traditions. His father had spent two years in England, where he had met Alexander Herzen, the famous Russian revolutionary emigré, and had become his ardent follower. Muralov worked for a time as a farm manager, came in contact with Socialist groups in Moscow in 1901–02, joined the Bolsheviks in 1905, and fought on the Moscow barricades in December of that year. In 1907 he was the manager of a "restaurant" where, in the back, Bolshevik leaflets and other "literature" were printed clandestinely.

During the first World War Muralov served in the Russian army, and in 1917 was one of the organizers of the Soldiers' Section of the Moscow Soviet. He fought as a high–ranking officer at various posts during the Civil War, helped Trotsky in the creation of the Red Army, and, in March, 1921, was appointed commander of the Moscow Army District. In 1922 he was delegated to "special assignments" for the Revolutionary Military Council.

As a member of Trotsky's group since 1923, Muralov was one of the most devoted and reliable opponents of Stalin's regime.

Leonid Serebryakov

Serebryakov, born in 1890 in Samara, was one of the six sons of a metal worker. Constantly in need, the family

[58] *Byulleten' Oppozitsii*, no. 54–55, (March, 1937), p. 11.

moved from one city to another as the father changed jobs. At the age of twelve Leonid was working in a brewery for one ruble twenty kopeks (sixty cents) a week. By 1905, the fifteen–year–old boy was in the Bolshevik Party.

Between 1905 and 1917 Serebryakov was arrested several times, deported, and for a time lived in exile. During the first years of the war (1914–16) he was active in Moscow and Leningrad; in 1917 he was already a leader of the Moscow Bolsheviks. Quiet, serious, stable, without systematic education and with little knowledge of world affairs, a man of "proletarian origin," a pure type of Russian leftist revolutionary worker, Serebryakov attracted the attention of, and was highly valued by the new leadership, especially after the November revolution. He advanced rapidly to become secretary of the Party's Central Committee and member of the Presidium of the All–Russian Central Executive Committee. From 1921 on he worked in the People's Commissariat of Transport as a member of the so–called Collegium. He was one of the first to join Trotsky's opposition, and was one of its staunchest members up to the rout in the late '20's.

Grigori Sokolnikov

Sokolnikov, born in 1888 in Poltava province, son of a physician, had received a good education in the high schools of Moscow. He joined a Marxist student group in his youth, and in 1905 the Moscow Bolshevik organization, becoming a "propagandist" among textile and typographical workers. Arrested in 1907 and exiled in 1908, he emigrated to France. During the war years he collaborated with Trotsky in the internationalist newspaper *Nashe Slovo* in Paris. Up to the revolution he lived abroad, where he acquired knowledge and experience. He was well–read, spoke several languages, and on the eve of the revolution was one of the best prepared of the Bolsheviks.

Sokolnikov returned with Lenin to Petrograd in April, 1917 and in that year was elected to the Central Committee; he also was, along with Stalin, a member of the editorial board of *Pravda*. Sokolnikov belonged to the Soviet delegation to the Brest–Litovsk conference and signed the peace treaty with Germany in March, 1918. Soon after, he carried out the nationalization of Russian banking institutions.

During the Civil War Sokolnikov occupied posts of command, first at the eastern front, then at the southern front, and in 1920 in Central Asia. From 1921 on he worked in the People's Commissariat of Finance; in 1922 he was appointed People's Commissar of Finance and held this post until 1926. Financial reforms and stabilization of the ruble were his outstanding accomplishments. He supported the "new opposition" (Zinoviev–Kamenev) in the mid–20's; as a result he was removed from his post in the financial agency and assigned to lesser ones in the Gosplan and in the Naphta Syndicate. He was not expelled from the Party, however, and in 1929 was appointed ambassador to London. He remained in England until 1932 and subsequently served in Moscow as Assistant People's Commissar of Foreign Affairs.

Despite his temporary "deviation," Sokolnikov was considered so loyal to Stalin's party that at the 15th, 16th, and 17th Congresses (1927, 1930, and 1934) he was elected to the Central Committee (in 1927 as a member and in 1930 and 1934 as an alternate). He was the last one against whom charges of Trotskyism, wrecking, and treason might be expected.

Mikhail Boguslavsky

Boguslavsky, born in 1886 near Kremenchug, son of a poor Jewish tailor, had had an unhappy childhood and youth. At the age of twelve, before completing his early schooling, he had to go to work. He began in his father's tailor shop, then became a typesetter in a printing plant, but he was unable to complete his apprenticeship. By the time he was thirteen he had descended to the depths of the social sea: himself a hunchback, he was guiding a blind man, the two earning their living by begging in the yards of the city. Their nights were spent in a cheap lodging house among the blind, the crippled, and the sick.

When he was about eighteen Boguslavsky finally completed his apprenticeship as a compositor. He soon joined an embryonic trade union in Kiev, and at the same time became a member of the non–Bolshevik Jewish Socialist Party. He was arrested several times between 1905 and 1917; when free, he was active in the trade union and cooperative movements. It was not until February, 1917 that he joined the Bolshevik Party.

His influence and rise to power in the Soviet era began at the fronts in the Ukraine. He fought the Germans in 1918, the Ukrainian Rada in 1919, and Denikin's White armies somewhat later. In 1922 he was elected Vice Chairman of the Moscow Soviet; in September, 1924 he was appointed chairman of the so–called "Small [Inner] Council of People's Commissars." This able, ranking Soviet official "of proletarian origin" would certainly have attained still higher posts had he not joined Trotsky's opposition. Despite his "capitulation," along with the other Trotskyites, his antagonism to Stalin cost him his career, his liberty, and, in the end, his life.

Yakov Drobnis

Drobnis, born in the North Ukraine in 1890, was the son of a shoemaker and at the age of twelve became a cobbler's apprentice. Since 1906 he was member of the Social–Democratic Party; he was arrested more than once and spent six years in prison.

Taking part in the Civil War in the Ukraine, Drobnis was "executed" by a Ukrainian guerilla troop (he had only been wounded, and eventually recovered). On three other occasions he was at the point of being executed; on one occasion he was held as a hostage.

Drobnis had been chairman of the "Small [Inner] Council of People's Commissars" in 1923. He joined the Trotsky opposition at its very beginning and was expelled from the Communist Party in 1927. He was restored to membership in 1929 and worked in the People's Commissariat of Communications.

IV THE INVESTIGATION

The methods and procedures of the NKVD investigation in the Pyatakov–Radek case were the same as those that had been applied in the long series of earlier Soviet political cases, except that as the investigation of this case was nearing its end, something new was added to the arsenal of NKVD weapons—the extracting of confessions.

Stalin viewed the confession—the main goal in this investigation—as the all-powerful weapon of the government against the defendants, and Vyshinsky carried out Stalin's instructions with servility though he was well aware that confessions could be proved false. In the assignment to each defendant of the particular role he was to play, a confession of having committed certain criminal acts was the most essential part. Various means were applied to extract the "confessions."

The Appeal to Loyalty

The demand of the investigators and the prosecutor that a defendant admit to having committed certain crimes was often coupled with an appeal to his loyalty as a Party member; if such confession meant self-degradation, admission of counter-revolutionary or dishonest, criminal, and terrorist activities, this was one of the sacrifices that a loyal Party member must bring to the altar of communism. We should not, however, exaggerate the effectiveness of this kind of appeal. In fact, an appeal to loyalty to the Party would have had no effect had it not been accompanied by other, more impressive, arguments. The first of these was that the defendants, all of whom had been expelled from the Communist Party and later pardoned and permitted to return (many had been twice expelled and rehabilitated), were in the position of criminals on parole, obliged to be docile and to supply ever new proofs of their loyalty. If they refused to testify in the manner suggested by the prosecution, their fate was sealed and their death imminent. If they complied, they might save their lives.

For a ranking Soviet Communist who has served the Party for years there is no such thing as resuming non-party status. If he is out of the Party, he has lost all the rights and privileges of a free citizen; he must go to a place of exile (as in the case of the members of the opposition in the late '20's), or a concentration camp, or pay with his life.

Membership in the Communist Party, however, deprived the defendants of important arguments and made self-defense difficult. The charges preferred against them were, of course, false, but was this fact of any importance? In the long years before they had joined the opposition, or in the years after they left the opposition, they had approved, more than once, the show trials organized by the Soviet government against other opposition elements. They had made speeches and written articles to prove how great was the danger to the Soviet system from these actually innocent men. Was their own case different in principle from that of the men accused in the old show trials? During these same long years they had maintained, in numerous speeches, articles, and books, that opposition to the Soviet regime is opposition to communism, that opposition to communism is counter–revolution, that counter–revolution is treason—and that treason is action in favor of international capitalism and restoration of capitalism in Russia. They held to the peculiar Soviet logic that in a dictatorial Communist system, opposition of even the mildest kind works in favor of restoration of capitalism and must be suppressed by every means.

The defendants were, of course, not guilty in the ordinary sense, but there were dark spots in their past that would suffice, according to this chain of Communist syllogisms, to prove their guilt. When they broke with the opposition, between 1927 and 1936, did they denounce their friends and co–oppositionists to the Soviet police? No, they simply turned their backs on Trotsky, Zinoviev, and Kamenev and took up work in a Soviet agency. They knew about groups representing anti–Stalinist trends that continued to meet to discuss Russian and world affairs. Did they inform the GPU (NKVD) about the dangers posed

IV The Investigation

by these groups and their leaders? Failure to denounce constitutes participation in a criminal act, and when the act is of such magnitude as to constitute treason to the state, those who fail to denounce are equally guilty and must be punished accordingly. The defendants had more than once in the past approved and promoted these very ideas when others were in the dock. Could they now deny this peculiar logic when it applied to themselves?

Self–defense was more difficult for party members than for those not affiliated with a political organization. Orlov, for example, reports the case of the non–Communist teacher Nelidov who refused to confess that he had collaborated with the Trotskyites. Kedrov, the cruel NKVD investigator,

> ... was unable to break Nelidov. Nelidov had one big advantage over the rest of the accused: coming from an aristocratic family which had been ruined by the revolution and being a non–party man, he was entirely free from any sense of duty toward the Party. No casuistical arguments could have persuaded Nelidov that he must kneel before the Party and testify falsely for the sake of its "monolithic unity."
>
> Thus, the intention of the chiefs of the investigation to demonstrate at the trial that there was a collaboration between the Trotskyites and the grandson of a czarist ambassador, on the basis of a terrorist program, failed.[59]

Compared to this attitude of a non–political and non–party man, the posture of the Communist leaders as defendants often lacked courage, vision, and self–respect. One of the defendants in the Bukharin–Rykov trial, Nikolai Krestinsky, tried to retract his confession, but failed. Two men among the scores of defendants in the trials, the trade union leader Mikhail Tomsky and General Yan Gamarnik, found the real answer to the accusations—they committed suicide.

Threats to the Family

Appeals to the loyalty of the defendants were often

[59] A. Orlov, *The Secret History of Stalin's Crimes, op. cit.*, p. 80.

coupled with threats of arrest, prosecution, and punishment of their wives or other members of their families. We must bear in mind that most of the defendants in this trial were in their forties and fifties, affectionate fathers of families. The thought that members of their families would share their fate in other cells and undergo the same ordeal of interrogation was a powerful inducement to "confession." Sometimes the defendant met his arrested wife "by accident" in the hallway of the prison or the NKVD building; in some cases he was compelled to listen to the terrible screams of women being interrogated by the NKVD in an adjacent room. More than a few of the defendants were broken (or, in Soviet police slang, "split") in this way.

Witnesses

The testimony of witnesses was also used to extract "confessions" from the accused and make it more difficult for them to try to retract their statements.

Witnesses were of two kinds. First there were the co-defendants who had already been broken and were willing to cooperate. Having signed confessions of their own crimes and having agreed to play their assigned roles in the "plots," they were prepared to "expose" the others and give the court "all the details." This was the most degrading and disgusting part of the trial—the lies, slander, and mud thrown against friends, relatives, superiors, and subordinates. It was the mass of damaging testimony incriminating him that convinced the more stubborn defendant that there was no sense in denying the charges: a multitude of witnesses would "expose" him again and again. We know, for example, that one group of defendants in the Zinoviev–Kamenev trial, by "revealing" the names of their collaborators, provided the impetus for the second trial. We also know of the confrontation between Kamenev and Sokolnikov following which Sokolnikov became one of the first of the defendants in the second trial to break and "confess."

Witnesses of a Special Kind

In addition to the defendants themselves accusing their

IV The Investigation

co-defendants, there was, in each of the great trials, a group of witnesses recruited from quite another milieu. To extract the confessions and to guard against possible retraction of statements in court, the prosecutor and the investigating agency assigned a number of NKVD men to play the roles of co-defendants and denouncers. These NKVD men were sent to jail, they signed "confessions" like the other defendants, and "exposed" their co-defendants in accordance with the requirements of the NKVD. Their names appeared in the indictments and they were present in court in the roles assigned to them—as Trotskyites, wreckers, German spies, killers, counter-revolutionists; they proved the thesis of the prosecution that opposition to Stalin leads "inevitably" to the most heinous crimes against individuals and the nation. In their fictitious personalities they combined all those characteristics that the prosecution needed to prove to demand death for the defendants. In the first trial, August 19–24, 1936, Fritz David, Konon Berman-Yurin, and Valentin Olberg played just such a role. In the Pyatakov-Radek trial there were at least two and probably more NKVD agents among the defendants.

It was not easy for Yezhov's agency to find persons suitable for this special job. The lower strata of NKVD men could not be entrusted with such a delicate and difficult task. What was needed were politically educated, intelligent men with real understanding of Party affairs, able to orient themselves in every court situation, parry possible attacks by their co-defendants, and never reveal to the public and the press their true status. One of their most important tasks was to impress foreigners with their sincerity and truthfulness.

This peculiar assignment was not the worst of the jobs given to these old hands of the secret police in the course of the years. Loyal Stalinists, they could be certain that once the trial was over they would be free to return to their police service. If a death sentence should be pronounced against them it would never be carried out. They were sadly unaware of what was in store for them. Because of the requirements made of such persons, the NKVD had a difficult task in their selection.

After the Zinoviev–Kamenev trial Trotsky was in a position to reveal the truth about Olberg, and show how he had tried over a period of years to penetrate Trotsky's personal and political secrets, win his confidence, and enter his organization.

The two NKVD agents among the defendants of the Pyatakov–Radek trial were Ivan Hrasche and Alexei Shestov.

Ivan Hrasche, a Czech by birth, member of the Russian Communist Party for about twenty years at the time of the trial, had served the Cheka–GPU since 1919. He was sent to Czechoslovakia in 1919 on a secret mission; on his return to Russia he took part, as a Czech delegate, in the second and third Congresses of the Communist International, and continued his police services throughout the '20's. In the late '20's, as an employee of the chemical industry (he was working there as a GPU man), he made trips abroad, in particular to Berlin, where his assignment was to recruit German engineers and workers for Soviet industry. He visited Denmark and made friends with a number of Danish Communists, but only those who were loyal Stalinists. When his name was mentioned in the press in connection with the Pyatakov–Radek trial, his friends abroad came out with numerous statements about his loyalty to the Soviet government and refutations of his statements made in court. His Czech and Danish Communist friends revealed part of the truth about him as far as they knew it. One of the Danish Communist leaders, the very loyal Tieger Tiegerson, stated, "I think what Hrasche said during the investigation is pure invention" (*Politiken*, January 28, 1937). This statement cost the unfortunate Tiegerson his job.

Hrasche mentioned three other Danish "Trotskyites" in his testimony in court—the engineer Windfeld-Hansen, the writer Sigward Lund, and the teacher Kierulf–Nielsen. The pro-Stalinist Danish Communist paper *Arbeterbladet* omitted the names of two of these, Kierulf–Nielsen and Lund, in its reports on the Moscow trials, because both

IV The Investigation

men were well known in Denmark as being completely devoted to the orthodox line of communism.[60]

The nature of the assignment given Hrasche in connection with the trial is seen from his testimony. Asked by Vyshinsky whether and when he was a member of the Trotskyite organization, he made a statement that had obviously been put in his mouth before the trial:

> I regard Trotskyism as a sum of certain convictions, and I, as a spy, am not entitled to have such convictions. ... I came in contact with Trotskyism on the basis of my espionage and wrecking activities.[61]

This statement was intended to prove not only that Trotskyites were spies for foreign powers, but also that professional non–political spies were attracted by the Trotskyites organization and joined its ranks.

Alexander Orlov, himself a high–ranking NKVD officer at the time, says about Hrasche:

> ... Hrasche worked officially in the Foreign Division of the Administration for Chemical Industry in Moscow. In his official capacity Hrasche was in charge of hiring foreign specialists for work in the USSR. His secret work for the NKVD consisted mainly in directing the secret informers among the employees of the Chemical Administration and in supervising the foreign specialists from the point of view of state security.
>
> The Economic Administration of the NKVD valued Hrasche very highly, because as a foreigner himself (a former Austrian subject) he spoke several European languages fluently and easily made friends with foreign engineers, some of whom he enlisted as secret agents of the NKVD.[62]

Alexei Shestov, the second of the two NKVD men among the defendants at the Pyatakov–Radek trial, had

---

[60] A well–documented article on Hrasche appeared in *Byulleten' Oppozitsii*, no. 54–55, (March, 1937), pp. 39–40. See also *The Case of Leon Trotsky*, (Harper and Brothers, New York, 1937), pp. 231–235.

[61] *Proceedings*, pp. 427, 430.

[62] Orlov, *op. cit.*, p. 174.

been a mining engineer in the Kuznetsk Coal Basin in Western Siberia and played a role in the Novosibirsk trial (see page 76). He testified about his "meetings" with Trotsky's son Lev Sedov abroad, about carrying their letters to Russia, preparing attempts on the life of Molotov, the killing of an engineer, the perpetrating of explosions in coal mines, assassinations of children, bank robberies, spying for foreign powers, and other activities. His "crimes" were so numerous and so horrible that prosecutor Vyshinsky on occasion tried to stop the eloquent flow of his recital of them.

Obligatory Torture

An innovation introduced by Yezhov soon after he took over direction of the NKVD was *obligatory* torture of people accused of political crimes who would not confess. On January 20, 1939, Stalin dispatched a telegram in code to NKVD agencies in the Union Republics and Communist Party leaders in the provinces:

> The Central Committee of the All–Union Communist Party (Bolsheviks) explains that the application of methods of physical pressure in NKVD practice is permissible from 1937 on in accordance with permission of the Central Committee of the All–Union Communist Party (Bolsheviks).... It is known that all bourgeois intelligence services use methods of physical influence against representatives of the Socialist proletariat and that they use them in their most scandalous forms.
>
> The question arises as to why the Socialist intelligence service should be more humanitarian against the mad agents of the bourgeoisie, against the deadly enemies of the working class and of the kolkhoz workers. The Central Committee of the All–Union Communist Party (Bolsheviks) considers that physical pressure should still be used obligatorily as an exception applicable to known and obstinate enemies of the people, as a method both justifiable and appropriate.[63]

We do not have the "explanation" of the Central Committee referred to in the telegram, but the telegram

[63] Khrushchev's secret report of February 24, 1956.

IV The Investigation

states that the method had been in force "from 1937 on," meaning that it dated from about the time Yezhov took over the NKVD post and the time of the investigation of the Pyatakov–Radek case.

These instructions given by Stalin must be taken literally, especially the wording relating to the *obligation* of the investigating agency to use "physical pressure." The Cheka–GPU–NKVD had never been among the more humane police agencies, and Stalin was well aware that there existed specific methods of "investigation," the use of which was permitted to enable the police agency to "reveal" non–existent crimes. On paper, torture in the inquisitional sense was forbidden, although beatings, excessively lengthy interrogations, withholding of food and drink during interrogations, and other measures were applied. Stalin's new order conveyed the meaning that from now on other and more effective methods must be used.

Many foreign students of Soviet affairs are inclined to minimize the role of physical pressure in the preparation of the Moscow trials; they view the "confessions" as a puzzle that they try to solve by means of psychological analysis. It is therefore significant that Khrushchev, in his secret speech at the 20th Congress, reverted no less than six times to the theme of torture as an explanation of the "confessions."

Referring to the grand–scale revision of the purge story by the Central Committee after Stalin's death, Khrushchev reported to the Congress: "Now, when the cases of these so–called 'spies' and 'saboteurs' were examined, it was found that all their cases were fabricated. Confessions of guilt of many arrested and charged with enemy activity were gained with the help of cruel and inhuman tortures."[64]

In his letter to Stalin, written on October 27, 1939, Robert Eikhe, a member of the Central Committee, said:

> I am now alluding to the most disgraceful part of my life and to my really grave guilt against the party and against you. This is my confession of counter–revolu-

[64] *Ibid.*

tionary activity. . . . The case is as follows: Not being able to suffer the tortures to which I was submitted by Ushakov and Nikolaev—and especially by the first one—who utilized the knowledge that my broken ribs have not properly mended and have caused me great pain, I have been forced to accuse myself and others.[65]

"And how is it possible," Khrushchev asked, "that a person confesses to crimes he has not committed? Only in one way—because of application of physical methods of pressuring him, tortures, bringing him to a state of unconsciousness, deprivation of his judgment, taking away of his human dignity. In this manner were 'confessions' secured."[66]

About the old case of Kossior, Chubar, and Kosarev, members of the Central Committee, the investigating officer Rodos stated, in 1956, that he had extracted confessions from them by abominable tortures.[67] In general, Khrushchev said, "It became apparent that many party, Soviet and economic activists, who were branded in 1937–38 as 'enemies,' were actually never enemies, spies and wreckers, etc., but were always honest Communists; they were only so stigmatized and often no longer able to bear barbaric tortures, they charged themselves (at the order of the investigative judges–falsifiers) with all kinds of grave and unlikely crimes."[68]

We must now consider it an established fact that torture of the accused played a primary role in the methods of NKVD investigation, although we may never know who among the defendants in the trials were tortured and to what kind of torture each was subjected.

V NKVD AGENTS ABROAD IN SEARCH OF MATERIALS FOR THE INDICTMENT

In its preparations for the new trial and its search for incriminating material against Trotsky and Trotskyism,

[65] *Ibid.*
[66] *Ibid.*
[67] *Ibid.*
[68] *Ibid.*

the NKVD carried out a masterful stroke abroad. In a daring night–time burglary it acquired fifteen bundles of Trotsky's papers. It had obviously been expected that names and addresses of Trotsky's correspondents in Russia and his ideas, plans, and schemes against Soviet leaders and the Soviet government would be found among the papers. The yield was not too abundant, and Yezhov must certainly have suffered some frustration when perusal of the documents was completed.

Here we must recall Trotsky's situation at the time. He had lived in France since 1933. In June, 1935 he was compelled to leave France and he went to Norway, where the Norwegian government had granted him political asylum on condition that he engage in no political activity. He lived in Weksal, a small place near Hoenefoss, not far from the capital, in the house of a Socialist editor, Konrad Knudsen, a deputy to the Norwegian parliament. He was far away from the centers of political life.

While Trotsky himself was condemned to inactivity (except, of course, for literary work), the activities of the center of his movement in Paris continued. In Paris there were two relatively large groups of French Trotskyites, one led by Pierre Naville and the other by Raymond Molinier; these two organizations were busy fighting the official Communist party and attacking one another. There also existed in Paris a small group of Russians around Trotsky's son, Lev Sedov. As editor and publisher of the *Bulletin of the Opposition*, Sedov was growing in political stature. In constant communication with his father, he held in his hands all the threads of the organization. All correspondence, secret and non–secret, was conducted by him; information arriving from Russia reached him first. Three or four personal and political friends of Sedov constituted the core of the Trotskyite movement as far as matters pertaining to Russia were concerned, and perhaps even in a larger sense.

Trotsky's voluminous archives, left behind in Paris and augmented since his departure, were stored in private apartments. "On the 10th of October [1936]," Trotsky said later, "I wrote my son, who was living in Paris:

'The NKVD will do its utmost to get hold of my archives. It would be better to place the archives in a respective scientific institute.' "[69] The Sedov group decided to transfer the archives to the International Institute of Social History in Paris. One day in October, 1936, members of the group transported the archives by taxi to their new location. On the night of November 7, a section of the back door to the Institute was cut out and the fifteen bundles of papers disappeared. That this was an act of political burglary was obvious from the fact that no money had been taken and no other papers had been removed. No one in the building had seen or heard the burglars; even the concierge had noticed nothing unusual.

A police investigation was initiated, but it led nowhere. Only four persons knew about the transfer of the archives, but they were all considered to be above suspicion. Some police officers and press organs suggested that the theft might have been an act of the German Gestapo, but no explanation was offered as to why the Gestapo should be interested in Trotsky's archives. The political climate of the time was so favorable to Russia that an accusation against the NKVD, without proof, would have been unpopular. The official investigation dragged on, with no results. Gradually the excitement abated and eventually the investigation was closed.

Sedov's group continued its activities as before. Trotsky continued to believe that Stalin and his police knew little about his own. Discussing the Moscow trials, he remarked contemptuously that all Russian knowledge about Trotsky and Trotskyism was based on "clippings from the newspapers." He was unaware that close to his son Lev there sat a Stalin agent, Mark Zborowski, nicknamed Etienne.

Zborowski might never have been exposed had it not been for one of those rare accidents that are the nightmare of every Soviet agent abroad. Another officer of the secret police defected and came to New York. This officer, Alexander Orlov, an Old Bolshevik veteran of the Civil War, and a silent admirer of Trotsky, broke away from the

---

[69] *Byulleten' Oppozitsii*, no. 54–55, (March, 1937), p. 15.

V NKVD Agents Search of Materials

police agency in the late 1930's. In New York he revealed to one of his new acquaintances what he had learned in Paris in the middle of the '30's, namely, that the man using the nickname Etienne was a paid agent of the NKVD and highly valued by his superiors in Paris and Moscow. This revelation was made in 1954, and the "Zborowski case" became public. Zborowski, who was then also living in New York, was interrogated by the FBI and summoned to appear before a Senate subcommittee; his statements were published.[70]

Mark Zborowski had been taken from Russia to Poland when his parents migrated there after the November revolution. According to his own story, he became a Communist in the '20's, was arrested, and in 1928 went to France to study in French universities. Whether or not he was connected with the GPU in the late '20's and early '30's is not clear, but his real services to the Soviet secret police began in 1933–34, when he was assigned to participate in the newly formed group of the "Union of Returnees to the Fatherland," a Soviet-financed emigré organization founded to promote repatriation. Other objectives of the "Union" were to recruit secret agents from among the emigrés, penetrate other Russian organizations, and serve as a reservoir of agents for many tasks in Europe, including kidnapping and murder. Zborowski entered this organization on instructions of the GPU.

His next assignment was to penetrate the Trotskyite organization in Paris. He started with the French group, to which admittance was easy, and reported on its activities to the GPU. There was, however, no sensational news about the group to report to his superiors. Among the French Trotskyites he met Sedov's wife, Jeanne, a French woman, who brought him in touch with Sedov

---

[70] The story of Zborowski given here is based on the report *Scope of Soviet Activity in the United States*, Parts 4 and 5 (U.S. Senate, Committee on the Judiciary, Subcommittee to Investigate the Administration of the Internal Security Act and other Internal Security Laws; hearings of February 29, and March 2, 1956), and on a detailed statement made by Zborowski to the writer on October 3, 1955.

himself. Soon he was able to move in the circles closest to Sedov; he was given Trotsky's letters to read; he knew about the contents of letters addressed to Trotsky, about secret conferences of the Trotskyites, and about all the plans of the Fourth International. To maintain the confidence of his "friends" in the Sedov group, he was obliged (and obviously permitted by the NKVD) to write articles for Trotsky's *Bulletin of the Opposition*. His articles were violently anti-Stalinist.

Zborowski met regularly with his superiors in the NKVD agency in Paris and reported to them on his collaborators in the Trotskyite group. The meetings, which occurred weekly or fortnightly, took place in a café. Zborowski never knew the real names of his superiors or their addresses—everything was according to the rules of "conspiracy." If something important had to be reported between meetings, he would telephone the Soviet Embassy and ask to speak to a person with an Armenian-sounding (and certainly fictitious) name. This routine of Soviet espionage continued for a number of months until, early in 1936, an important agent arrived from Moscow to give a new impetus and direction to Zborowski's activities. Of this event Zborowski later told the author:

> The man from Moscow was, as I understand, [Mikhail] Shpigelglas, the second man in the Foreign Department of the NKVD, a well-known Chekist [with a number of criminal affairs on his record]. He strongly reprimanded us—my superior and myself: "What are you doing here? You are gathering information on the unimportant French Trotskyites and on the printed *Bulletin of the Opposition*. Our enemies are the Russian Trotskyites; they plan to overthrow the Soviet government; they are connected with the Nazis; they are ready to combine forces with anyone in order to achieve their goal—the overthrow of Soviet power. Who is interested in the stories you are reporting to us about the Navilles and the Moliniers? They don't interest us; you better tell me whether you know anything about 'such-and-such' people, " and he pulled out of his pocket a long list of names. Among them were the names of Ivan N. Smirnov, Zinoviev,

and, if I am not mistaken, also Valentin Olberg. Then Shpigelglas gave me the order to find in Sedov's correspondence and elsewhere traces of ties with the above mentioned people as well as material that could help to expose the conspiracy.

Zborowski was in the right spot to comply with the new instructions; he became one of Stalin's most important tools in the fight against Trotsky. His pay and rank in the Soviet service were raised; had he chosen to go to Moscow, a bright new medal would have been pinned to his chest. Simultaneously he was rising higher and higher in the Trotsky group.

In July, 1936 a secret conference of Trotsky's Fourth International met in Paris. Ironically, Sedov assigned Zborowski to meet the arriving delegates and escort them to the secret meeting place. Zborowski now admits having reported on the conference to the NKVD. When the Norwegian government, in December, 1936, put Trotsky on a tanker bound for Mexico, great secrecy was maintained concerning the event; only Sedov in Paris was notified. There were no other passengers aboard the ship and the press was not informed, yet it was probably only a matter of hours before the news reached Stalin's security agencies.

In the fall of 1936, when Zborowski helped to transfer the fifteen bundles of Trotsky's archives to the Institute of Social History, he reported the matter to his NKVD superiors. Zborowski says—and we must believe him— that he did not take part in the burglary. It would be hard to believe that this slight, bespectacled, soft-spoken man could have been of help in a burglary or a killing or that he knew how to shoot a gun or pick a lock. He was by nature rather an infiltrator, an informer, a "fingerman"; he was able to report on where documents could be stolen, but he had to leave the stealing to professional criminals. This is why Zborowski was unhappy about the theft of the documents, for it could have exposed him. He later stated to the author:

> When I heard about the burglary I rushed to my NKVD chief and protested vehemently, because this

could expose me as a spy. Only four persons knew of the whereabouts of the archives. I was one of them. The three others could not have been suspected. The answer I received was: "We never inform our agents about a forthcoming operation because, being nervous, they might betray us. Besides, we had to get hold of the documents that night to make our present to Stalin." [The Trotsky archives were to be a gift to Stalin on the anniversary of the Bolshevik revolution.]

With Zborowski's numerous reports and the fifteen bundles of Trotsky's archives in their possession, Stalin–Yezhov and Vyshinsky were well aware that the activities of the Trotskyites in Russia had been reduced almost to zero. They knew that no correspondence was being exchanged between Trotsky or Sedov and their friends in Russia, and that since 1933 there had been no contacts between Trotsky and former friends of his on their visits to the West.

To complete the Zborowski story, in 1937 he supplied information to the NKVD on the whereabouts of Walter Krivitsky, the former Soviet military intelligence man who had defected in the fall of 1937. When Krivitsky left Stalin's service he turned for assistance to Sedov, who promptly appointed Zborowski Krivitsky's bodyguard. Zborowski now admits that he was reporting on Krivitsky's whereabouts to the NKVD as usual, but before Moscow could take action, the French government assigned police to guard Krivitsky. An unsuccessful attempt on Krivitsky's life was later made in Marseilles.

Zborowski's hand is also seen in the case of the high–ranking NKVD man Ignace Reiss, who not only defected in the summer of 1937 but tried to organize abroad a group of anti–Stalinist Old Bolsheviks, including several NKVD officials. Moscow decided to liquidate Reiss at once. According to Swiss and French police reports, two gangs of assassins were dispatched to waylay Reiss—one on September 4, 1937 in Lausanne, Switzerland, and another the next day in Reims, France, in case the first attempt failed. Zborowski was the only person who could have told the NKVD about Reims; he knew that a meeting between

V NKVD Agents Search of Materials

Reiss and Sedov had been scheduled there on that date. Reiss was killed in Lausanne. A ticket to Reims was found in his pocket.

Another bloody affair was that of Erwin Wolf, Trotsky's former secretary, who left Paris for Spain to fight for the Loyalists. Zborowski knew that Wolf was going to Spain. Wolf never returned; he was murdered in Spain by the NKVD.

The NKVD intended to kidnap Sedov and bring him to Moscow, obviously to become a defendant in one of the trials. Zborowski was to arrange the kidnapping. Somehow, perhaps because this was a risky operation, the not too courageous Zborowski shirked the assignment.[71]

Lev Sedov died under strange circumstances in February, 1938. He fell ill, and Zborowski called an ambulance. No doubt Zborowski gave the NKVD the address of the hospital to which Sedov was taken, which was staffed by Russian emigrés. The young and vigorous Sedov died after an operation.

In 1941 Zborowski, with his family, came to the United States, where he has been living since. One of his exploits in the United States was surveillance of Victor Kravchenko, who had defected from the Soviet service in April, 1944 Although not a top–ranking Soviet official, Kravchenko's defection was extremely embarrassing to Moscow. At a time when sympathy for "our great Soviet ally" was widespread throughout the United States, he had published a statement in the *New York Times* stressing that the Soviet political system was still based on terror and that Soviet foreign policy was aggressive and imperialistic. Zborowski was given the job of discovering Kravchenko's whereabouts and watching his movements. He was also ordered to meet and report on a number of Russian emigrés in America, which he did as a matter of course.

Zborowski was perhaps the most important, but far

---

[71] "It was told to me the idea was to lure him [Sedov] to a place where he and me together would be kidnapped and brought to Soviet Russia." (Zborowski's testimony before the U.S. Senate Subcommittee of the Committee on the Judiciary, February 29, 1956, part 4, p. 89.)

from the only secret agent among the Trotskyite groups. There were others, for example Valentin Olberg, who tried to win Trotsky's confidence and was rejected but somehow managed to meet Sedov from time to time in Berlin. During an earlier period there were the two Sobolevizius brothers (nicknamed Senin and Wel') who likewise mixed with the Trotskyites and reported on them to the GPU.[72]

Stalin and his NKVD possessed abundant information about Trotsky and the "secrets" of the Trotskyite groups, owing to the extent and depth of the police penetration of the Trotskyite organizations. Moscow was thus fully aware that the activities of the Trotskyites in Russia represented no danger to the government. This fact throws an even worse light on the proceedings.

VI THE TRIAL IN NOVOSIBIRSK

With the advent of Yezhov to the leading post in the NKVD, the whole country became engulfed in a maelstrom of large and small local purge trials at which the defendants were, as in the Moscow trials, "Trotskyites," "wreckers," "diversionists," and "terrorists." The trials were mentioned in the local press, but only one case was reported extensively by the press of the capital. This was the trial of the "counter–revolutionary Trotskyite wrecking group at the Kemerovo mines."[73]

The Kemerovo affair in Novosibirsk was to serve as a sort of introduction to the forthcoming Pyatakov–Radek trial in Moscow. In the Novosibirsk trial a "German Fascist" sat on the defendants' bench along with the "Trotskyites" and "wreckers." The trial was obviously intended to prove that the "opposition" was tied up with the Nazis as well as with the Japanese government.

Thousands of German engineers and workers were

[72] *The Case of Leon Trotsky*, (New York: Harper & Brothers, 1937), p. 138. One of the brothers Sobolevizius (Senin) is Jack Soble, sentenced in New York on October 8, 1957 to seven years' imprisonment; the other (Wel') was Dr. Robert Soblen, who was given a life-sentence in New York on August 7, 1961. He escaped abroad and finally committed suicide in London. (*Ed.*)

[73] *Pravda*, November 20-23, 1936.

VI The Trial in Novosibirsk

holding jobs at the time in Russian industry. Since the beginning of the "industrialization era," from about 1930 on, the high salaries offered to foreign engineers and workers attracted many; later, during the depression, thousands of unemployed Germans wanted to go to Russia. Their written applications were processed in Berlin by the GPU section of the Embassy, their political views were checked and rechecked, and only if the findings were satisfactory were they given jobs. It was from among this body of loyal, or at least non–political, German engineers that Stalin now tried to draw the contingent of "Fascist wreckers" for his trials.[74]

In early November, 1936, a number of German engineers and workers were arrested. Although the Soviet press did not report the arrests for two weeks, the German Embassy in Moscow learned about them, and on November 16 the German ambassador lodged an official protest with Maxim Litvinov, the People's Commissar. Litvinov informed the German ambassador, of course, that the Germans charged with creating a Fascist organization in the Soviet Union must be prosecuted; several of them, Litvinov said, had already confessed. The Soviet government then published an official statement accusing the arrested Germans of intent to overthrow the government, espionage, wrecking, and attempts on the lives of Russian leaders. The situation turned serious when the German press began to use belligerent language, and *Angriff* hinted at retaliation against Soviet citizens in Germany. It became obvious that Moscow had begun to regret the whole affair. In a face–saving maneuver, and without withdrawing the charges entirely, it was decided to make only one of the German engineers a defendant in the trial.

The trial took place on November 19–21, 1936 in Novosibirsk.[75] In the dock were nine defendants: the

---

[74] Defendant-engineer Stroilov testified:" . . . for six months I was in charge of engaging specialists for the U.S.S.R. . . . about 250 men passed through my hands, but only 70 were engaged" (*Proceedings*, p. 264).

[75] The proceedings are summarized in a purely factual manner; their analysis is given in the other chapters.

German "engineer–Fascist," "agent of German intelligence" Emil Stickling, who had worked at the Kemerovo mines since 1933; four "Trotskyites"—Ivan Noskov (head of the Tsentral'naya pit), Feodor Shubin, Mikhail Kurov, and the engineer Vladimir Andreev; the "counter–revolutionists and wreckers" engineers Ivan Lyashchenko, Ivan Kovalenko, and Nikolai Leonenko; and the "White Guardist" chief engineer Ivan Peshekhonov, one of the "wreckers" sentenced at the Shakhta trial of 1928. Actually Peshekhonov had been working since 1928 at the Kemerovo mines and was recognized as a first–class engineer. G. K. Roginsky, assistant to Vyshinsky and a man of inferior abilities, was the prosecutor in this trial. "Hundreds of toilers" were among the spectators, *Pravda* reported. (As always in these trials, the majority of these "toilers" were officials of the NKVD.)

The indictment was based on two actual facts—the death by gas poisoning of two miners on December 28, 1935, and an explosion in the second section of the Tsentral'naya mine on September 23, 1936, in which ten miners lost their lives and fourteen were seriously injured. The charges were as follows: since 1935 the defendants had been members of a counter–revolutionary organization in Kemerovo, whose aim was to fight the Soviet state "by diversionist and wrecking acts." The crimes committed in 1935–36 were directed toward "disorganization of the mines, disruption of coal production, disorganization of transport, disruption of safety provisions and working rules in endangered mines." The leaders in the organization were the "Trotskyites" Noskov, Shubin, Kurov, and Andreev, and the "White Guardist" Peshekhonov. The Trotskyites acted on instructions of Ya. N. Drobnis, one of the leaders of the "Trotskyite" underground in the West Siberian region. (Drobnis was later to be tried in Moscow as one of the defendants in the Pyatakov–Radek case. Two witnesses at the Novosibirsk trial, Stroilov and Shestov, were also to appear in the dock in the Moscow trial.)

"The accused perpetrated their criminal deeds with the personal assistance of the German subject, engineer E. I.

VI The Trial in Novosibirsk

Stickling, who penetrated the Kemerovo mine under the guise of a specialist and acted upon the direct instructions of an intelligence organization of a foreign power." The indictment cited the deposition of Noskov to the effect that Drobnis, the leader, had encouraged collaboration with the Fascists, since "Trotsky himself at present makes use of the services of Fascist Germany." And a gas explosion in the mine, even "if some workers should be injured, would be very effective in its results," testified Kurov. The eight Russian defendants were indicted under sections 58–7 (wrecking), 58–8 (terrorism), and 58–11 (forming secret criminal organizations) of the Criminal Code, and Stickling was indicted under sections 58–8 and 58–11. All the defendants pleaded guilty to the charges, including the most impossible and absurd ones.

The first session of the tribunal dealt with the testimony of workers who confirmed that working conditions in the mines were appalling. "These intolerable conditions were intentionally brought about" by the defendants. Ivan Noskov was the first of the defendants to testify. In 1929–30, he said, he was already "hostile to the Party line, but by concealing his opposition he became a double-dealer." Noskov was the man who in 1935 organized the counter-revolutionary Kemerovo group in accordance with Drobnis's instructions. First he enlisted the Trotskyite Shubin, who had been present in 1927 at two "underground Trotskyite meetings" in Moscow; next he recruited the wrecker Peshekhonov and his group; and finally he made contact with Stickling. All of them, the Trotskyites, the Fascists, and the White Guardists, testified Noskov, were united in a program of "restoration of capitalism in the U.S.S.R. and the establishment of a Fascist regime."

The "Trotskyite" Shubin (who had perhaps belonged to the Trotskyite opposition years before and had later "capitulated"),[76] "actually" did not cease to fight the Party and became "one of the most cruel and cynical bandits" among the members of the gang. He told the court how

[76] The *Byulleten' Oppozitsii*, no. 54–55, (March, 1937), p. 45, insisted, however, that among the defendants in this trial there was not a single Trotskyite or former Trotskyite.

he prepared the physical destruction of workers. Drobnis, to whom he submitted a report, was "very much satisfied" with his work and ordered him to continue. Answering a question of the prosecutor as to whether he was a murderer of workers, Shubin said: "It is hard to admit, but I have to confess that it was so."

The defendant Kovalenko stated that as early as 1934 he had "made friends with the German engineer–Fascist Arimont," who instructed him to "disrupt coal production in order to undermine the basis of the Bolsheviks." He admitted that he had poisoned workers.

Leonenko, a former member of the Komsomol, stated that he "sold himself to the Fascists" because they promised him "a car, an apartment, a record player and a camera. I received only a camera."

Lyashchenko, the former supervisor of ventilation of the Kemerovo mines, deliberately caused malfunctioning of the ventilation system and the result was the explosion of September 23. He confirmed that only twenty–four per cent of the funds allocated for safety measures and devices had been spent for this purpose; the other seventy–six per cent had been used for production. (During those years, and to some extent today, managers of Soviet mines and industrial plants, with the knowledge and consent of their superiors in Moscow, often used money appropriated for housing, food, and the general welfare of the workers for production purposes. This is done in an attempt to fulfill or over–fulfill the program and earn recognition and rewards.)

Engineer Andreev testified that the German Fascists directed the work of the organization and gave him his instructions. "We on our part have tried to cover up their Fascist activities."[77]

After witness Stroilov had testified that he had organized the Kemerovo wrecking group, Alexei Shestov, a ranking official in the Kuznetsk Basin, was called to the stand. He testified that while working in Berlin he had received an order from Pyatakov to get in touch with Muralov[78] and to work out with him the plan of attempts on the lives of Party and government leaders.

Drobnis testified that in 1934 Pyatakov had ordered

VI The Trial in Novosibirsk

him to get in touch with Muralov and Boguslavsky for purposes of terroristic work and particularly arrangements for attempts on the life of Eikhe. In the spring of 1935 Pyatakov conferred with Drobnis about an attempt on Stalin and other members of the government. As far as wrecking was concerned, Drobnis testified that his instructions were to center "attention on the basic industries—coal, metal and chemistry; to destroy and paralyze plants and weaken the defense potential of the nation."

The German engineer and "Fascist" Emil Stickling was the last to testify. *Pravda* reported that he "looked with unconcealed hatred at the judges, the prosecutor and the whole audience of toilers." The court went into a closed session to hear Stickling's testimony about the German consul in Novosibirsk, Grosskopf, under whose instructions he had committed diversionist and wrecking acts. The new German consul, Meyer–Heydenhagen, who replaced Grosskopf on the latter's transfer to Kiev, attended the trials as an observer. Stickling admitted his guilt; at first he denied his connection with the Gestapo, but finally gave in and admitted everything.

The trial ended on November 21. All the defendants were condemned to death. There was no appeal from the

[77] In how primitive and awkward a manner the performance had been prearranged is seen from prosecutor Roginsky's questions and Andreev's answers:
Roginsky: Tell me who are your friends?
Andreev: Fascists.
Roginsky: What kind of ideology do you have?
Andreev: Fascist.
Roginsky: What are the methods of your undermining work?
Andreev: Fascist.
Roginsky: Hence who are you?
Andreev: A Fascist.
(*Pravda* November 22, 1936).
Andreev and Peshekhonov had been highly praised by the Soviet authorities. *Pravda*, on June 5, 1933, printed a front-page appeal to all miners and engineers of the mining industry of the USSR to follow the example of Andreev and Peshekhonov at the Kemerovo mines to achieve the best results in mining.

[78] At the time of this trial Muralov had not yet "confessed"; Shestov's testimony was necessary to "split" him.

sentences. "Crush the reptiles!" *Pravda* demanded.[79] Hundreds of resolutions demanding similar treatment of the defendants were adopted by crowded meetings.

When Stickling was condemned to death along with the others, the German ambassador in London, Joachim von Ribbentrop, called on British Prime Minister Stanley Baldwin to inform him that Germany would break off diplomatic relations with Moscow if Stickling were executed. Anthony Eden, the British Foreign Secretary, immediately informed Soviet Ambassador Ivan Maisky of the situation. The Central Executive Committee, which had received pleas for clemency from all the defendants, commuted the Stickling sentence to ten years' imprisonment. Since it was impossible to spare the life of the German Fascist alone, the sentence of two Russians, Leonenko and Kovalenko, were likewise commuted to ten years' imprisonment.[80] All of the other defendants were executed.

The protective attitude of the Nazi government proved effective; no Germans were added to the group of defendants in the Pyatakov–Radek trial. This was certainly a major disappointment to the Kremlin.

VII   THE CONFESSIONS

At the outset of the investigation of the Pyatakov–Radek case the situation seemed unfavorable for the prosecution. No evidence and practically no confessions were at hand. There was Nikolai Muralov, in jail since April, 1936, whose stubborn refusal to confess had made it risky to try him along with Zinoviev and Kamenev There were in jail several less prominent men, such as. Mikhail Boguslavsky (arrested August 5, 1936) and Yakov Drobnis (arrested August 6, 1936); although the first started to confess almost immediately (a week later), he and his confessions were of secondary importance. Sokolni-

[79] *Pravda*, November 24, 1936.
[80] *Pravda*, November 26, 1936.

VII   The Confessions

kov and Serebryakov had been officially charged in August, 1936. This was too little and too slow.

With the arrival on the scene of Yezhov (September 27, 1936), a peculiar new spirit came into the case. Ten days after Yezhov's appointment, a number of additional prospective defendants were already in jail, among them Pyatakov and Radek; Valentin Arnold broke down on September 21, and Gavriil Pushin, arrested on October 22, "confessed" on October 26. Still there was not enough on which to base the prospective trial. November proved to be the crucial month. The Novosibirsk trial had furnished the basis for accusations and "evidence" against a number of prisoners in Moscow, in particular Muralov, Pyatakov, and Drobnis. At this point the specific NKVD tactics described above must have been applied. By early December most of the defendants had been "split." Sokolnikov had "confessed" on the 30th of November; Boris Norkin had started to "confess" on the 3rd of December, Muralov on the following day, and Knyazev on the 14th.

We must bear in mind that of the seventeen accused in the Pyatakov–Radek trial, only two (defendants of lesser importance) were under forty years of age; the majority were men in their forties and some were between fifty and sixty, an age at which the power of resistance has weakened and the fighting spirit has waned. By Russian standards this was a group of old men. They had gone through some grueling experiences in their lives and now were prepared to compromise on any basis.

The story of Karl Radek's confession is somewhat unusual. In his interrogation by the NKVD he had refused to admit to any of the crimes charged and did not confess for several months.

> First Radek was interrogated by the investigating officer Kedrov, son of an Old Bolshevik, a man of about 27. . . . The interrogation consisted of insults and threats. "Counter–revolutionist," "reptile," alternated with threats of shooting him down. The second stage of questioning is conducted more cleverly: the accused, who is not yet broken, is presented with

the depositions of those of his co-defendants who have "confessed." Usually the accused starts to waver and finally also "confesses."[81]

But why should Radek admit his guilt? He was innocent, and there could be no evidence, not a single document, that could prove he had been disloyal to Stalin and the Soviet government in the last seven or eight years; his former crimes, those of the '20's, had been forgotten since he had been officially pardoned when he was readmitted to the Party. Radek held out longer than his co-defendants— denial and defiance seemed to him the best way to save his life. But then he began to realize how truly desperate his situation was. He was shown testimony of co-defendants as well as of men unknown to him, some of them agents of the police, about his dishonesty, his crimes, his participation in underground organizations. Would it help to continue to deny everything? He was aware that a number of former friends, as innocent as he, had been executed a short time before on similar charges because a battery of witnesses giving so-called evidence had turned against them and "proved" their guilt.

In early December Radek decided to reverse his tactics. He would not only collaborate with the NKVD and the prosecutor, not only confess to the crimes with which he was charged, but he would go beyond that and give evidence that no investigator of the NKVD could invent, that exceeded the ability of the prosecutors, including Vyshinsky himself, to extract. He would testify in court about "letters from Trotsky" that he had received from abroad, letters in which Trotsky would repeat all the accusations Stalin wanted to put in his mouth. Now Trotsky's collaboration with German Fascists, his expectation of Russia's development toward capitalism, wrecking activities, etc. would be proved not by witnesses but by Trotsky himself as the author of letters written to one of the most intelligent of the former Trotskyites.

[81] W. Krivitsky, *Iz vospominanii sovetskogo kommunista* (Recollections of a Soviet Communist), *Sotsialisticheskii Vestnik* (Socialist Courier), No. 8, (April 29, 1938), p. 6.

VII The Confessions

Radek could offer no better gift to Stalin, and Radek knew Stalin well. In his prison cell he invented all the details of his correspondence with Trotsky. He added some "facts" about his conversations with German diplomats to confirm that Trotsky and the German government were already in contact and even in agreement. The stories that he told his investigators and, in refined form, presented in court, sounded less absurd than the crude stories invented by the small minds of the NKVD. Radek's testimony was subtle; it partly corresponded to actual events. His conversations with the German diplomats were connected with their actual visits to the Foreign Office, and the expressions used in these conversations were on a diplomatic, not a gangster, level. Once in possession of Radek's testimony, the NKVD was in a position to induce Pyatakov to confirm Radek's story and to testify that he had known from Radek about these letters. The circle of evidence was closed; Radek had won a point.

As we shall see in the story of the trial itself, Radek continued to use these techniques in court. He always tried to exceed the prosecutor and prove that his knowledge of the subversive activities of the Trotskyites went farther than what the security agencies knew about.[82] He implicated Marshal Tukhachevsky. He made the point that he would be useful to the prosecution and the NKVD in the Bukharin–Rykov trial and other trials that might take place in the future, and hinted that therefore his life must be spared. He was not unsuccessful in this effort.

During the investigation, probably some time before the trial started, Pyatakov and Radek were brought before Stalin.[83] No details of the conversation have become known. A few months earlier Stalin, at a similar point in their trial, had received Zinoviev and Kamenev and promised to spare their lives. This promise was necessary in order to persuade them to testify according to plan. There can be little doubt that in his meeting with Pyatakov

---

[82] Radek referred to these services of his in court, when he shouted at Vyshinsky:" ... you learned about the program and about Trotsky's instructions only from me...." (*Proceedings*, p. 135.)
[83] *New York Times*, January 20, 1937.

and Radek Stalin employed the same tactics. Whether or not he intended to keep his promise was, of course, another question.

Because of the extreme haste with which the preparations for the trial had been conducted, a haste obviously ordered by Stalin, the indictment as well as the details of the role of each of the defendants could not be carefully worked out. The investigating agency had a difficult task to perform; if it were to be done well it would have required many months. The legend called for the depicting of four of the seventeen defendants as leaders of a "Center," and the other thirteen as carrying out orders to wreck, spy, and assassinate. The NKVD and the prosecutor had to invent the organizations in which the men were grouped, their relationship, methods of communication with Trotsky abroad, conversations with agents of Germany and Japan, political programs, etc. The story, if it was to sound truthful, would have to be elaborated in detail, with every person fitting logically into the pattern. Neither Vyshinsky nor Yezhov, nor their investigators were of the type suited for such a task. In the end the formal indictment, which was widely publicized, proved to be a mass of inconsistent statements and unconvincing accusations.

To begin with, given the story presented by the prosecution, it would have to be assumed that Pyatakov, Radek, Sokolnikov, and Serebryakov, the four members of the "Parallel Center," the underground leadership of a prospective upheaval, had been meeting regularly and frequently. But the indictment did not mention any meetings of the four, nor were such meetings alleged by the prosecutor or the "confessing" culprits. Only from time to time, and casually and infrequently, one would meet another, and meetings of the leaders of the conspiracy with subordinates outside of Moscow occurred by accident only. No underground conferences were alleged. The reason why Vyshinsky and the NKVD could not present a more logical type of activity was, obviously, that names, addresses, dates, and other details are dangerous additions to a fictitious story; if checked, they could not be corroborated.

Neither the confessing defendants nor the prosecutor

were in a position to produce documents in court. A number of letters allegedly exchanged with Trotsky were testified to. These were quoted by Radek from memory; they were not shown in court. Concerning an alleged trip by Pyatakov from Berlin to Oslo to see Trotsky, the name Pyatakov had used on his false passport was not brought out nor were other details of his trip. A number of government witnesses testified. No explanation was made of why those among them who had implicated themselves in the crimes had not been indicted—*Izvestia* correspondent Vladimir Romm, the German engineer Stein. Had the NKVD promised them liberty if they played the game? Or had they been previously connected with the NKVD?

An impossible amount of foolish loquacity on the part of Trotsky, Radek, and the others was alleged by the prosecution. Obviously unaware of the code of revolutionary "conspiracy," the NKVD investigators had the actors in their play narrate their murder and wrecking plans to a large number of "third persons."

Terroristic acts against Soviet leaders were the alleged program of the organization, but no such acts (except the one against Kirov) were carried out, despite the fact that many occasions had presented themselves. Terrorist organizations allegedly existed all over the country (see the list of these organizations given on page 43), but these bands of assassins remained unknown to the vigilant Soviet police. One defendant stated that the "Parallel Center" had been organized in 1932, another 1933, and so on.

While the charges against the accused were fabricated, they were usually tied to some actual occurrences. However, it was precisely the imaginary "events" that were used by the prosecution to prove the guilt of the defendants.

When Pyatakov testified about his flight to Oslo to see Trotsky in December, 1935, he took as a basis for this story a fact—his visit to Berlin in December, 1935; he assumed, as did Vyshinsky, that the minor detail of the flight to Norway could never be disproved.

Radek testified about a visit to his summer home, in August, 1934, of two Germans, Professor Oberländer of

Koenigsberg and press attaché Baum. Bukharin, Radek said, was present during the visit. In the conversation the subject of better Soviet–German relations was stressed, because, Radek said, the Germans knew he was a Trotskyite. There is no doubt that this conversation took place, and that Bukharin was present (Bukharin was co-editor with Radek of *Izvestia*).[84] Radek testified to two other talks in 1935 with the German attaché about an improvement in relations between Germany and the Soviet Union. There is no reason to doubt that the latter two talks also took place. In court, however, Radek added a few "details" that changed the whole picture: the bringing of Trotsky into the incident and the nostalgia for the better relations that had existed in Trotsky's time between the armies of the two nations.

Meetings between the members of the "Center" had actually taken place, as admitted in court. The defendants, ranking Soviet officials, had met by accident or by appointment for business purposes. Conversations had taken place. How could anyone prove that in these conversations no plots had been forged?

This, then, was the general pattern of the plots. It was better than inventing a story from whole cloth and risking refutations and alibis. The indictment, the confessions, and all the testimony were built on such a *sui generis* factual basis. Train wrecks and mine explosions had occurred; Molotov's car may have really overturned. That there had been no criminal plots behind these events could not be established in the face of the "evidence" and the "confessions."

Nor was the peculiar terminology used by all participants in the trial—"terror," "wrecking," etc.—the product of invention. There was behind it a peculiar kind of logic that both sides agreed on.

It was the view of the opposition, the prosecution maintained, that Stalin's regime could not be altered by constitutional means, and that consequently it must be removed by force. A removal by force, in the absence of a

---

[84] *See* Gustav Hilger and Alfred G. Meyer, *The Incompatible Allies*, (New York: Macmillan, 1953), pp. 267–268.

popular revolution, means assassination of the leaders. Consequently, every oppositionist adhered to terroristic tactics. This logic explains the origin of the multitude of "terror organizations" suddenly found to exist all over the country. In simple language, "terror group" means Communists opposed to Stalin's course. A mysterious "algebra" and "dialectics," of which neither the public nor the press understood the meaning, were mentioned by both the prosecution and the defendants in court:

> Pyatakov: I gave the instructions in a more algebraical formulation, in a general form, without being specific, because I also had in mind the remnants of the former wrecking groups among the specialists and other....
> Vyshinsky: ... I know what you mean by algebra, but I must now deal not with algebra but with facts.
> Pyatakov: I cannot be concrete on everything on every occasion. But I confirm this.[85]

According to the NKVD version, the defendants were "recruited" into the "terror groups." They, in turn, recruited others, this recruiting being one of their main "subversive" activities. Here again factual items become part of the picture. If a people's commissar, revealed to be a Trotskyite, had appointed ten or fifty persons to various jobs, these appointees are his protégés, his friends, his supporters; and since he is a "terrorist," he chose these people with special intent. They are co–plotters, co–members of the "terror organization." To hire an employee means, according to this terminology, to "recruit" him. Thus every Soviet agency in which an important chief had been "exposed" is infested with subversives. The Pyatakov–Radek case, for example, involved two Assistant People's Commissars of Transport, an Assistant People's Commissar of Heavy Industry, an Assistant People's Commissar of Foreign Affairs, and a number of high–ranking officials of the coal and chemical industries. They, of course, "recruited" a large number of other "terrorists," the majority of whom were punished outside of court.

[85] *Proceedings*, pp. 188–189.

Strange as it may now seem, many foreign visitors and correspondents during the trial failed to understand either the peculiar terminology or the twisted logic.

VIII THE MILITARY TRIBUNAL

On January 4, 1937, *Pravda* came out with a fierce article against the accused and those members and leaders of the Communist Party who were too lazy or too passive to recognize symptoms of treason. *Pravda* lumped together those opposition leaders who had been executed, such as Zinoviev and Kamenev, with the defendants of the forthcoming Pyatakov–Radek trial, who "hoped to restore capitalism in Russia, bringing it back on the bayonets of the imperialists." The campaign was on.

The trial opened on January 23 at noon and lasted for seven consecutive days without interruption, with two sessions daily. Throughout the trial the press and the Party committees tried to incite the public against the "mad dogs" in the dock. Mass meetings were held, resolutions were "unanimously" adopted; "no mercy" was the slogan. "We demand execution." "Death." As the trial approached its end *Pravda* (January 28) printed a large picture of Yezhov and congratulated him on his new title of General Commissar of State Security. This was a reward for the preparation of the Pyatakov–Radek case.

The first of the daily trial sessions was from noon to 4:00 P.M., the second from 6:00 P.M. to 10:00 P.M. These odd working hours were arranged to fit in with Stalin's habits and to make it possible for him, if he wished, to observe the proceedings. (Rumor in Moscow had it that Stalin followed the proceedings from his office and that he was present, in a private room, during the closing session.) The radio broadcast daily two news reports on the trial.

Among the prominent persons present in court were the ambassadors of the United States and France and the German press attaché; among the Soviet and foreign writers and Communist leaders there were Alexei Tolstoy, Leon Feuchtwanger, Paul Vaillant–Couturier, and Marcel

VIII The Military Tribunal

Cachin. Forty foreign correspondents sat in the center of the courtroom.

Several hundred alleged "workers," most of them employees of the NKVD and Party leaders, made up the audience. The seventeen defendants, guarded by four soldiers, sat in four rows in a separate box, microphones in front of them. Vyshinsky, displaying his two medals, sat opposite the defendants.

The President of the Tribunal was Army Military Jurist Vasili Ulrikh; the other two members of the Tribunal were I. O. Matulevich and N. M. Rychkov. Three of the less important among the accused were defended by counsel; all the others had declined the services of lawyers. The four leading defendants, Pyatakov, Radek, Sokolnikov, and Serebryakov, in particular, preferred to do without the services of lawyers. They knew how little weight legal arguments have in a Soviet court and how poor the performance of a defense counsel is in a Soviet political trial.

The indictment followed the form established in preceding years—in the Shakhta and Ramzin trials, the trial against the Mensheviks, the Zinoviev–Kamenev trial, and others. A few political leaders accused of underground activity were combined with leaders of Soviet economy into one conspiracy of wreckers and spies. According to the indictment, the program of the "Parallel Center," organized on instructions of Leon Trotsky, "was to direct criminal anti–Soviet, espionage, diversive and terrorist activities for the purpose of undermining the military power of the U.S.S.R., of accelerating an armed attack on the U.S.S.R., of assisting foreign aggressors to seize territory of the U.S.S.R. and dismember it, and of overthrowing the Soviet power and restoring capitalism and the rule of the bourgeoisie in the Soviet Union."[86] To carry out this program, two members of the "Center," Sokolnikov and Radek, entered into communication with the representatives of "certain foreign states" [Germany and Japan]; the "Center" undertook to grant these states a number of political and economic privileges and terri-

[86] *Proceedings*, p. 18.

torial concessions; members of the "Center," as well as the other defendants, engaged in espionage on behalf of the two states and supplied secret information of the utmost importance. The "Center" carried out a number of wrecking and diversionist acts at industrial enterprises and on railways that caused loss of human life and destruction of state property. The "Center" intended to carry out a number of attempts on the lives of leaders of the Communist Party and Soviet government.

In addition to the four chief defendants, thirteen other persons were accused of having committed crimes covered by sections 58–1a (treason), 58–8 (terrorism), 58–9 (diversion), and 58–11 (forming of secret criminal organizations) of the Criminal Code. Of the thirteen, five were ranking railway officials: Leonid Serebryakov, Assistant People's Commissar of Transport; Yakov Livshitz, Assistant People's Commissar of Transport; Ivan Knyazev, Assistant Chief Administrator of the South Urals Railway; Yosif Turok, Assistant Chief of Exploitation of the Perm' Railway; Mikhail Boguslavsky. Seven were ranking leaders of the coal and chemical industries: Stanislav Rataichak, head of the Chemical Industries; Boris Norkin, Chief of Construction of the Kemerovo Combined Chemical Works; Yakov Drobnis, Norkin's assistant; Alexei Shestov, Manager of the Kuzbass Coal Mines; Mikhail Stroilov, Chief Engineer at the Kuzbass Coal Mines; Ivan Hrasche, of the Chemical Industry; Gavriil Pushin, of the Chemical Industry. Valentin Arnold was head of the garage in Kemerovo.

The Testimony of the Chief Defendants[87]

Pyatakov, the man of highest rank among the defendants and depicted by the prosecution as the real head of the conspiracy, was the first to testify. Evidently in no doubt

[87] The purpose of this section is to give the reader a picture of the trial proceedings. The proceedings, and the terminology employed in them, are reported matter-of-factly and in general without dispute or criticism; criticism of various details in the proceedings are contained in other sections.

VIII The Military Tribunal

as to his fate, almost reconciled to the prospect of imminent death, Pyatakov testified for four hours, quietly, in a colorless voice, and as if he were repeating from memory a prepared speech. With his greying hair and beard, tall, with a high forehead above black-rimmed glasses, he looked more like a professor lecturing on medieval history than a defendant confessing to the most heinous crimes. Even the members of the Tribunal and the prosecutor treated him with a certain respect which they did not accord most of the other defendants.

Pyatakov's testimony was a "wholehearted" confession. In his position as chairman of the General Administration of Chemical Industries in 1931, he had had more than one opportunity to travel abroad and make contact with Trotsky and Trotsky's organization in Western Europe. He met Trotsky's son, Lev Sedov, in 1931, he said, and Sedov asked him point-blank: "Do you intend to take a hand in this fight?" "I gave my consent," Pyatakov testified. Sedov went on to outline the new tactics: Trotsky was in favor of the forcible overthrow of the Stalin leadership by methods of terrorism and wrecking. Trotsky also maintained that a struggle confined to one country would be absurd and that the "international question" (which in this case meant collaboration with the other governments) could not possibly be avoided.

In this first alleged conversation as well as in the correspondence between Trotsky, Sedov, and their friends inside Russia, Trotsky's position was that of an undisputed dictator, an autocrat whose every word was an order that must be blindly obeyed.[88] Trotsky, Sedov "told" Pyatakov, had arranged the financial problem of the opposition in the most simple and logical way: the money was to come from the Germans.

> Sedov said that only one thing was required of me, namely, that I should place as many orders as possible with two German firms, Borsig and Demag, and that

[88] Those who know the real situation inside the Communist opposition in Russia will understand how absurd this notion was, how much dissension there was within those groups, how much freedom of opinion there existed, and how much fighting was going on.

he, Sedov, would arrange to receive the necessary sums from them, bearing in mind that I would not be particularly exacting as to prices.[89]

In December of the same year, when Pyatakov was in Moscow, engineer Shestov arrived from Berlin and brought with him two letters secreted in shoes. One, marked with the letter "P," was meant for Pyatakov; the other was marked with an "M" for Muralov. In the letter to Muralov Trotsky said: "The first task was to use every means to remove Stalin and his immediate assistants."[90] Of course, Pyatakov added, "every means" was to be understood as violent means.

The next year (1932) Pyatakov was again in Berlin and again "met" Sedov. Trotsky was extremely dissatisfied, Sedov told Pyatakov. He was "roaring and raving, burning with impatience to have his instructions carried out as quickly as possible, and nothing concrete is visible from your report."[91] Back in Moscow Pyatakov proceeded to organize the "Parallel Center." He contacted Kamenev and through him received the consent of the rightists (Bukharin, Tomsky, Rykov); he met with Serebryakov in the Gagra resort (this was not until the end of 1933), and met Sokolnikov in the middle of 1935. (Somehow the audience did not grasp the absurdity of this organization, whose members did not meet and whose contacts with one another were sometimes separated by years.)

Correspondence with Trotsky was carried on by Radek, while wrecking operations were conducted by Pyatakov. Pyatakov reported about his activities in great detail, implicating himself as well as other defendants. He testified about deliberate waste in industry, about defective construction, about deliberate delaying of plans of industrial expansion. In case of a war, preparations had to be made to put enterprises out of action by means of fires and explosions. Loss of life was inevitable since "it was impossible to commit acts of diversion without sacrificing human lives."

[89] *Proceedings*, p. 26.
[90] *Ibid.*, p. 32.
[91] *Ibid.*, p. 36.

VIII The Military Tribunal

A new phase in the activities of the Center started in mid–1935, after the arrest of the members of the main Center, Zinoviev and Kamenev. In December of that year Pyatakov made his famed "flight to Oslo" from Berlin. When he started to tell the tribunal about this trip the audience seemed to sense that the testimony was approaching a peak of sensation. "A great movement in the hall," the correspondents cabled their papers. The flight to Oslo, Pyatakov said, was organized by Bukhartsev, the *Izvestia* correspondent in Berlin. Dmitri Bukhartsev was in touch with a German, Gustav Stirner, allegedly a friend or representative of Trotsky in Germany, a man who was in a position to procure a false passport for Pyatakov, arrange for a plane to fly him from Berlin to Oslo, etc. (This was the hint, of course, at the connection of Trotsky with the Gestapo without whose help the trip would have been impossible.) During his two–hour conversation with Trotsky, Pyatakov testified, he came to understand the views and intentions of the former Soviet leader.

> ... we should now go into the service of the Stalin state, not, however, to help to build the state, but to become its grave–diggers—therein lies our task.[92]

To effect this, cooperation with the "Fascists" was necessary. In a war (which Trotsky expected to break out in 1937) the opposition would have to assume a defeatist position. Wrecking and diversionist cadres were to be trained "in order to draw a line of demarcation between the Stalin state and the Trotskyite organization"; also, in the event of war, diversionists and those who would engage in destruction, "helpers for the Fascist attack on the Soviet Union," would have to be trained. Trotsky told Pyatakov about his lengthy negotiations with Rudolf Hess and the agreement he had reached with him: territorial concessions to Germany, economic concessions, and realignment of the Soviet social system to the needs of Germany. " ... German capital would be allowed to come in and obtain a necessary

[92] *Proceedings*, p. 61.

economic complement, but the definite forms which this was to assume would evidently be worked out later."[93]

When Pyatakov had finished this part of his testimony, Vyshinsky asked him:

> And so, what was there new in what Trotsky said in 1935, compared with what you were told before, and what you had been guided by in your criminal activities?
>
> Pyatakov: What was new, if you like, was formulated distinctly enough: in essence, the Trotskyite organization was being transformed into an appendage of fascism.
>
> Vyshinsky: Did you learn that only at that time?
> Pyatakov: To me it became clear only then.[94]

When the report on this session of the trial reached the Western press, Vyshinsky suffered a heavy blow. The administration of the Kjellere airfield, near Oslo, where Pyatakov had allegedly alighted, stated that not a single plane from abroad had landed there during the entire month of December, 1935. In the haste of its preparation, the NKVD had obviously not taken the time to investigate local conditions; they had made again the same blunder they had committed a few months before in connection with the Hotel Bristol in Copenhagen.[95] Without mentioning the contents of the Norwegian refutation, Vyshinsky, in a face-saving effort, made a lame statement in court quoting a note from the Commissariat of Foreign Affairs:

> 'The consular Department of the People's Commissariat of Foreign Affairs hereby informs the Procurator of the U.S.S.R. that according to information

[93] *Ibid.*, p. 65.
[94] *Ibid.*, p. 66.
[95] One of the accused in the Zinoviev-Kamenev trial of August, 1936, Eduard Goltsman, testified that he met with Lev Sedov in November, 1932, at the Hotel Bristol in Copenhagen. While a Hotel Bristol was mentioned in the old edition of the Baedecker, it no longer existed in Copenhagen in 1932. It had been closed down in 1917 and the building was demolished. (*Sozial-Demokraten*, Copenhagen, September 1, 1936, quoted in *Byulleten' Oppozitsii*, No. 52–53, September–October, 1936, p. 34). Furthermore a German re-entry permit was not issued to Lev Sedov; he never went to Copenhagen.

VIII The Military Tribunal

received by the Embassy of the U.S.S.R. in Norway the Kjellere Airdrome near Oslo receives all the year round, in accordance with international regulations, airplanes of other countries, and that the arrival and departure of airplanes is possible also in winter months.'[96]

Vyshinsky implied that despite the fact that technically "arrival and departure of airplanes is possible," the administration of the airport in Oslo did not know about the secret plane from Berlin (which was highly improbable).[97]

What has been said above about Trotsky's organization and its contacts with Russia since 1932 must be borne in mind if we are to be able to evaluate the testimony of the second witness, Karl Radek.

[96] *Proceedings*, p. 443.

[97] Both Trotsky and Sedov denied the whole Pyatakov story. Sedov declared that he had last seen Pyatakov on a Berlin street in 1931, when Pyatakov, noticing him, hurriedly turned and crossed to the other side of the street: "I shouted a few insults at him," said Sedov. And that was all.

In fact, the ties between the Trotsky group and their former friends in Russia had been all but broken since 1932–33. Ivan N. Smirnov in 1931, and Eduard Goltsman in 1932, were the last Trotskyites from Russia whom Sedov met; as far as Trotsky himself was concerned, he had not seen a single Russian friend since 1930. Here is what Natalia Sedov-Trotsky told the writer:

"So long as we were in Soviet exile, in Alma Ata (1928–29), a lively correspondence was carried on, at least in the beginning, between Trotsky and a number of friends in the country. When we were deported to Turkey there was still at first a slight possibility of writing letters; but no Russian visitors (except one, Yakov Blyumkin) arrived. After a short time, for obvious reasons, all correspondence became impossible and personal contacts ceased altogether. Trotsky could see no Russian friends any more. A few non-Russian Communists with Trotskyite sympathies who had visited Moscow came to see us on their way back to the West. They had not met any of our friends in the Soviet Union, and they brought no messages. All correspondence was conducted by Sedov, but even he had no personal contacts with friends or sympathizers inside the Soviet Union after 1932. I was getting two letters or postal cards a year from my son Sergei until 1935, then even these ties were broken."

Unlike Pyatakov, Radek appeared in court in a fighting mood; he talked much on sociological and historical problems and shouted at Vyshinsky; the general impression was that, in intellect, he towered over the prosecutor. But he failed to win the sympathies of the audience; his methods of self-defense, his implicating of other people, his denunciations of men still at liberty, his obvious intention to fight tooth and nail for his life sometimes made him repulsive.

Radek started his testimony with a history of his deviation from Stalinism and his subsequent reconciliation. In 1928 he was exiled from Moscow when the opposition was suppressed and dispersed. In July, 1929 he surrendered and was permitted to return and resume his work. At the time he accepted all of Stalin's political ideas, except one, that concerning the situation in the Party: Radek thought that more democracy in the Party was needed. But he bowed to Stalin and for a number of years continued to work with the Soviet machine. Among his friends was Pyatakov, who had likewise been pardoned by Stalin and the Politburo.

Radek started to doubt again about 1931, when the collectivization of farming was bringing disaster to the peasantry and the general economic situation was deteriorating. He thought that the best thing to do was to "hold back the Socialist offensive," perhaps revert to a kind of NEP. At this point Radek proceeded to tell a fantastic story of his new orientation toward terrorist tactics, and he implicated a number of other leaders, a few of whom had been executed after the trial of August, 1936, but others of whom were still alive. He mentioned Mrachkovsky, Dreitzer, Bakaev, and Smirnov as opposition leaders with whom he had conferred about the resumption of the fight against Stalin's course; he also mentioned Bukharin and other rightist leaders. (This had obviously been prearranged with the NKVD; on the same day, Rykov, Uglanov, Moskalev, and several others were arrested.)

Having joined the "terrorist" underground, Radek became a member of the "Parallel Center." He spoke eloquently about the working habits of the Center. He

VIII The Military Tribunal

had joined the "movement" in 1933, but did not meet Kamenev and Zinoviev at all in that year. As far as the members of his "Parallel Center" were concerned, "... there was one meeting in the summer of 1934 with G. Y. Sokolnikov.... I saw Pyatakov in December, 1932, a second time at the end of 1933; in 1934 I saw him in the summer, in July; in 1935 I saw him in July and December; in 1936 I saw him in January. Serebryakov I saw in 1933, in 1935 and in 1936. I saw Sokolnikov three times."[98] (This terroristic organization that intended to assume power in Russia must have consisted of escapees from a lunatic asylum!)

Radek then testified about "letters" he had received from Trotsky from 1933 to the end of 1935. (We mention these letters and give some quotations from them not because they were real or constitute historical material of any importance, but because they played such a prominent role in the Pyatakov–Radek trial.) The first letter, Radek said, was received in February, 1932. It was the first attempt on the part of Trotsky to resume political relations with Radek. Trotsky concluded from information he possessed that Radek was coming over to Trotsky's position: "Either we shall be destroyed together with the Soviet Union or we must raise the question of removing the leadership." Commenting on this letter in court, Radek said: "The word terrorism was not used, but when I read the words 'removing the leadership' it became clear to me what Trotsky had in mind."

In April, 1934 another letter arrived from Trotsky. Trotsky said that in his view a war had become inevitable and that in this war the Soviet Union would be defeated. It could be saved only if the Trotskyite–Zinovievite bloc assumed power. A Soviet defeat in war would help the opposition. Trotsky told his correspondent that, drawing the necessary inference from this thesis, he had established contact with the governments of Germany and Japan and that certain concessions would of course have to be made to these powers.

Radek testified to various conversations with Germans.

[98] *Proceedings*, p. 92.

About a conversation with the German military attaché in Moscow, Radek told the court:

> "Our leaders ... know that Mr. Trotsky [the German diplomat said] is striving for a rapprochement with Germany. Our leader wants to know, what does this idea of Mr. Trotsky's signify? Perhaps it is the idea of an emigré who sleeps badly? Who is behind these ideas?" It was clear that I was being asked about the attitude of the *bloc*. ... I told him that realist politicians in the U.S.S.R. understand the significance of a German–Soviet rapprochement and are prepared to make the necessary concessions to achieve this rapprochement. This representative understood that since I was speaking about realist politicians it meant that there were realist politicians and unrealist politicians in the U.S.S.R.: the unrealist politicians were the Soviet government, while the realist politicians were the Trotskyite–Zinovievite *bloc*. And he also understood that what I meant was: if the *bloc* comes into power it will make concessions in order to bring about a rapprochement with your government and the country which it represents.[99]

A third letter from Trotsky arrived in December, 1935. It was more outspoken, more defeatist, demanded more concessions to the foreign powers; and it was explicit as to the contemplated reversal to capitalism. Coming to power, Radek said, would mean for Trotsky and the Trotskyite–Zinovievite group the making of territorial concessions—Trotsky specifically mentioned cession of the Ukraine to Germany and on another occasion he had mentioned the cession of the Maritime Province to Japan; it would mean partition of the U.S.S.R., granting of concessions in industrial enterprises to capitalist states, admission of foreign capital for the exploitation of Soviet factories, disbandment of collective farms, and restoration of capitalism in general.

> ... There can be no talk of any kind of democracy [Trotsky said in this letter]. The working class has

[99] *Proceedings*, pp. 108–09.

VIII The Military Tribunal

lived through eighteen years of revolution, and it has vast appetites; and this working class will have to be sent back partly to privately–owned factories and partly to state–owned factories which will have to compete with foreign capital under most difficult conditions. That means that the living standard of the working class will be drastically lowered.[100]

Wrecking and terror were other points in Trotsky's program; here Radek did not add anything new to the statements made by Pyatakov on the preceding day.

Radek now was permitted (obviously by prearrangement with the prosecution) to tell the court how he had become "disappointed and disillusioned" about Trotsky. The economic and military situation in the Soviet Union had considerably improved in the meantime, Radek said, and defeat was no longer an inevitability. The Soviet Union could be victorious in a war, Radek now thought, and Trotsky's insistence on cooperation with and concessions to Germany and Japan would merely be service to foreign powers without any justification. This is why, Radek said, he started, in 1935, to move more and more away from the "Parallel Center."

Among other persons implicated (also, of course, on the insistence of the NKVD) by Radek was Marshal Mikhail Tukhachevsky. (The trial of Tukhachevsky and the other generals, which actually took place a few months later, was already being contemplated by Stalin.) Vyshinsky interrogated Radek about Tukhachevsky: "Do I understand you correctly . . . that your reference to Tukhachevsky was made in connection with the fact that Putna [the former military attaché in London, who had been in jail since August, 1936] came on official business on Tukhachevsky's orders?" Radek responded:

> I confirm that, and I say that I never had and could not have had any dealings with Tukhachevsky connected with counter–revolutionary activities, because I knew Tukhachevsky's attitude to the Party and the government to be that of an absolutely devoted man.[101]

[100] *Proceedings*, p. 114.
[101] *Proceedings*, p. 146.

Radek grinned maliciously as he made this statement, and the impression that he created, and intended to create, was that Tukhachevsky had been under suspicion.

Vladimir Romm, the *Izvestia* foreign correspondent, was interrogated along with Radek. Romm, well-known in Paris, Geneva, and the United States, had allegedly served as messenger between Trotsky and Radek. He had spent some time in jail; flanked by two uniformed guards, he testified for forty-five minutes. Well-dressed, apparently in good health but extremely nervous at the outset, he confirmed all Radek's statements and allegations. Between 1932 and 1935 he had carried five messages from Trotsky and Sedov, and on one occasion had met Trotsky in the Bois de Boulogne in Paris. This was at the end of July, 1933. Although Trotsky was meeting Romm for the first time, he confided to him his secret thoughts about terrorism and wrecking activities; it must be understood, Trotsky said, that loss of life is inevitable in carrying out wrecking operations.[102]

Defendant Sokolnikov, Assistant People's Commissar of Foreign Affairs, followed Romm on the stand. He testified that he had one talk with Kamenev in the beginning of

---

[102] Trotsky, in Mexico, made an immediate retort to this story: "I can only repeat that I did not send any letter to Radek and I did not have any idea that Vladimir Romm existed." Pointing out the absurdity of the whole story about his meeting with Romm, Trotsky said that at that time (July, 1933) he lived in a small provincial town in France about two hundred miles from Paris; moreover, he was then ill. He had a large number of visitors every day and any absence of his from home would have been noticed. A secret meeting with a Soviet correspondent for the purpose of establishing ties with the Soviet underground, to be held in the Bois de Boulogne, where hundreds of people could observe him and Romm, would have been the height of foolishness.

Members of the "newspaper corps" in Washington requested the U.S. Ambassador in Moscow to intervene in favor of "our colleague" Vladimir Romm. Ambassador Joseph E. Davies took the matter up with Kalinin, Molotov, and Litvinov; later he was told by Konstantin Umansky that Romm's life was saved by this action of the American journalists. Some doubt is cast on the accuracy of this story by the fact that Romm has never been heard of since.

1934, and started to work in the "Parallel Center" in the summer of 1935. Kamenev told him about Trotsky's defeatist course; "incidentally... Kamenev warned me that someone might approach me with inquiries." Indeed, in the middle of April, 1934, even before Sokolnikov joined the "Parallel Center," he had an important conversation with an official "of a certain country"; the meeting took place in Sokolnikov's office.

> ... While I was showing my visitor to the door he asked me whether I knew that Trotsky had addressed certain proposals to his government. I confirmed that this fact was known to me. He asked further whether these proposals were serious. I confirmed this too. He asked whether this was my own personal opinion. I said that this was not only my opinion but that of my friends as well.[103]

Later Sokolnikov was informed about Trotsky's letters as well as Pyatakov's visit to Trotsky in December, 1935, and he testified about the two alternatives allegedly mentioned by Trotsky—one, to achieve power without war; the second, to achieve power as the result of a war; in either case the opposition would have to establish friendly relations with the governments of Germany and Japan. If there was no war, the other side (meaning Germany or Japan) was "to give the government of the *bloc* its friendly support." In the event of war, "the *bloc* undertook to conclude peace immediately and recognize territorial concessions."

Sokolnikov reported in detail about a number of wrecking plans and activities, in line with the testimony of the other defendants. He also asserted that restoration of capitalism was the actual result to be expected from the realization of the program of the *bloc*.

Serebryakov testified that he had met Pyatakov in the Gagra resort in the fall of 1933 and that this meeting was the start of his activities for the Center. An old railway man, he devoted himself to preparation of wrecking acts

---

[103] *Proceedings*, p. 149.

in the railway system, in particular the preparation of sabotage in war. Quoting the testimony of Serebryakov the President of the court said:

"... Livshitz and I discussed the matter and came to the conclusion that in addition to the actions of the organizations in the center and in the provinces, the effect of which would be to cause confusion and chaos on the railways, it was also necessary to ensure the possibility of blocking the most important railway junctions in the first days of mobilization by creating on them such jams as would lead to the dislocation of the transport system and reduce the capacity of the railway junctions."[104]

Serebryakov also denounced a number of Communist leaders in the Caucasus, among them Budu Mdivani, whom he accused of preparing a plan of collaboration with non–Communist parties, namely, the Dashnaks in Armenia, Mussavatists in Azerbaidjan, and the Mensheviks in Georgia. (Mdivani was arrested, tried, and executed in July of the same year.)

The Testimony of Heads of the Coal Industry and Railways

Vladimir Loginov, manager of the Coal Trust in Khar'kov, was then called as a witness. (It is a mystery why this man, no less guilty than the others in the dock, was not among the defendants.) Loginov testified about numerous meetings he had with Pyatakov and about their discussion of wrecking plans in Loginov's area. He reported further on wrecking in the coal and chemical industries in the Ukraine. He mentioned attempts to contact German intelligence agents in Russia, particularly engineers in the coke industry. Loginov's testimony was related to the defendants Rataichak and Livshitz, who were accused of terror and wrecking.

Loginov was followed on the stand by Mikhail Boguslavsky. Boguslavsky testified, not altogether untruthfully,

[104] *Proceedings*, pp. 172–173.

about the Trotskyites in Siberia in the late '20's, after they had been exiled from Moscow. What he depicted as a Trotskyite underground organization was actually—and this became obvious from his testimony—an arrangement for mutual help to exiles. He told the by now standard tale in the court about the Trotskyite underground work, wrecking, and terrorism. According to his own testimony, he had met with Pyatakov, the leader in these operations, once in 1932, once in 1933, once in 1934, and not at all after that; in the crucial years 1935–36 he had not seen his Trotskyite boss at all. He confessed to having planned terroristic acts, in particular against Stalin, Kaganovich, Molotov, and Eikhe; the plans were never carried out. At the end of Boguslavsky's testimony, Vyshinsky perpetrated one of his hypocritical tricks. Well aware that no defendant would dare tell the truth about his interrogation by the NKVD, Vyshinsky addressed Boguslavsky:

> At first you would not testify at all, and then you began to testify. Perhaps this is to be explained by some specific conditions of your arrest, perhaps pressure was brought to bear on you?
> Boguslavsky: No.
> Vyshinsky: Perhaps it was suggested that you should testify in the way you subsequently did, in return for which your sentence would be mitigated?
> Boguslavsky: No.
> Vyshinsky: Consequently you began to give this testimony quite voluntarily and sincerely, because of your internal personal convictions?
> Boguslavsky: Quite true. . . .[105]

Yakov Drobnis, also of Western Siberia, confessed to extensive wrecking and efforts to hamper the Stakhanov movement in his economic region. A special point was made of the explosion in the Tsentral'naya pit. This, the main crime charged against Drobnis, had been discussed in the Novosibirsk trial. Drobnis told the court about his alleged conversation with engineer Noskov.

Noskov said that such a wrecking measure as allow-

---

[105] *Proceedings*, p. 203.

ing gas to accumulate in the mine would result in explosion and would cause loss of life. I replied: well then, we must be ready for this, too. It would even be a good thing, because it would arouse the resentment of the workers which will enable us to win their sympathies.[106]

Drobnis later tried to retract the most horrible part of this statement—his intention to cause the greatest possible number of deaths in the explosion. The following colloquy between Vyshinsky and Drobnis then took place:

> Drobnis: You are exaggerating a little.
> Vyshinsky: Let us make this clear, let us recall the facts. Did you say to Noskov that the more victims, the better?
> Drobnis: Yes.
> Vyshinsky: What then am I exaggerating?
> Drobnis: I did not mean by this that he should kill more.
> Vyshinsky: Did you think that if you said "more," he would understand you mean "less," that he would understand you to mean that you wanted to reduce the loss of life?
> Drobnis: I wanted to reduce....
> Vyshinsky: Yet you said, let there be more, and even explained why more deaths were necessary. You said, let there be more victims, since that would arouse the resentment of the workers. The greater the number of victims, the less the resentment?
> Drobnis: No, on the contrary.
> Vyshinsky: The greater the number of victims, the greater the resentment?
> Drobnis: Yes.
> Vyshinsky: Is that what you wanted?
> Drobnis: Yes, in effect, that is what I wanted.[107]

At the very end of his testimony Drobnis suddenly brought out the fact that the explosion had taken place on September 25, 1936, whereas he had been arrested six weeks before, on August 6. Vyshinsky did not find it easy to explain why Drobnis was to be punished for the explosion.

[106] *Ibid.*, p. 212.
[107] *Ibid.*, p. 213.

VIII The Military Tribunal

The next to be called was Muralov, the staunch Trotskyite. Having for eight months refused to confess, he had now been completely broken and admitted all the terrible crimes with which he was charged. He testified that he had received three letters from Sedov in 1932 and had been in contact with Pyatakov in Moscow. In accordance with the instructions contained in Sedov's letters, he assigned Shestov and others to organize attempts on the lives of Molotov and Eikhe. His wrecking and terroristic activities were no different from those engaged in by his co-defendants, but a new item emerged when he reported that his correspondence with Sedov was carried on via German engineers working in Western Siberia. This was an allusion to the Nazi police serving Trotsky and the Trotskyites inside Russia.

Muralov was followed on the stand by two high-ranking Soviet officials from the Kuznetsk Coal Basin, Alexei Shestov and Mikhail Stroilov, both connected with German firms and allegedly involved in a conspiracy with German intelligence. Both Shestov and Stroilov had spent much time abroad and had allegedly had occasion to contact both the Trotskyites and the German secret service.

Shestov was a talkative man with a lively imagination. He gave so many details and invented so many fantastic stories that there was danger that he might become entangled in contradictions. Vyshinsky requested him more than once not to go into detail, although it would seem that the prosecutor and the tribunal should have been interested in obtaining a complete picture. Shestov testified that in June, 1931 he was in Berlin along with Pyatakov and Ivan Smirnov. In his capacity as member of the Board of the Eastern and Siberian Coal Trust, he was brought in touch, by Smirnov, with Sedov, and met Sedov more than once. Sedov explained to him the new political situation, gave him Trotsky's new instructions, and advised him to contact Director Dehlmann of the firm Fröhlich–Klüpfel–Dehlmann. Dehlmann made it possible, through his representatives in the Kuzbass (in Western Siberia), for Trotsky's mail to be forwarded to the Soviet Union; on the other hand, the Trotskyite organization in Siberia supplied secret information to the German firm and helped it in its transactions. Shestov produced the names of many Russian and German engineers who allegedly were members of his ring and accomplices in his criminal undertakings.

Back in Russia at the end of 1931, Shestov went to Prokop'evsk, where he worked at one of the main Kuzbass mines. With the help of German engineers working for Dehlmann, actually agents of German intelligence, he transmitted letters from Trotsky to Muralov; the letters contained instructions about wrecking and terrorist operations. Shestov then proceeded to recite his exploits in his area: preparation of terroristic acts against Ordzhonikidze and Molotov; setting fire to industrial enterprises (1933); stealing dynamite (1934); causing explosions, with loss of life; assassination of engineer Boyarshinov, a former "wrecker" who had reformed and become a devoted Soviet patriot; theft of 164,000 rubles from a state bank and distribution of the money among terrorist groups (he himself, Muralov testified, received 70,000 rubles). Shestov's whole story was one of the most improbable and fantastic heard during the trial.

Stroilov might at first have seemed an exception among these Communist defendants, for he had not been a member of the Communist Party. As his testimony developed, however, it became obvious that he belonged to the group of "non–party" intellectuals who are intentionally kept out of the official Communist Party so that they can be paraded as objective, dispassionate supporters of the Soviet regime. As such, Stroilov had been elected an alternate member of the Central Executive Committee. He testified that in the early '30's he was sent to Germany, where he spent two years. His main task was the recruitment of German specialists, technicians, and workers for Soviet industry. (Such an assignment could be entrusted only to someone in the complete confidence of the GPU.) In the course of his duties he was in touch with a large number of Germans, among them, he said, men serving German

VIII The Military Tribunal

intelligence. After two years in Germany he decided not to return to Russia, and on the advice of one of his German contacts formally requested the German authorities for permission to remain in Germany. No sooner had he presented this request to his new friends than German intelligence began to blackmail him, and he became a traitor to his fatherland. Soon after he was recalled to the Soviet Union. His German "commercial" contacts requested him to carry out some assignments: to receive German engineers being dispatched to Russia and to assign them to suitable jobs. (The engineers would use the password "greetings from Wüster"—a strange choice since Wüster was the actual name of Stroilov's German contact.) Stroilov was to see to it that the Germans were enabled to do their intelligence work; in addition he was to carry out wrecking operations in the coal industry.

As a matter of fact, Stroilov testified, among the large number of Germans who arrived between 1932 and 1934 there were six intelligence agents whom he helped to penetrate Soviet industry, and he himself gathered information for Germany and transmitted it through these intelligence agents. It was he, Stroilov, who sent the German engineer Emil Stickling (tried and sentenced in the Novosibirsk trial) to Kemerovo. He testified at some length about his wrecking activities and furnished a number of details.

Boris Norkin, head of the Kemerovo Combined Chemical Works Construction, testified that he had joined the Trotskyite underground in 1931; in 1932 Pyatakov sent him to Kemerovo, principally to begin wrecking operations there. Norkin's main aim was to retard the development of the chemical industry and to freeze the invested capital. He set the stage for three explosions at a power station in February, 1936. In general, his activity was "diversion" and violating of technical regulations. Once again Vyshinsky plied the mouse in his trap with hypocritical questions, knowing that Norkin could not say anything detrimental to the NKVD or the prosecution:

Vyshinsky: How were you kept? What were your prison conditions like?

Norkin: Very good. Are you asking me about outward pressures?

Vyshinsky: Yes.

Norkin: There was no pressure whatever.

Vyshinsky: A man can be deprived of good food, deprived of sleep. We know this from the history of capitalist prisons. He can be deprived of cigarettes.

Norkin: If that is what you are talking about, there was nothing like it.

Vyshinsky: Did they feed you well?

Norkin: They were extremely attentive.[108]

Valentin Arnold began his testimony with an involved biography. He had been a citizen of Finland and of the United States and was now a Soviet citizen. He had been educated partly in Russia and partly in Finland and had traveled all over the world as a worker, sailor, and soldier; he had served in the Russian army since 1915, had deserted and been punished for desertion; in 1917, in New York, he was drafted into the American army. While in the United States he joined the Communist Party. In 1932 he returned to Russia and became a member of the Soviet Communist Party. Working in the Kuzbass, under Shestov, he was ordered to carry out wrecking jobs in the coal mines. In addition, as the boss of a garage, he planned and almost perpetrated two terroristic acts. In the spring of 1934, when Ordzhonikidze arrived in the Kuzbass, he was assigned to drive the car carrying Ordzhonikidze and two other important passengers (Eikhe and Rukhimovich) and to engineer an accident. Everything was prepared, but at the last moment Arnold lost his nerve. When Molotov arrived at the Kuzbass, Arnold was assigned to drive him, too, again with instructions to cause an accident in which all the passengers, including Arnold himself, would be killed. He again lost his nerve, and Molotov was spared.

Yakov Livshitz, the next defendant to testify, had had a rapid advance in the Railway Department. He was chief

[108] *Proceedings*, p. 288.

of various railways between 1932 and 1934, and in 1935 was appointed Assistant People's Commissar of Transport. He admitted having deliberately disrupted the transportation of coal, allowing cars to remain empty, and in general having tried to frustrate Kaganovich's efforts to improve the railway system. He furnished a large number of names of wreckers and Trotskyites involved with Soviet railways, among them his co-defendants Knyazev and Turok. He had also had knowledge of the preparation of terroristic acts against Stalin, Kossior, and Postyshev. Through Knyazev and Turok he was in touch with Japanese intelligence agencies, and he supplied Knyazev with secret information for the Japanese intelligence service.

Ivan Knyazev, another of the heads of the Soviet railway system, who had been traffic manager on a number of railways in the '30's, followed the Assistant People's Commissar on the stand. Knyazev had risen "from below"; he had worked as a carpenter and tailor; in 1917–18 he at first was sympathetic to the Leftist Socialist–Revolutionaries, but later joined the Communist Party. He confessed to having perpetrated wrecking acts on the South Urals Railway and sabotaging repair of tracks and locomotives. He and his group caused a number of train wrecks in which lives were lost, and gave their superiors a false explanation; he depicted them, he said, as purely non–political, although they were engineered by the Trotskyites. He cited shocking figures about train wrecks during the preceding few years. Asked by Rychkov, a member of the Tribunal, how many train wrecks had been engineered under his leadership, Knyazev answered:

> From thirteen to fifteen train wrecks were organized directly by us ... the increase in train wrecks was undoubtedly connected with the wrecking activities of the Trotskyite organization in the other branches of industry as well. I remember in 1934 there were altogether about 1,500 train wrecks and accidents.[109]

Knyazev testified also about his dealings with Japanese

[109] *Proceedings*, p. 371.

agents, most of them with the Japanese railway expert S. Hiroshima; he admitted having done intelligence work for Japan and having turned over to the Japanese information on Soviet mobilization plans. At this point Vyshinsky produced a photocopy of a letter written by Hiroshima to Knyazev. Now Vyshinsky had a real document in his hands, not a "confession." He did not, however, show the letter to the press, nor did he read it to the Tribunal. He merely asked the defendant a few questions, from which it was obvious that the letter was an innocent one in which Hiroshima said that he wanted to see Knyazev in Moscow and that he hoped an opportunity for a meeting would soon present itself. Whether or not the Japanese expert had other things in mind, he was cautious enough not to mention them; this was the reason the "document" produced by Vyshinsky, had it been published, would have made no impression. The "document," however, made Knyazev the most prominent among the "Japanese spies" at the Pyatakov–Radek trial.

Yosif Turok was the last of the group of railway men among the defendants. He had served as assistant manager of the Traffic Department, of the Perm' and Urals Railway, had been recruited into the Trotskyite underground in 1934, and had been engaged in wrecking activities for the last two years. He testified that about forty railway accidents had been deliberately engineered by his Trotskyite organizations during that time, beginning with the end of 1934. His group had also organized attempts on the lives of Molotov and Kaganovich. He started to work for Japan in 1934, and since then some funds had been received from the Japanese intelligence service.

The Testimony of Heads of the Chemical Industry

Stanislav Rataichak, chief of the Central Administration of the Chemical Industry, member of the Communist Party since January, 1918, followed the group of railway men on the stand. He testified that he had engaged in espionage for Germany and had conducted these criminal activities with the help of his two assistants, the co-

VIII The Military Tribunal

defendants Pushin and Hrasche, who delivered secret material to German intelligence. In addition, he had engaged in diversion: three breakdowns in production were arranged by him and his organization. Rataichak gave a number of names of Soviet citizens and Germans working in the chemical industry as wreckers and spies.

Ivan Hrasche and Gavriil Pushin were alleged members of the subversive Trotskyite organization and important men in the Soviet chemical industry. They followed Rataichak on the stand. Hrasche testified first. His biography and activity have already been described (see pp. 60, 61). A member of the NKVD, he now revealed that he had been a Czech intelligence agent in the '20's and a German intelligence agent since 1932. Pushin confessed to having committed three acts of diversion on the instructions of his boss, taken part in wrecking, and turned over three secret documents to a German agent.

The fourth and last man from the chemical industry to testify was Leonid Tamm, a non–party man who had been brought into court from jail under escort, but not as a defendant in this trial; he was involved in another case. He testified against Pushin, but for most of his testimony he requested a session behind closed doors: his testimony was to reveal names of German diplomats working in Russia, and such revelations could not be made in an open court session. The session behind closed doors took place the same day. The court report issued after the session was non–committal.

When the testimony of the defendants and witnesses was completed, the so–called "experts" announced their findings. This was another component part of a primitive show trial. The experts were invited to give their opinions about the causes of the explosions and other accidents, and to answer the question whether the accidents could have been avoided. Their findings, of course, were such as to support the position of the prosecutor and show that the loss of life and property in these accidents was due to intent on the part of certain persons.

Vyshinsky's summation lasted five hours, but it was a

poor performance. Since the defendants had confessed to all the crimes, Vyshinsky's task was an easy one. He was not obliged to prove or dispute any statements of the defendants or their lawyers. Part of his speech was an excursion into the history of Trotskyism before the revolution and since, in which he repeated the story of Trotsky's ties with the Gestapo and quoted and referred to Stalin endlessly. Despite the fact that the speech had been prepared in advance and that Vyshinsky read it, it was badly organized, repetitious, and conceived in a style of hypocritical pathos; he used so many bloodthirsty expressions that they lost their impact; he was loud and dull. He concluded his summation with a demand that the court pronounce one penalty for all the defendants—"death by shooting."

Fourteen of the seventeen defendants had no counsel. Their strategy had been to admit all the charges, not to dispute the indictment, and not to defend themselves. The performance of the attorneys for Knyazev, Pushin, and Arnold was lamentable. Unable to deny any of the charges, they threw all the guilt on the "contemptible Trotsky" or on other defendants, without even making an attempt to dispute Vyshinsky's accusations.

On the last day of the trial, January 29, the defendants were permitted to make their final pleas. By that time all of them had begun to realize their true situation. If some of them had expected or hoped for a favorable outcome, they now looked worried and unhappy; some wept, others held their heads in their hands in despair. But it was too late to change their strategy; in their final pleas most of them threw themselves on the mercy of the court; the others declared themselves undeserving of mercy, obviously expecting pardon or leniency if they played their roles to the very end.

The only exception was Radek, who again made a lengthy speech lasting forty minutes. His tactic was to save his own life by implicating others and by hinting that he would be able to reveal other phases of the conspiracy and name other leaders of the underground. In his plea he included a statement that General Putna "had connections

VIII   The Military Tribunal

with leading Japanese and German military circles." (General Putna was executed a few months later.) He also stated: "Something remains hidden both from us and from the authorities and could be disclosed." He mentioned the name of Bukharin more than once, and hinted that in addition to the Zinoviev–Kamenev Center and the Parallel Center there existed a third organization, which had not yet been entirely exposed. Even people sympathetic to the government and to the prosecution felt revulsion at this performance of Radek's.

Radek's final speech [wrote Walter Duranty from Moscow on January 30] produced a strange and not wholly pleasant impression. He dragged in somewhat unnecessarily the names of Nikolai Bukharin, former *Izvestia* editor, and General Vitovt K. Putna—both under arrest—as Leon Trotsky's conspirators and seemed to be trying to suggest in an ambiguous fashion that other centers of Trotskyite activity of which the authorities were ignorant still existed here.[110]

IX   AFTER THE TRIAL

The last session of the Tribunal closed at 7:00 P.M. on January 29; the Military Collegium retired to deliberate. The conference behind closed doors lasted eight hours, and it was not until 3:00 A.M. that the court returned to the nervous defendants and excited audience to announce their decision.

Eight hours were needed not because the deliberations concerning the fate of the defendants were protracted or because there was any disagreement among the members of the court. The writing of the lengthy verdict (almost three thousand words) may have taken some time. But the main reason for extending the deliberations was that the proceedings must create the impression of a genuine, objective judgement; that in a case in which seventeen human lives are involved a Soviet court does not make hasty decisions; that all the pros and cons are taken into consideration. The government and the court were aware

[110] *New York Times*, January 30, 1937.

that at this moment the eyes of the world were upon them, that these hours would be decisive, or at least influential, in the forming of a judgement as to the standing of Soviet justice.

Actually the sentence in all its details was ready before the court retired. To understand this final stage of the trial as well as the other purge trials of those years, it is important to understand the real nature of this Military Collegium of the Supreme Court. Its title as well as its place among the supreme Soviet constitutional agencies was intended to produce the impression that, as far as justice is concerned, the Soviet Union is not inferior to the democratic countries; that a high degree of independence is a sacred virtue of the Soviet court system.

Actually the institution called the Military Collegium of the Supreme Court is nothing but a subsidiary of the NKVD, one of the most abject agencies of the Stalinist system; Vasili Ulrikh, its President, was actually dependent on instructions from above—from the Kremlin and from Yezhov. Sentences in important political trials all over Russia were prepared by the NKVD in advance,[111] and lists of defendants and the projected sentences were sent by the NKVD to Stalin. Stalin approved or amended them, and they were then carried out by the prison wardens and executioners. Here is what Khrushchev says now about the role of this Military Collegium of the Supreme Court:

[111] "The fate of the defendants in counter-revolutionary cases," says Nikolai Semionov, a former Soviet jurist, "is always *decided before the opening of the trial*. Therefore the superfluous court proceedings, complicating and delaying the decision, are considered undesirable, even politically harmful. Observation of the procedural formalities in these cases is considered necessary *only in show trials*. They have, however, no influence whatever on the predetermined fate of the defendants: the formal observance of the procedure on the part of the tribunal serves exclusively *propaganda purposes*, and not at all the purpose of aiding the defendants. The investigation of such a case in court is based on material presented by the MGB. The situation of the defendant in such cases is that of utter helplessness, and the performance of the prosecutor and the defense serves, as a rule, only *propaganda purposes*" (N. Semionov, *Sovetskii Sud i Karatel'naya Politika*) (The Soviet Court and Punitive Policy) (Munich: Institute for the Study of the History and Culture of the USSR, 1952), p. 99).

IX After the Trial

The vicious practice was condoned of having the NKVD prepare lists of persons whose cases were under the jurisdiction of the Military Collegium and whose sentences were prepared in advance. Yezhov would send these lists to Stalin personally for his approval of the proposed punishment. In 1937–38, 383 such lists containing the names of many thousands of Party, Soviet, Komsomol, Army and economic workers were sent to Stalin. He approved these lists.

... from 1954 to the present time the Military Collegium of the Supreme Court has rehabilitated 7,679 persons, many of whom were rehabilitated posthumously.[112]

Stalin himself was the agency that actually pronounced sentences, and in pronouncing them he often broke promises given to the defendants. In this trial the sentence, at least for a majority of the defendants, was a foregone conclusion. To Stalin, the danger was that the trial would be seen for what it actually was—a fake and a frame-up. If no death sentences were pronounced, the impression would be given that the proceedings had been merely propaganda against the Communist opposition. So much fanfare had been indulged in both before and during the trial, so many demonstrations had been held all over the Soviet Union, and so many articles on the trial had been published all over the world that nothing short of the death sentence was possible.

There was, however, in all of the purge trials, one consideration that could work against the imposition of the death sentence. If on the basis of earlier trials defendants were convinced that nothing could save them, that no promise of leniency would be kept, then how could confessions be obtained from the accused? The prospect of escaping the death sentence and the "solemn promise" were among the strongest arguments used by Stalin and his henchmen in trying to obtain confessions. Hundreds of prospective defendants had already been groomed for new trials in Moscow and the provinces; it was important to be able to point out to them during the investigation of

[112] Khrushchev's secret report of February 24, 1956.

their case that some—the most loyal and "sincere" ones—would be let off with a prison sentence.

The possibility that some defendants would retract their confessions in court was a spectre for the prosecution; the embarrassment would be great and Stalin's anger terrible. This was the reason why, five days before the end of the Zinoviev–Kamenev trial, a special order granted the defendants the right to appeal to the Supreme Soviet; in this way the defendants were being told that in case the sentence should be death, they still had a possibility of saving their lives; thus any prospect of embarrassing the authorities by the retraction of a confession was avoided. The appeals, when they were made, were rejected as a matter of course; the executions were hastily carried out.

When the tribunal returned at three o'clock in the morning, Ulrikh read the long sentence. Thirteen of the accused, including Pyatakov and Serebryakov, were sentenced to be shot; the other four were sentenced to prison terms: Sokolnikov, Radek and Arnold to ten years, Stroilov to eight years. The thirteen sentenced to death were shaken; several of them wept. All the thirteen signed petitions for mercy addressed to the Presidium of the Central Executive Committee.

If any had to be spared, Radek, Sokolnikov, Arnold, and Stroilov were the logical ones. It would have been unwise to execute Sokolnikov, the former ambassador to London, who was well known in the West; Stroilov and Arnold had given great help to the prosecution both before and during the trial; and Radek saved his life by his hints and promises. This shrewd scoundrel had succeeded where so many before him had failed.

The Soviet press hailed the "verdict of the people," but stressed that "Judas Trotsky is still loose in the world!" *Pravda* quoted Henri de Kérillis, writing in *Echo de Paris*: "I agree with [Jacques] Duclos that the closest tie exists between Hitler's Gestapo and the Trotskyites. The French General Staff is well informed about this." *Pravda* also quoted *Ere Nouvelle:* "They turned over secret documents to foreigners."

IX After the Trial

Lion Feuchtwanger, the non–Communist German writer, who happened to be in Moscow at the time, stated in the press that the "crimes of these men deserve punishment by death."

Joseph E. Davies, the United States Ambassador to the Soviet Union, who also was present at the trial, reported to the State Department:

> I arrived at the reluctant conclusion that the state had established its case, at least to the extent of proving the existence of widespread conspiracy and plot among the political leaders against the Soviet government, and which under their statutes established the crimes set forth in the indictment.[113]

Walter Duranty cabled the *New York Times* that "this trial does stand up and the evidence rings true," and that Vyshinsky "is serious minded and an earnest seeker after truth."[114]

Demonstrations were going on all the time all over the country. At the close of the trial resolutions adopted at meetings of children ten to sixteen years of age, couched in bloodthirsty terms, demanded "shoot the bandits," "destroy these hounds," etc. After the sentences were announced, a huge street demonstration in Moscow carried banners calling on the government to show no mercy; among the speakers was Nikita Khrushchev, who addressed a crowd of 200,000 in Red Square. It was not yet known whether the pleas for mercy would be granted, when Khrushchev shouted:

> We have gathered here, in the Red Square, to say our proletarian word, the word of full approval of the verdict pronounced by the Military Collegium of the Supreme Court against enemies of the people, betrayers

---

[113] Joseph E. Davies, *Mission to Moscow* (New York: Simon and Schuster, 1941), p. 43.

Four years later the ambassador reached the conclusion that: "The story which was unfolded in these trials disclosed a record of Fifth Columnist and subversive activities in Russia under a conspiracy agreement with the German and Japanese governments that were amazing" (p. 276).

[114] *New York Times*, January 27, 1937.

of the fatherland, traitors to the cause of the toiling masses, spies, diversionists, agents of fascism, base, despicable Trotskyites. . . .

These assassins aimed at the heart and brain of our Party. They raised their vicious hand against Comrade Stalin. By raising their hand against Comrade Stalin they raised it against all of us, against the working class, against the toilers! Raising their hand against Comrade Stalin, they raised it against the teachings of Marx–Engels–Lenin!

Raising their hand against Comrade Stalin they raised it against all the best that humanity possesses; because Stalin is the hope, the expectation, the beacon of all progressive humanity. Stalin is our banner! Stalin is our will! Stalin is our victory![115]

On the evening of February 1st at 8:25, it was announced that all pleas of the condemned men had been rejected and that the thirteen sentenced to death had been executed.[116]

Meanwhile Stalin's offensive was growing in size and ruthlessness. The great purge was embracing the whole country and devouring thousands and thousands of human beings. Previous decisions of the highest Communist bodies were ignored and those who were inclined to doubt the virtues of Stalin's terrorism were to pay with their lives. Bukharin, Rykov, and their friends were again in jail.
[1958]

---

[115] *Izvestia*, February 1, 1937, p. 1.
[116] It is reported from Moscow that Pyatakov and Radek have been rehabilitated. However, the rehabilitation is purely legal, that is, the charges of espionage, terrorism, and sabotage have been quashed, while no political rehabilitation has followed (*New York Times*, October 19, 1962). (*Ed.*)

AUSTRIA: WHERE STALIN FAILED

Though Stalin's initial ideas about the settlement in East Europe after the second World War were quite definite, their realization depended on which armies reached the area first. It seemed likely that the American and British armies would occupy Berlin, Czechoslovakia, and western Poland long before the Soviet armies. Stalin's first and tentative plan was to place Poland, Czechoslovakia, and Hungary under Soviet tutelage; as to Austria, he insisted, from 1941 on, that it simply be re-established as an independent and sovereign country. Cordell Hull, in his memoirs, mentions, for example, Stalin's conversation with Anthony Eden in December, 1941 in Moscow, in which Stalin "proposed the restoration of Austria as an independent state."[1] In October, 1943 Stalin agreed to the Moscow Declaration, which stipulated the restoration of an independent Austria as an Allied objective. In 1945, Stalin's program and the statements of his generals were all to the effect that Austria must be separated from Germany and be an independent state.

With the rapid advance of the Soviet armies, Stalin's plans began to change. During the last stage of the war it appeared likely that Austria would be invaded from the east and at least partially, "liberated" by the Red Army.

[1] *The Memoirs of Cordell Hull*, (New York: The Macmillan Company, 1948), II, 1167.

Now Austria appeared as one more of those countries that, after the military invasion, would take the path of political and social transformation and be forced to develop into a people's democracy. As Russia's ally, Austria would, along with Czechoslovakia, acquire importance as a "Western" type culturally advanced, industrial nation. Moreover, because of its geographical location it would extend the Soviet sphere to its westernmost limits—the borders of Switzerland—and open the way to the establishment of a Soviet military base only a short distance from Milan and Munich and only some 300 miles from Paris. In the new era of missiles such a base would immensely enhance Soviet power; as for France and Italy, with their sizable Communist Parties, it might mean the difference between victory and defeat for a Soviet-type socialism there. But even the inclusion in the Soviet sphere of eastern Austria alone would help substantially to round out the future realm of communism.

The Austrian situation naturally had its peculiarities, as indeed was to be the case in each of the people's democracies. Unlike Poland and Rumania, Austria does not border on Russia, and its strategic importance is relatively minor. But this is also true of Albania and Yugoslavia. On the other hand, if Austria was to be occupied by Western troops, so was Rumania. From still another point of view, Austria had been a part of Germany since 1938: why could it not go the way of East Germany?

Stalin made a complete right-about-face on the question of Austrian independence, and in the aftermath of the Moscow Conference of October, 1943 the Soviet periodical *War and the Working Class* attacked all Western proposals for an independent non-Communist Austria; it attacked not only the "Hapsburg monarchists" but also the Socialists, "who are now hastening to undertake the distribution of the leading posts in a future Austrian state"; it also opposed all plans for Austrian membership in a Danube federation "which is to spread from the Baltic to the Aegean."[2]

---

[2] *Voina i Rabochii Klass* (War and the Working Class), Moscow No. 12, (November 15, 1943), pp. 14–17.

Austria: Where Stalin Failed

For ten years after the war the Soviet government clung to the scheme of a satellite Austria. The history of Soviet policy toward Austria during that era was, as we shall see, the history of a sustained effort to continue Soviet expansion to the European west from advanced bases. And Austrian history in the postwar decade was that of a small nation that succeeded in extricating itself from a tight net of dependence and in ideologically joining the West, while in the strict political sense observing neutrality.

II

Soviet plans for postwar Austria were laid before the end of January, 1945. A number of ranking Communists among Austrian emigrés in Moscow, were assigned to move into Vienna as soon as the Red Army occupied the capital. The leading intellectual of this emigré group was Ernst Fischer, who in Moscow served as head of the "Free Austria" radio. Johann Koplenig, a man of "proletarian descent," was the tireless organizer. Friedl Fürnberg and Franz Honner were two other experienced and, in Moscow's view, reliable leaders. Honner, likewise a "proletarian," a veteran of the Spanish Civil War, who had been sent to Yugoslavia in 1944 as organizer of an "Austrian army," had his own ties with the Soviets.

It became known in the West that "Moscow has also chosen a Committee to become the provisional government in Austria in place of the Free Austrian Group in Paris and London who are backed by the Western Allies."[3] This did not mean, of course, that a purely Communist regime would be set up in Vienna. The plan, similar to those for Hungary and Czechoslovakia, was to institute a government without emphasizing the Communists' role in it; to appoint a flexible non–Communist as Premier; to have a member of the Communist Party occupy the post of police minister; to approach the Socialists for "labor unity" under Communist guidance; and gradually to eliminate other political groups from governmental collaboration, the press, and public prominence.

[3] *New York Times*, February 2, 1945.

Collaboration of the Austrian Communist leadership with the Soviet Army was imperative. General Alexei Zheltov, later (until January, 1958) chief of the Main Political Administration of the Soviet Army, was the senior political officer in General Feodor Tolbukhin's army and in charge of political operations in Austria. No government could emerge until Zheltov, after consultation with Moscow, had approved it. For the returning Austrian emigrés Zheltov served as the Austrian end of the Moscow–Vienna channel.

At the end of March, 1945 General Tolbukhin's army crossed into Austria, and on April 1, on their way to the capital, detachments of Soviet military forces reached Gloggnitz, where the aged Karl Renner lived with his family. For the people, conditions were extremely bad. Food was scarce, looting and rape had reached enormous proportions; the police were impotent. In an effort to put an end to these troubles, Renner appealed to the Soviet military command.

Karl Renner, formerly the leader of the Austrian rightist Socialists, now seventy-five years old, had served as Chancellor and Foreign Minister of Austria after the first World War and as President of the Austrian Parliament in the '30's. As a writer, speaker, and political leader, he had played an important role in Austrian politics; although opposed to the Nazi methods of *Anschluss*, he had stated his view that the unification with Germany was a "progressive" act. Lenin and his group had hated Renner, considering him a "social traitor." Renner, Lenin wrote, was "one of the most abject lackeys of German imperialism."[4] Lenin had attacked "the traitors of socialism, who supported the war of rapacious imperialists, all these Scheidemanns and Eberts, Austerlitz's and Renners."[5]

In 1943, Moscow's mouthpiece, *War and the Working Class*, violently attacked Renner for his "capitulation to the Fascists" in 1938. The success of Hitler's *Anschluss* policy "was furthered by the decision of influential Aus-

[4] Lenin, *Sochineniya* (Works), 4th ed., XXIII, 261.
[5] *Ibid.*, XXVIII, 345.

trian politicians, like the former Social Democratic Chancellor Karl Renner, to capitulate to the German Fascists and to declare the *Anschluss* an act of 'historical progress.' "[6]

The Soviet intelligence officers whom Renner contacted in Gloggnitz had heard about him in Russia and read of him in Communist textbooks and in Lenin's works. They were greatly interested in this intriguing figure. In their search for non–Communist collaborators and, in particular, a possible candidate for a new premiership or presidency, they had to contact and report on political leaders, past and present, who had never embraced either National Socialism or communism, persons who would represent the "plain people," the "man in the street," as well as the formerly large Socialist Party. Thus a political bloc could emerge that would serve as the first stage toward another kind of state. "Such a man [as Renner]," said Adolf Schärf, "no longer young but seriously compromised in the eyes of the Communists, ought to be a docile tool in the hands of the occupation power and of those close to it!"[7]

As Renner later described it,[8] his conversation with the Soviet officers touched at first on the local situation but was soon extended to the area of general politics. Renner was polite and friendly. On the one hand, Russia was a member of the great democratic coalition, a fact that made the rapprochement easier for him. On the other hand, Russia's power in Austria was at that moment absolute, and Renner, the flexible "opportunist," deemed it reasonable to maintain a sympathetic tie with the Soviet Union and, in particular, with Stalin. "I was not worried about the danger of our country falling prey to the dictatorship of the Bolsheviks. Allied with the United States and Great Britain, Russia could not attempt any attack against the social and economic structure of Austria."[9]

[6] *Voina i Rabochii Klass*, No. 15, (November 15, 1943) p. 15.

[7] Adolf Scharf, *Oesterreichs Erneuerung 1945–1955*. (Vienna: Verlag der Wiener Volksbuchhandlung, 1955), p. 30.

[8] Karl Renner, *Denkschrift uber die geschichte der Unabhangigkeit Osterreichs und Bereicht uber drei Monate Aufbauarbeit*. (Zurich: Europa-Verlag, 1946), p. 9.

[9] *Ibid.*, p. 15.

The Soviet generals informed Moscow about their contact with Renner. Anastas Mikoyan has related that Stalin was surprised and pleased. "Why," he exclaimed, "is the old traitor still alive? He is just the man we need!" General Zheltov asked Renner about his attitude toward the Soviet Union and the Red Army, and inquired whether he would be willing to head the new Austrian government under Soviet occupation. Renner reports: "I deliberated for a long time and made the decision: I have confidence that the Red Army does not want anything from Austria except what is imposed on her by its victory over Hitler's armies and what is granted to it by the rules of war. I believe myself capable of undertaking the task of freeing Austria from fascism."[10]

In his memoirs Renner mentions the fact that General Zheltov proposed that he (Renner) write a memorandum on the political situation; Renner says he refused. He had, however, on April 12, written by hand a long and important letter to Stalin (which he omits to mention in his memoirs). Following is the text of this friendly, humble, somewhat pro–Stalinist and anti–Western communication:[11]

His Excellency Marshal Stalin
Moscow

 Esteemed Comrade:

 In the early days of the [labor] movement I was connected by personal ties with many Russian leaders, but I did not have the pleasure of knowing you personally, dear Comrade.

 I met Lenin at the Stockholm Socialist Peace Conference in 1917.* I was associated with Trotsky in the years of his stay in Vienna; I worked together with Ryazanov on the Vienna *Arbeiter-zeitung*. Many of the comrades who fled tzarism stayed with me, or at

---

[10] *Ibid.*, p. 16.

[11] A photostatic copy of the original letter is in the archives of the President of the Austrian Republic.

*Renner obviously was in error. There was no peace conference when Lenin passed through Stockholm on April 13 (March 31), 1917, on his way from Switzerland back to Russia.

least spent a night in my flat on their way to Switzerland; some of them I provided with passports.

And now, by a whim of history, it has so happened that, at an age when I thought to have completed my political activities, I have come into personal contact with you in such an unusual and significant way.

At its entry into Vienna, the Red Army found me and my family at my residence in Gloggnitz (near Wiener-Neustadt), where I, along with my Party comrades, was looking forward with confidence to the occupation. The Russian commanders promptly and respectfully offered me their protection and gave me full freedom of action, of which I had been painfully deprived since 1934, during the reign of Dollfussism and Hitlerism.

For this I now express to the Red Army, and to you, its glorious Commander, my sincere and devoted gratitude as well as that of the working class of Austria.

It so happens that I was the first of the members of the Presidium of the Social Democratic Party who remained in Austria thus to regain my freedom of action. It is fortunate that I, as the last President of the then free Parliament, can declare myself entitled to speak for the Austrian people. It is another advantage that I, as the first Chancellor of the Austrian Republic, have had experience in forming a state as well as in organizing an administration, and therefore believe myself capable of taking up and carrying out the task of reawakening Austria.

I consider it, therefore, my absolute duty to make myself fully and completely available for this task. Competent organs of the Tolbukhin army group have declared themselves ready to put the necessary means at my disposal. This was essential, since we did not even possess the stationery to draft our first proclaimations, or railways, mail service, or cars to distribute them. Without the Red Army none of the steps I took would have been possible, and therefore not only I but also the future "Second Republic" and its working class will be forever grateful to you, Mr. Marshal, and to your victorious army.

The Hitler regime left us here absolutely helpless, and we shall remain helpless before the barriers of the world powers when the new order in Europe comes into being. I beg of you now to think of Austria benevolently at the council of the Great Powers, and to take us, as far as the tragic circumstances permit, under your mighty protection.

We are threatened at present by starvation and epidemics. We are threatened with loss of territory in the showdown with our neighbors. Even now we do not have enough arable land in our stony Alps to provide even poorly for our daily bread, and if we lose more land we shall be unable to live! It cannot be the intention of the victors to let us perish helplessly, but the West knows, as 1919 proved, too little of our situation and is not interested enough in us to assure us the prerequisites of independence.

But I do not wish to bother you prematurely, esteemed Comrade, with questions of the future. I only ask you to take notice now of the following:

Thanks to Russia's surprising display of might, our entire people has become aware of the lies of the twenty years of National Socialist propaganda, and is full of admiration for the tremendous achievements of the Soviets.

The confidence of the Austrian working class, especially in the Soviet Republic, has become boundless.

The Austrian Social Democrats will come to a brotherly understanding with the Communist Party and will cooperate with them as equals in the founding of the Republic. There is no doubt that the future of our country belongs to socialism. This is beyond question and needs no emphasis.

Respectfully yours,
Dr. Karl Renner

Wiener–Neustadt
April 15, 1945

Meanwhile Renner moved along with the Soviet military staff. On the way to Vienna he wrote leaflets and appeals to the population. In Vienna he was put up in a district that had been completely taken over by the Soviet forces and from which the Austrian population had been evacuated. A Russian bodyguard and a Russian colonel, who acted as interpreter, lived with him. Renner's connection was solely with the Russians, since no contact was possible with the British and Americans, who had not yet moved into Vienna. In being asked to form a government he believed that his regime would be approved by Britain and the United States and that its jurisdiction would embrace the whole of Austria; he was mistaken. Moscow had simply placed before the Western Allies the accomplished fact of the establishment of an Austrian regime; Renner was left in the dark as to his own position.

These were, in a sense, the "Russian months" of Vienna, and of eastern Austria in general: there was no non-Communist press during this initial phase and news came mainly through Soviet channels; whatever authority existed was Russian-appointed or at least Russian-tolerated; the British forces were still in the southwest of the country, and the Americans had entered through Salzburg; but the east, including Vienna, was, contrary to Allied plans, strictly in Soviet hands.[12]

The situation was the result of a deliberate, well-prepared and thought-through course of Soviet policy. Whenever possible—an occupied territory such as Korea in 1945 and Manchuria in 1945–46—Stalin tried to gain time for a peculiar set of operations: to enable a group of leaders, upon their arrival from Russia, to set up the framework of a reformed Communist Party; to establish a government, ostensibly non-Communist but actually under Communist guidance; to take over the press and the radio; to reorganize the police and the armed forces.

III

Following the Red Army's entry into Vienna came the Communist leaders from abroad: Fischer and Koplenig directly from Moscow, Honner and Fürnberg via Yugoslavia. On April 23, 1945, the leaders of the Christian-

[12] Adolf Schärf, *Zwischen Demokratie und Volksdemokratie*. (Vienna: Verlag der Volksbuchhandlung, 1950), p. 7: "Anyone who visited or lived in Lower Austria, the Burgenland or Styria in the months following the entry of the Red Army into Vienna, might have gained the impression that this part of Austria had become Communist and Russian."

Social (*Volkspartei*), Socialist, and Communist parties agreed to form a government and to submit its list of ministers to the Red Army's political branch. Approval arrived promptly, and on the 27th the new government, officially established, issued its first proclamation to the nation.

During this period the Communist Party appeared to be strong and growing rapidly; because of the tremendous energy and efficiency of its members, public opinion greatly overestimated its size. Communists as well as non–Communists believed that the Communist Party could win twenty–five to thirty per cent of the votes. Entitled, therefore, to about a third of the ministerial posts, the Communist Party claimed and obtained the Ministry of Internal Affairs, including the police (Franz Honner) and Education (Ernst Fischer). Col. Franz Winterer, a Communist, was appointed Under–Secretary of Defense; he was soon elevated to the rank of major general. Johann Koplenig was included in the five–man supreme "political cabinet." Renner, as Premier, and the other ministers were well aware of the special relationship that existed between the Red Army and the Communist Party.

Although the Soviet generals did not take part in meetings of the government, they were kept informed, officially, on all issues and decisions.[13] On April 28 Renner sent a circular letter to all ranking members of the government, stating: "The document regarding the formation of the Provisional Government has been duly sent, along with the list of prospective cabinet members, to Moscow, to be forwarded to London and Washington."[14]

The formation of the Renner government took London and Washington by surprise. Viewing it as a Soviet puppet, they refused to give it recognition, since it had been intended that Vienna should become a city of three (or four) occupational zones and not a Soviet capital. Renner's regime was more worried about this situation than was the Soviet government; Renner's limited jurisdiction did not go beyond the eastern (Soviet) zone, but Renner considered

[13] *Ibid.*, p. 18.
[14] Schärf, *Oesterreichs Erneuerung 1945–1955*, p. 37.

his government an all–Austrian government. In the Allied view, Moscow, in fact, wanted to see the Vienna regime develop into a satellite, but not before it had extended its authority over the entire country. By breaking Austria in two (as was done later in the case of Germany), Moscow could become the unilateral ruler in Vienna. At that time, however, Stalin was not prepared to go to such lengths.

In mid–May, 1945 Renner received Stalin's reply to his letter of April 15:

> His Excellency the Chancellor of the State of Austria, Mr. K. Renner.
>
> I thank you, dear Comrade, for your message of April 15.
>
> You need have no doubt that your concern for the independence, integrity and welfare of Austria is likewise my concern.
>
> Any assistance which may be necessary to Austria, I am ready to accord you to the best of my power and ability.
>
> I apologize for my delay in replying.
>
> I. Stalin[15]

It would be wrong to consider this short note merely a polite gesture, for its implications touched upon an important problem of the time. In his letter Renner had, among other things, expressed the hope that Stalin would support Austria against a possible loss of territory to her neighbors. Offering Stalin *"das grenzenlose Vertrauen der öesterreichischen Arbeiterklasse"* (the unlimited confidence of the Austrian working class), Renner tried to win the help of his new "comrade" against territorial claims that were certain to be voiced, especially on the part of Tito's Yugoslavia. Stalin was no doubt aware of this issue when he promised Renner to take care of Austria's *"Gänzlichkeit"* (integrity).

It was a strange united front: Stalin and Renner against Tito.

[15] *New Times*, Moscow, No. 37, (September 7, 1949), Supplement, p. 1.

IV

The Yugoslav regime, headed by Tito and Dr. Ivan Subasich, claimed Istria and Trieste from Italy and southern Carinthia from Austria, Carinthia to be incorporated in the adjoining Yugoslav province of Slovenia. A number of German–built aviation plants in the area made this part of Carinthia doubly important in Yugoslav eyes. The Yugoslav government notified the Big Three of its claims. Since Carinthia lay in the prospective British zone of Austria, the Yugoslav program primarily affected Churchill's government. It was expected in Belgrade that, in order to support his protégé, Yugoslav Foreign Minister Subasich, Churchill would accede to the demand, and that Stalin, in view of his ties with the Yugoslav Communists, would do likewise. Tito must have discussed the matter with Stalin in April, 1945, when he came to Moscow to sign the Soviet–Yugoslav treaty.

Stalin's position was not an easy one. His Yugoslav allies were enthusiastic and aggressive; they certainly deserved a reward in the form of territory. But Stalin's course could not be dictated by a specific situation in the Balkans, and Stalin could not at that time defy the British. Nor could he repudiate his friends in Austria, which appeared to be on the way to becoming a people's democracy. It was not generally known at the time that disagreements between Stalin and Tito had started as early as 1942, and that Tito's anti–British course during the war had been opposed and rejected by the Soviet leadership.[16]

Stalin could not and did not promise Tito that he would support Tito's drive into Carinthia. Tito had to go it alone.

On May 8 the British army moved into Klagenfurt, capital of Austrian Carinthia, and began to organize the occupation of the zone. At about the same time the Yugoslav "partisans" appeared in Klagenfurt, bringing with them the embryo of a government. The formation of a regime under Hans Piesch, with two Communists among

[16] Mosha Piyade, *About the Legend that the Yugoslav Uprising Owed Its Existence to Soviet Assistance*. (London: A. Quick & Co., Ltd. 1950).

its members, was announced. There arose the paradoxical situation of two occupation armies that did not recognize one another, with each claiming dictatorial powers. The result was confusion and chaos; the situation was further complicated by Churchill's strong course against Tito in which Churchill had the support of President Truman. Field Marshal Earl Alexander was instructed by Churchill to "have a solid mass of troops" in the Trieste area and to make it clear that territorial issues would have to be decided at the peace conference. Truman sent Churchill a strong message to the effect that "we should be prepared to consider any necessary steps to effect Tito's withdrawal."[17]

Churchill instructed the British ambassador in Belgrade to join the American ambassador in making strong representations to Tito. Under these conditions Tito decided on a different course of procedure in Trieste and Carinthia: he replied in the negative on the Trieste issue, but withdrew his forces, after two weeks of occupation, from southern Austria. It was reported that he had been instructed by the Russian general to do this and had immediately obeyed. That orders from Stalin were behind this humiliating defeat was seen from the fact that on May 22, 1945 *Izvestia* reported on a statement of Field Marshal Alexander, part of which read as follows: "Marshal Tito obviously intends to enforce his claims by means of arms and by military occupation. Such action is too reminiscent of the methods of Hitler, Mussolini and Japan. . . . I did my utmost to reach a friendly understanding with Marshal Tito, but I did not succeed. Therefore the governments of the United States and Great Britain have put the question directly to Marshal Tito. The Soviet government is fully informed."[18]

Marshal Tito issued an indignant reply, but he withdrew his forces.

At the opening of the Potsdam Conference of the Big Three on July 20, 1945, Churchill charged Stalin with not permitting British and American forces to occupy their

[17] Winston S. Churchill, *Triumph and Tragedy*, (Boston: Houghton Mifflon Company, 1953), pp. 551 ff.

zones in Austria. In his answer Stalin took the offensive. Field Marshal Alexander (whom he detested) had behaved, Stalin said, "as if Russian troops were under his control." A few days later, however, Stalin informed the Conference that the Soviet troops were withdrawing to their own area.[19] It was several weeks before the Western armies entered their sectors in Vienna and the Allied administrations could be set up.

Still acting as protector of the Renner government against Western suspicions and malevolence, Stalin proposed to Churchill and Truman the extension of the powers of the new Vienna regime to all of Austria. The proposal was not accepted. It was decided instead to study the question again after the entry of troops into Vienna, when the Western representatives would be in a position to acquaint themselves with the situation.

Acting consistently as friend and protector of Austria, Stalin reiterated that Russia was claiming no reparations from Austria; he wanted this made clear in the official protocol. Actually he did not intend to refrain from taking from Austria what Russia used to call "contributions" (war indemnities), and what, after the first World War, had been called reparations.[20] It was Molotov who did most of the talking on this point—the issue of "German external assets"—which was to play an important role in the developments of the next decade. The Soviet government claimed and obtained the right to German property in a

[18] *Izvestia*, May 22, 1945, p. 4. A month passed before Stalin reverted to the sharp wording of Marshal Alexander's statement. On June 21 he wrote to Churchill: "I cannot accept the supercilious tone with regard to the Yugoslavs which Field-Marshal Alexander has occasionally adopted in these conversations. It is absolutely unacceptable that Field-Marshal Alexander in an official and public message allowed himself to compare Marshal Tito with Hitler and Mussolini. Such a comparison is unjustified and offensive to Yugoslavia." Churchill answered on the 23rd, saying, among other things: "I do not see any reason to make excuses for Field-Marshal Alexander, although I was not aware that he was going to draft his telegram exactly in this way." (Churchill, *Triumph and Tragedy*, pp. 560–61).

[19] James F. Byrnes, *Speaking Frankly*. (New York: Harper & Brothers, 1947), p. 161.

number of territories, including eastern Austria, as part of its reparations.

The Western delegates were not aware of the meaning and scope of the "German assets" claimed by the Soviet government. During the years of German dominance over Austria (1938–45) Germany had not only invested in the Austrian economy but had also forcibly taken over Western industrial and commercial companies and had by various means, including anti–Jewish policies, seized the property of Austrian citizens. The value of this property was relatively high; to impoverished Russia it represented a boon; to the West, the matter of restoration of this property to its legitimate owners was a moral issue as well.[21]

In the discussion of this problem at Potsdam, Molotov proposed a sum of $250 million as the amount of Austria's future payments to the four Allies (the Big Three and Yugoslavia). Britain and the United States rejected this suggestion outright. Had Molotov's proposal been accepted, the Soviet Union and Yugoslavia would have received about $150 million (since the Western powers renounced their claims). This sum was far less than what Austria had to supply to Russia in the course of the next ten years, in addition to the $150 million it paid after the signing of the *Staatsvertrag* of 1955. The British and Americans had not been equal to their task at Potsdam.

In the meantime an agreement on zones of occupation in Austria had been reached; soon Allied armies started to move into their assigned areas. At the last minute, a slice

---

[20] Since Lenin had been violently opposed to the system of war indemnities, Stalin had to draw an artificial line between the system of imperialist "indemnities" and that of reparations: "Indemnities are of a compulsory character and in their essence represent plundering of the population of an occupied territory or a defeated nation. Indemnities are one of the forms of pillaging the colonial and dependent countries by the capitalist states. . . .

A distinction must be made between indemnities and reparations, i.e., compensation by a defeated state which was responsible for the outbreak of the war, of damages suffered by the victorious nation. . . ." (*Large Soviet Encyclopedia*, 2nd ed., XXII, 461.)

[21] On January 5, 1943, the Allied governments had declared this type of forcible dispossession to be invalid. The Soviet government was among the signers of this declaration.

of Austrian territory previously allotted to the Americans was claimed and obtained by the Soviet forces.[22] The importance of this territory was that it bordered on Czechoslovakia; the Soviet government wanted no direct contact between Czechoslovakia and the American forces in Austria. In size and economic potential the Soviet zone was by far the most important.

Vienna, occupied by all four powers, was situated in the heart of the Soviet zone, and overland access to the city was through Soviet-occupied territory. An Allied Council was set up as the supreme legislative and executive power. The only concession made to liberated Austria was the omission of the word "Control" from the name of the Council (unlike the Allied Control Council established for Germany). In this governing body the Soviet representatives had the strongest position. Because of the extent of its zone, the size of its army in Austria, the proximity of Austria to its borders, its role in the neighboring countries, and in general its predominance in Central Europe at the time, Russia had its way. Rarely inclined to make concessions, helped by the local Communist Party, defying the other powers, it often assumed a position of unilateral control. In direct negotiations the Soviet military and political leaders on the spot were affable and friendly; not so in the conduct of state affairs, for which they were responsible to Moscow.

Once the Allies were in Vienna, new ties began to develop between Renner and the Westerners. Despite his public statements, the West was closer to Renner's heart than was Russia. Privately the Western representatives advised him on how to resist Soviet pressure in important matters. While repeatedly declaring his profound gratitude to "Generalissimo Stalin" for what Russia had done for Austria, he at the same time took advice on how to oppose Soviet demands.

Early in September, 1945, for example, the Soviet Deputy Minister of Foreign Trade, P. N. Kumykin, arrived with a delegation to organize the Austrian-Soviet

---

[22] Mark W. Clark, *Calculated Risk*, (New York: Harper & Brothers, 1950), p. 455.

Oil Corporation which was to exploit the rich Zistendorf oil fields. Moscow was certain that Renner's "satellite" government would not oppose this organization. The day before the Allied Council met for the first time, Renner was called from a cabinet meeting to Soviet headquarters to sign the contract for the oil company. Advised in advance by the Americans, he refused to sign, arguing that he could not yet speak for the whole of Austria and that, moreover, he would have to consult with the other members of the Allied Council. The Russian threats were unavailing. The contract was not signed. This action did not basically change the situation, since the Soviets took over the Zistendorf oil fields—and much more. But the course of the Renner government had changed: although still obedient, it ceased from then on to follow blindly the satellite road.

Another slight deviation from satellite behavior was the reform of the Communist–headed Ministry of the Interior (police) at the end of September, 1945. At conferences of Austrian representatives from provinces in all four zones, leaders from the western, non–Communist provinces refused to submit to the Vienna government because the police organization was in Communist hands and the Communist Party was thus in a position to falsify the results of the forthcoming elections. As a concession, a committee of five, representing various groups, was formed to supervise the elections. Meanwhile Minister Honner remained at his post. Since this was a way of extending Renner's jurisdiction to all of Austria, Moscow acquiesced. As to more far-reaching reforms, the Communists emphasized that "the Soviet government will not permit substantial changes in the government." Delegates from other zones threatened to leave and form a separate government, which would have split Austria into two parts.[23] Finally, on October 20, the four Allies gave *de facto* recognition to the reorganized Provisional Government headed by Karl Renner. Control over the government remained in the hands of the Allied Council (in which each of the occupying powers

[23] Karl Gruber, *Zwischen Befreiung und Freiheit* (Vienna: Verlag Ullstein, 1953), pp. 28, 36ff.

had the right of veto). In addition, the size of the occupying army in each zone remained unlimited.

In preparation for the elections scheduled for November 25, the three main political parties (the conservative People's Party, the Socialists, and the Communists) became very active; the press was practically free; meetings were held without interference by the police. In Vienna anti-Communist propaganda was cautious; in the Western zones the slogans were hard-hitting: "He who loves the Red Army votes Communist!" The general situation was bleak: food was scarce, shipments to Russia massive. Russia was making itself unpopular, and thereby paralyzing the Communist Party of Austria.

The election proved this beyond all expectations and predictions of even the most extreme anti-Communists. The People's Party's vote was 1,602,000 (eighty-five deputies); the Socialists', 1,435,000 (seventy-six deputies); the Communists', 174,000 (four deputies). It was perhaps the worst defeat suffered by any Communist Party in the immediate postwar era.

Renner's government was not purged of Communists, however; after all, the two Communist ministers represented the strongest of the occupying powers. The important Ministry of the Interior, however, was taken from the Communists and entrusted to a Socialist. To Moscow it must have appeared that Austria intended to cast off her satellite status. Relations between Austria and the Soviet Union began to deteriorate.

The closing weeks of 1945 marked the end of the first post-war phase of Soviet-Austrian relations. The trend toward satellite status for Austria was reversed; Austria entered on a path leading away from a people's democracy. These unusual developments were caused by three circumstances: first, Austria's geographical position, which made her less important from the Soviet strategical viewpoint; second, the presence of Western military and diplomatic forces in Vienna, which might have meant a large-scale war if the Soviet Union had attempted to revamp the Austrian political system; and third, the lamentable showing of the Communist Party in the elections. Stalin was never guided in his plans and decisions by the results of free balloting or public opinion, but even so he could not base a new regime in Austria on a party that had polled only five per cent of the vote in an election. Had the country been Poland or Germany, Stalin would have drawn no conclusions for his policy from the vote, but Austria was less important.

Neither the Communist Party of Austria nor its Soviet protectors were as yet entirely discouraged. Ascribing the vote to temporary and accidental causes, they hoped to regain influence and strength. Moscow still pretended that the majority of Austrians were in sympathy with the Soviet Union:

> There can be no doubt that progressive intellectuals, as well as the masses of the Austrian people, are anxious for understanding and closer relations with the Soviet Union. That these wishes have not yet found support among many prominent leaders of Austria's two largest parties—the People's and the Socialists— only goes to show that they are ignoring the national interests of their country for the sake of definite political tendencies and as a result of outside influence.
>
> Austria stands now at the parting of the ways. The cardinal issue is being decided, namely, whether she is to be a plaything in the hands of international reaction, or will take the road of free and independent democratic development.[24]

In the next five years at least two attempts were made by the Communists, with the tacit knowledge and cautious support of the Soviet authorities, to subvert the regime by a clumsily organized "popular uprising"—one in 1947, the other in 1950. (See pp. 138-41) Both failed. But the attitude of Moscow toward Vienna had changed markedly.

To the Soviet leadership and the Soviet press, Austria, in 1945, was a "democracy" on a level, for example, with Poland; it was evolving toward a people's democracy. The Soviet Union was the first to accord *de jure* recognition to Austria, in October, 1945; the other powers withheld such recognition until January, 1946. Since 1946 Soviet hostility

[24] *New Times*, Moscow, No. 13, (July 1, 1946), p. 12.

toward the political system and government of Austria has been manifest. The Soviets' delaying action in connection with the peace treaty, the large number of Soviet occupation forces, Soviet economic operations, the embryo Communist army disguised as an industrial guard, the propaganda against allegedly "reviving fascism" and pro-German sentiments—on all these issues and problems the Soviet side took an anti-Austrian political line. The defense of Austrian interests, quite naturally, fell to the West. It was a continuing cold war; at times it seemed to be reaching the freezing point.

The Soviet side insisted on the forcible repatriation of alien displaced persons (about 750,000 after the war, and 437,000 in 1946, and about 400,000 in the spring of 1947). All were escapees from countries of the Soviet bloc—Russia, Poland, Yugoslavia—to which they were afraid to return. With the permission of the American authorities, two Soviet repatriation commissions were sent to Austria to persuade the Soviet refugees to return home. The commissions caused unrest among the refugees; they sometimes tried to force DPs to repatriate; sometimes they tried to recruit spies from among them. After two Soviet efforts, the Americans refused to permit the commissions to operate.[25]

The Soviet government insisted on a more severe procedure against Austrian Nazis and on a policy of "denazification." The charge that the Americans and British had been slow in this respect was standard in Soviet policy and propaganda from the end of 1945 on. In 1946 *New Times* wrote:

> ... Soon after the end of the war a law on the punishment of active Nazis was passed. According to this law, persons who had been active in the ranks of the Fascist Party were liable to the death sentence. A special People's Court was set up to try the former Hitlerites. But what actually came of this? Of 6,874 Nazis arrested in Vienna after the liberation, 2,025 were indicted for trial. In all this time, however, only

[25] Clark, *Calculated Risk*, p. 475.

119 cases have been examined and in these, nine of the accused have been exonerated. Furthermore, 2,559 former Nazis have been released from prison on formal juridical grounds, and of the 1,934 Nazis interned in prison camps 1,001 have also been released.[26]

In fact, the Western powers were less severe than the Soviet authorities in their prosecution of former Nazis.

The situation was the same with respect to the so-called repatriation of Germans, including the so-called *Volksdeutsche* and others. The deportation of Germans was carried out with great cruelty on the part of the Soviet authorities: families were ordered to move on a few days' notice and were not permitted to take their belongings with them. Again, the Soviet government and its press were violent in their accusations that the Western powers were too lenient toward the Reich Germans.

The Russian armies demanded from the Austrian government substantial funds as "occupation costs." The Western powers either claimed nothing or exacted much less than did the Soviets. While the Soviet forces lived off the Austrian land, the United States and Britain supplied food not only to their military forces but to the civilian population of Vienna as well.

At the beginning, the formal relationship between the Austrian government and the Allied Council was simple: to come into force, a decision of the Austrian government required the approval of the Allied Council. Since unanimity on the Council was required, the Soviet delegate in effect could veto laws promulgated by the Austrian government. Not until June 28, 1946 was this situation remedied: from that date on, simple legislative measures became automatically effective if they were not vetoed by the Allied Council. The reform was significant. In their own zone, however, the Soviet authorities maintained unilateral rule and demanded obedience on the part of the Austrian zonal agencies.

This was, in particular, the case with regard to the police after the Communist Minister of the Interior was forced

[26] *New Times*, Moscow, No. 2, (January 15, 1946), p. 26.

to quit (see p. 134) and the personnel had been gradually purged of Communists in ranking positions.[27] Arrests and kidnappings on a large scale continued, however, especially in the first postwar years. Hardly a day passed without a report of at least one case of kidnapping.

V

Soviet industrial and trade enterprises assisted the Austrian Communist Party in several ways. Among the Soviet employees a large number had been recruited from among Austrian Communists. The "plant guards," the Communist armed force, consisted to a large extent of politically reliable men. To attract the Austrian intelligentsia, a "progressive" theater was established, pro–Soviet and pro–Communist books were published, a luxurious building to house the Communist paper *Volksstimme* was to be erected. The membership of the Communist Party was claimed to number about 120,000, but many had joined the Party only in order to keep their jobs. The population viewed the Communist Party as a well-paid representative of the Soviets—a fact that substantially lowered its prestige.

The plan to turn Austria into a people's democracy was not definitely given up until 1950. Two forcible attempts were made to achieve this goal.

On May 5, 1947, while negotiations over a "state treaty for Austria" were under way and the conclusion of a treaty appeared to depend on the good will of Moscow, the Communist Party arranged political strikes and street demonstrations ("hunger demonstrations") in Vienna; the demonstrators gathered in front of the government building on the Ballhausplatz with the slogan "The Government

[27] The most sensational case (April, 1954) was that of Soviet agent Nikolai Khokhlov. Khokhlov arrived in Frankfurt, Germany, with the assignment to assassinate a leader of a Russian anti-Soviet organization. He defected, reported to United States authorities, and showed an Austrian passport in the name of Josef Hofbauer. The passport was genuine. It had been delivered by the Austrian police on orders of Soviet officers, despite the fact that the Austrian police were aware that it was to be used illicitly.

Must Go!" A group of demonstrators invaded the building, where the ministers sat in conference, and for a time the situation appeared dangerous. The police advised the members of the government to escape. "From our windows," Minister Karl Gruber reported, "we saw Soviet liaison officers moving at the edge of the crowds."[28] The government appealed to the Allied Council for help. The Soviet element refused to intervene. But before the other members of the Council could take any action, the crowd dispersed. It was obvious that the Soviet members of the Allied Council had conveyed the appropriate orders to the leaders of the demonstration.

This attempt at a "putsch" was followed by secret negotiations for the formation of a new government more sympathetic to Moscow. The initiative for these negotiations was taken by the Communists, but a number of ministers of the conservative People's Party were among the negotiators. Ernst Fischer held out the prospect of Soviet concessions if a greater role in the regime were given to the Communist Party; the socialists were to be eliminated; as the prospective head of the government, Dr. Josef Dobretsberger, a pro-Soviet ("fellow traveler") professor of economics, was proposed. Although himself a member of the People's Party, Minister Karl Gruber saw the far-reaching implications of the negotiations and reported them to the Vienna agency of the Associated press. When the story became public, the negotiations were temporarily abandoned.[29]

A few months later the Marshall Plan became a cause of discord. The Communist Party, of course, opposed participation in the Plan, and its representatives quit the government in protest.[30] When the government nevertheless decided, on April 16, 1948, to participate in the Plan, the Soviet side issued a formal protest charging that such action was contrary to the system of Allied control over Austria. In its reply the Austrian government stressed its

[28] Gruber, *Zwischen Befreiung und Freiheit*, pp. 162–65.
[29] *Ibid.*, pp. 162–69; Schärf, *Oesterreichs Erneuerung 1944–1955*, pp. 161–68.
[30] Schärf, *Oesterreichs Erneuerung*, pp .173–174.

right to take this action. Thereupon a new Soviet note informed the Austrian government that the Marshall Plan would not be put into effect in the Soviet zone.[31]

The second Soviet–sponsored attempt to overthrow the Austrian government coincided with the first stage of the Korean war, in October, 1950. This second attempt had been well prepared in advance. It was far more dangerous than that of three years earlier. To the outside world the active force appeared to be the Austrian Communist Party and the Communist–controlled strike committees; in fact, the active element were groups of workers from the Soviet–operated enterprises in Austria. The Soviet occupation forces themselves pretended to be neutral, though in fact they lent substantial support, at least in the beginning, to the subversive campaign.

The movement was centered in Vienna and its suburbs, in certain cities of Lower Austria and in Styria. Demonstrations started on September 25; the movement lasted until October 4. Groups of striking Communist workers, brought in by trucks to other industrial plants, tried to stop work everywhere. Demonstrators demanding "Down with the government!" again gathered in the Ballhausplatz. In an effort to aid the Vienna police, the government tried to get assistance from the loyal gendarmerie of the Soviet zone, but the Soviet authorities prohibited this. In Wiener–Neustadt, where the post office had been occupied by Communist groups, the police at first succeeded in routing the occupants, but Soviet officers ordered them to return the building to the strikers.

A formal protest was addressed by the Austrian government to all four occupation powers. In addition, Minister Gruber asked to see the Soviet Ambassador, Mikhail Koptelov, and told him: "If the Soviet occupation authorities really intend to assist lawbreakers in Austria, the

---

[31] When the Plan was put into effect the Moscow *New Times* (no. 3, January 14, 1948) reported that a small quantity (two per cent) of Marshall Plan supplies bearing the American label "Sixty per cent of this food is American aid" reached the Eastern zone, where a rubber-stamp inscription, stating "Contrary to the facts," was placed beside the American label.

government will not only ask all international organs for help but will also resist such action."[32] Koptelov's reply was that, although the incident in Wiener–Neustadt was "unknown" to him, he and his government would observe strict neutrality in internal Austrian affairs. The movement did, in fact, abate and finally died out.

In the following years no similar attempts were made. The Communist voting strength never exceeded five per cent, and their representation in Parliament amounted to from four to five deputies: since the election of 1959 they have not obtained a single seat.

VI

Thus, since the end of 1945 the roles have been reversed: the Soviet government has ceased to play the part of Austria's protector, while the Western powers have tried to assume it. Negotiations concerning a future "state treaty" with Austria were greatly influenced by this new situation: the Soviet Union, the strongest of the four powers in Austria, was not interested in a speedy consolidation and pacification of the country; on the contrary, it discriminated against Austria, which was now considered a "capitalist" nation. Peace treaties with Italy, Rumania, Bulgaria, and Hungary were prepared and signed in 1947. Despite American insistence, however, Molotov refused to sign a treaty with Austria at that time. Moreover, the Hungarian and Rumanian treaties gave Russia the right to maintain troops in those countries to guard the "lines of communication" with Austria so long as Soviet troops were stationed in the latter country; no time limit to this privilege was provided for; Moscow was now interested in prolonging the period of "transition" in Austria in order to keep its armies in the Balkans.

After a long delay, Big Four negotiations for a peace ("state") treaty with Austria began in January, 1947 and continued, with interruptions, until 1955. A detailed description of these prolonged parleys would be tiresome and unrewarding. The most important Soviet considera-

[32] Gruber, *Zwischen Befreiung and Freiheit*, p. 234.

tion—a purely Stalinist one—was to hold on to territory in Europe, cling to advanced positions for the great Soviet move to the West, and, eventually, transform Austria into a people's democracy—in short, to consolidate the "Socialist camp" instead of weakening it by an unnecessary withdrawal. To this end, negotiations were dragged out, pretexts for delays were invented; disputes over terminology and legal notions were extended almost *ad infinitum*. All in all, over 260 meetings were held to discuss the Austrian treaty. It took years for most of the Western delegates assigned to these meetings to realize that there was no sincere desire on Stalin's part to sign a treaty with Austria and throw the small but rich country into the "capitalist" fold.

The negotiations started in London on January 14, 1947 and continued in Moscow during the session of foreign ministers in March–April, 1947,[33] where German assets in Austria that were to go to Russia constituted one of the main issues in the discussion. Subsequently a committee of deputies of the four foreign ministers continued to negotiate. Between May 12 and October 11, 1947, eighty-five meetings were held. From February until May, 1948 the negotiations were carried on in London; they were broken off when the Soviet delegates insisted on recognition of the Yugoslav demands. In 1949 Moscow ceased to support Tito's claims to Carinthia; some progress was made during that year, and in December only five items (out of fifty-three) of lesser importance remained to be settled. Then Moscow demanded compensation for certain supplies and services previously rendered to Austria. This brought a new stalemate. In the spring of 1950 the Soviet side began to tie the Austrian treaty to the difficult Trieste problem, obviously a delaying maneuver. The new Soviet position was maintained and emphasized during the first stage of the Korean war, in 1950.

[33] For more detailed reports on the negotiations *see* Philip E. Mosely's *The Kremlin and World Politics. Studies in Soviet Policy and Action*, (New York: Vintage Books, 1960), pp. 263–88; *see also*, Gustav E. Kafka, in *Osteuropa*, Stuttgart (Germany), June, 1953, pp. 171–77, and August 1953, pp. 257–263.

Austria: Where Stalin Failed

The year 1951 passed without further negotiations. Early in 1952 the three Western powers prepared a new, "abbreviated" treaty consisting of only eight paragraphs, on the assumption that it would facilitate negotiations. They were mistaken: the Soviet government rejected it and somewhat later demanded, as a precondition for further talks, that the new proposal be formally withdrawn.

Stalin's death had no immediate effect on the negotiations. For many months there was disorientation and lack of guidance in Moscow. It took some time before the first act under a new policy, an armistice in Korea, could be achieved. Germany and Austria then appeared as the great issues, and the Berlin Conference of Foreign Ministers was convened in January, 1954 to discuss them.

When the Austrian issue came up for discussion on February 12, 1954, Molotov raised new conditions, which were rejected by the three Western foreign ministers. Nevertheless the conference marked the start of a new phase in Soviet–Austrian relations.

The Plenum of the CPSU Central Committee in January, 1955 brought about a change in Soviet leadership that was rapidly reflected in Soviet foreign policy. Outwardly at least, Molotov bowed to it. On February 8, he delivered to the Supreme Soviet his report on the international situation, in which he dwelt at length on the Austrian issue. On March 11; the Soviet Foreign Ministry, in a lengthy statement, announced the change of policy.[34] This marked the turn of the tide for Austria; it was clear that the Soviet government was launched on a new course.

The State Treaty was signed in the Belvedere Palace in Vienna on May 15, 1955, and became effective on July 27; by October 25 of the same year all occupation forces were withdrawn from Austria.

[1959]

---

[34] *Pravda*, March 12, 1955

Part Two:
TRENDS AND PORTENTS

THE COMING ERA*

I AFTER THE REVOLUTION

The "outlook for the future," which has always figured so prominently in the thinking of our Socialist parties, has never been an idle or a purely academic question. Unless the objective conditions that shape the course of events are clearly understood, politics is merely the sum of separate "actions" and not a logical chain linked together by a unifying principle. In party struggles, victory belongs to the party that foresees future developments most accurately. The coming era in Russia will be discussed with particular reference to its mass ideology.

Ideology grows slowly, imperceptibly; it is rooted in the general conditions of the preceding epoch. Upsets in

---

* This article appeared in May, 1919, in the Khar'kov *Mysl'* (The Thought), a bi-weekly theoretical review. It was written in Moscow at the height of the Civil War, amidst political and economic chaos, and at the time attracted wide interest among Russian Socialist groups. It is one of the few attempts of the period to forecast the further development of the Soviet regime, an attempt whose main elements were later to be confirmed by the course of events. Most of the ideas explored in this article, except for the threat of a military coup and the growth of a new Soviet bourgeoisie, were developed more amply in the author's subsequent writings. (*Ed.*)

ideology do not come about in the same way as in politics, where a revolution or a conspiracy can change a political system in a single day. In mass ideology there are no such swift revolutions. Here the fruit takes a long time to ripen, and the most interesting and most important problem is precisely to discover in the revolutionary period the seeds of the coming, post–revolutionary trends—to discern in the seething cauldron of revolution the particles that will float to the top when the fire goes out and the popular movements subside.

That is the task I have set myself. I shall be blunt and ruthless—with myself, my own wishes and hopes, as well as with my own Party. If the resulting picture is not the one I should like to see in Russia's future, the fault is not mine. It is time for all of us to discard our habit of "scientifically" demonstrating that history, by a strange coincidence, is leading exactly where we should want it to lead, and by the very paths we would choose!

II HOW IT WILL HAPPEN

We must first examine the general conditions in which the post–revolutionary era will take shape.

The Red Army will defeat Kolchak, Dutov, and Denikin. The Don, the Kuban' and Siberia, Lithuania and Finland will be reunited with Russia. The Soviet government will win the civil war, and its victory will be complete, final, unquestionable. The Allies and other foreign powers will once and for all give up supporting border armies, and no general will again get the idea of raising troops to make war on Moscow.

The Allies will recognize the Soviet regime. Whether they will do so all at once, or retreat one by one from the old principles, sooner or later ambassadors from England, France, America, and Germany, too, will arrive in Moscow.

Long before recognition, however, the blockade will be lifted. Trade will resume, at first in a trickle, then grow steadily. The factories will get the machinery parts they need; repairs on railroads will resume; scythes, sickles, and other scarce implements will pour into the rural areas.

II How It Will Happen

Another few months, and Russia will be over the worst. Industry will revive, production expand, stocks grow, distribution improve; the famine will pass; the exchange of goods between country and city in Russia, and between Russia and the outer world, will increase, expand, and assume impressive proportions.

Strange as it may seem, it is then that the Communist government will face its most critical moment. Those who, ever since November 7, 1917, have been expecting that the growing hunger and disorganization would spell the ruin of the Soviet power, are sadly mistaken. They are drawing analogies between the fate of the Communist government and that of all the preceding regimes. They reason, perhaps, as follows: when Russia became very badly disorganized, tsarism fell and was replaced by a liberal government; when hunger became still worse and prices kept climbing, the government of the Kadets and Octobrists collapsed; under the coalition regime Russia continued downhill, and that was the end of Kerensky and his semi–Socialist government. How then, runs the argument, can the Soviet regime survive? Must it not perish, too, like all its precursors?

This reasoning is radically wrong. As long as power remains in the hands of the upper classes or of some intermediate groups, the lowest popular strata are excluded from it. The harder their life, the more they fume and seethe, and when it becomes unendurable they revolt and overthrow the government. But when they themselves are in power, when the most destitute elements of the urban proletariat have taken over the power fallen from the hands of the propertied classes, who is left to rebel? There can be only occasional outbursts of despair, without any political thought or plan behind them, and relatively easy to squash.

That is the lesson world history teaches us. The popular masses submit to exploitation as long as their usual living conditions remain the same. When life becomes mercilessly crushing, they explode in a revolution. *But when the hardest time is over, there is another period of "calm"—and millions of former rebels put their necks back under the yoke and drag forward the heavy chariot of social progress.*

When the cost of bread in Petrograd rose to three rubles a pound, Kerensky's government was overthrown. But later the price rose to ten, fifteen, thirty, and forty rubles—and Lenin's government became all the stronger. The same holds true for political developments. Reverses in the war toppled tsarism. The abortive offensive decided the fate of the coalition. But neither the peace of Brest-Litovsk nor the endless humiliations and the reduction of Russia's territory by half were able to shake the Soviet power.

Now suppose that the situation begins to change: the internal enemies have been defeated, the outer world is willing to compromise, Russia is reunited under the aegis of the Moscow government and is recognized by all as a force to be reckoned with. Life gets just a little easier. The depopulated cities require less food and, as rail service is restored, prices climb less madly, there are more provisions in the markets, epidemics subside, child mortality drops. Things improve, if only a little.

On the heels of the slight improvement comes a measure of calm. If the appalling defeat in the World War and the unbelievable famine aroused in the lower classes the stupendous energy that carried them to the crest of power, the incipient improvement makes them sink back into their usual apathy. Weary, drained by the hardships and the intense labor of several years, they surrender the sword without protest as soon as living conditions become at all bearable. *Their energy grows as conditions deteriorate, and diminishes as they improve.*

After this, only bourgeois forces remain in the arena of contest: the prosperous peasantry, longing for free trade; the Soviet bureaucracy; the new bourgeoisie of big and small speculators, of the new contractors and the new purveyors to the army; finally, the Red Army itself, demanding better supplies and hence disposed, at the moment, to make all kinds of concessions to capitalist principles. All these forces are thoroughly bourgeois, in their outlook, though they all have severed their ties with the old Russian bourgeoisie. These groups are all new. They have no familial or financial ties with the nobility or with the big wheels of our former business world. They have not a shred of sympathy for the expropriated elements among the well-to-do classes, and nothing to gain from having the land returned to the gentry, the banks to the old financiers, and the factories to their former owners. The question of compensating the "victims of the revolution" for their losses does not interest them much. The reason for all this is that they themselves are the offspring of the revolution, nurtured on its milk; they have become "somebodies" thanks only to the revolutionary upheaval. All of them are *parvenus; it is the revolution that has made them statesmen and generals, landlords and millionaires.*

Among them, a special role belongs, of course, to the new urban bourgeoisie. It consists of new people, with a poverty-stricken ancient past and many blemishes on their own recent past. They do not want to remember their origins; no portraits of noble ancestors hang in their halls. They began to live only yesterday, and they hurry to do so with all the maniacal energy necessary to outdo their likes in the struggle for survival. They never went to high school or college but they know their arithmetic very well. They are adventurers on a grand scale—aggressive, tenacious, stopping at nothing in the pursuit of their goals. They are a cross between the American billionaire and the Russian black marketeer. They despise democracy, for they know that with money they can buy anything and anyone.

Yet all four groups—the rich peasants, the new bourgeoisie, the new army, and the new bureaucrats—are "revolutionary." They have no use for Purishkevich and Sazonov, Milyukov and Nabokov. *They hail "the conquests of the revolution."* They would gladly introduce an annual holiday in honor of it; on that day no memories will darken their revolutionary brows. That is why their victory over today's communism will be accomplished facilely, without undue noise: their platform will be *the recognition of the November revolution.*

That is the kind of *coup d'état* that will take place when Russia's situation improves. Then and only then can we speak of a victorious counter-revolution since a counter-revolution always strengthens and consolidates the power of the well-off.

Their victory will be an out–and–out counter-revolution. *Not a restoration*, however, and that is the crucial point. That is the distinction between their victory and the kind of counter-revolution we now observe on the outskirts of Russia. Kornilov's or Kaledin's, Denikin's or Krasnov's, Kolchak's or Dutov's victory would bring in its wake the restoration of the old social relationships in Russia, and in the first place the dominance of the gentry. A Soviet victory will puncture these dreams. *Subjectively*, Moscow's victory is the proletariat's victory over the bourgeoisie. *Objectively*, Moscow's war with the Don and Siberia is a war of the new bourgeoisie against the old gentry and against the old bourgeoisie reared on tsarist grants and subsidies. Lenin's victory will mean the victory of the new bourgeois Russia.

The *coup d'état* in which the revolution will end will be quite unlike the March and November revolutions. It will not be a popular rising, and no loyal army will fight it. It will be the conspiracy of a clique, and it will no doubt be headed by some "open–minded Bolshevik"—energetic, adroit, well known, probably an army officer. He will have no trouble entering the Kremlin with a group of armed men, and in half an hour the *coup d'état* will be accomplished.

And that will be the end of the revolution.

III RUSSIA, EUROPE, AND AMERICA

Outwardly, events will follow the direction they have taken under the Soviet regime. Russia's position among the nations, which began to improve toward the end of 1918, will continue to grow stronger. In this, two decisive factors will come into play.

An agricultural country with primitive methods of cultivation, Russia was the first to succumb in the World War. In a "war of attrition" the first one to be starved out was, of course, Russia, already underfed to begin with. But the same primitive conditions will enable her to

III Russia, Europe, and America

recover more easily and quickly than any of the other great European nations. A young organism is more susceptible to infection but recuperates faster than a mature one. So, too, young Russia, having keeled over after less than three years of war, will recover sooner than the complex, older body of Western Europe.

The backbone of Russian rural economy is its manpower. Synthetic fertilizers, steam plows, modern inventions play no important part in Russian farming. When the war removed ten million men from our fields, that was a very telling blow. The end of the war and the return of the rural labor force have already done more for Russia's recovery than the mere fact of peace can do for any other country. In addition, with the blockade lifted, factories and railroads will be able to replace the most needed items of their worn-out inventory. Thus the requisites for Russia's economic recovery will be at hand.

For Western Europe the prospect is not so promising. Though less disrupted by the war, it will find it harder to return to normal. It suffers from a disease known as "the problem of raw materials." In Russia their shortage is due to the civil war and to the breakdown of transport, not to lack of raw materials in the country. In the West the situation is different. The local production of raw materials is so inadequate that Western industry cannot function without imports. And importing raw materials is difficult because they have to be paid for in merchandise or in gold, neither of which is available. Foreign loans can help only to a certain extent. It will be quite some time before this problem is solved.

America alone is free of the disease and strong in both agricultural and industrial production. That is why it is at the moment the master of the situation.

For Europe, the time will come when the more speedily recuperating East will surpass the West in power—when Russia will be the master of the situation, with the United States its only rival. Russia and America are the principal sources of raw materials; this gives them a mighty weapon for exerting pressure on Western Europe. The Hungarian and Bavarian revolutions which have already been launched, and the German Spartacus revolution, if it materializes, are the outposts of Russian influence in the West—and a war on the Rhine between a Russo–German and a British–French coalition is not a fanciful notion but a very real possibility.

I do not know whether or not there will be such wars; but in a series of ripening international conflicts the new Russia will stand up for itself and *force* its own recognition.

Even if wars break out, they will be far removed from the territory of Russia; besides, depleted Europe will be unable to throw on the battlefields such great numbers of men as it did in the past war. In spite of militarism, therefore, Russia's national economy will gradually become stronger and its industry will get back on its feet. An alliance with some European country, Germany for instance, would render a blockade virtually harmless.

External successes and a developing national economy will further contribute to the relaxation of domestic tension that begins when a country sets out on the road of large-scale development.

IV THE MEAT-GRINDER OF THE REVOLUTION

A profound and long revolution has the effect of a meat-grinder on a nation's millions. The first revolutionary explosion snatches up people like a cyclone and flings them into the giant maw of the revolutionary meat-grinder, while naughty History stands by, turning the handle and watching with a mischievous smile to see what emerges at the other end.

A whole nation is churning and boiling. In every soul, a new torch is lit. Eyes blaze, and hearts flame. No one harbors doubts, and there cannot be any: analysis and skepticism are entirely out of place. It is a time of wild words and of foolhardy deeds. The "common man"? Oh, that piteous contemptible breed! Who can be a philistine in the turmoil of revolution? He no longer exists: today it is all for one, one for all. "The good life," "home and hearth," "comfort"—how trite, how disgusting! One thing

IV The Meat-grinder of the Revolution

alone is great and worthy of man: the revolutionary struggle! Time passes. The meat-grinder does its work. Behold, at the other end of our machine there emerge strange new beings: withered, shrivelled little men with a slow pulsebeat and mournful sing-song speech, pedantic and practical, cowardly, harmless, neither honest nor dishonest, neither intelligent nor stupid, and as alike as a pair of twins. Tsarism? It was bad, yes. The revolution? Sure ... but it isn't so good either! A counter-revolution? No good either!

The propertied classes are the first to pass through the grinder. After only three or four months of it they are squeezed dry. Their parties begin to dissolve, to divide into factions and sub-factions; they lose the stamina for political activity; what political meaning they had soon evaporates. They are unable to fight; they have become *passive*—for such is the fate of all who have gone through the revolutionary meat-grinder.

Next comes the intelligentsia. It kicks and resists longer. For a long time, it refuses to leave the womb of the revolution; the revolution repeatedly applies forceps to extract the intellectual from the machine. But God, look at him! Where are the noble speech, the lofty pride, the kingly valor? Can this miserable creature be the heir of Belinsky and Pisarev, Chernyshevsky and Mikhailovsky?

Have you seen a "Soviet employee"? He is the very type of the intellectual who has passed through the revolutionary meat-grinder. He is hungry, as the Russian intellectual has always been, but now he never forgets his hunger for a minute. His head is full of thoughts about food, his talk is all about food, and so are the deepest longings of his heart. He has suddenly realized how handy and pleasant it is to be rich and powerful, to be able to afford whatever one wishes and to take from life all it can yield. He counts pennies but now he refers to millionaires no longer with hatred but with envy and respect. For an extra hundred rubles or so he will discover the necessary "principles" to justify a suitable job. His mind is a jumble, only tatters remain of the old principles and theories, and they are for sale to the first jobber at a reasonable price. What can you expect of him? His child has just died of malnutrition, his brother has typhus, his wife is at the end of her rope—and everyone tells him that all this is the work of the revolution which he had been worshiping for so many years!

A complete change has come over the intelligentsia. What it wants is no longer an "integrated *Weltanschauung*" but a comfortable berth. By now we have a European type of intelligentsia—bourgeois to the core, valuing "law and order," free of that adulation of "the people" that made it a menace to any established regime.

Finally comes the turn of the working class. Again the process is gradual. First the highly skilled and best paid, the intelligentsia's immediate neighbors: workers in the printing trade, in commerce and industry, technicians of various kinds, and so on. Then the "semi-skilled" worker. As he, too, gives up active struggle, he leaves the power to the nethermost stratum: illiterates, unskilled laborers, women, etc. This seems to be the period we are living in now. In the end, however, even the last contingent still faithful to the revolution and still believing in it is caught up in the machine—and the process is completed. The grinder has done its work. At the other end, there is a crowd of "common men"—the new look of the nation, once revolutionary but now plain tired. All they want is bread and a peaceful life, with no talk of socialism and revolutionary struggle for a long, long time. And as soon as economic conditions improve they will retire into their shells and live like snails—in peace, not too hungry, and pleased enough with their peaceful and not-too-hungry lives.

The "Pan-Russian philistine" is the name of the new type of man, the man of the post-revolutionary period. The ingredients of his philosophy have been forming under our eyes. We can see him spread and multiply, filling everything—from bourgeois apartments to workmen's basements, from confiscated town houses to the Kremlin's penetralia.

At present he is still grumbling, complaining, and criticizing the government. In retaliation, the government calls him a counter-revolutionary. How unfair to any counter-revolution! Counter-revolutionists are men of action, not windbags. As for these spineless weaklings, clearly they wear the badge of "philistine impotence."

V THE VICTORIOUS TRIAD

Old Hegel would feel very pleased with himself if he could take a look at our revolution: it follows the "Hegelian process." If we take the pre–revolutionary conditions and trends as the point of departure (the thesis), then the revolution represents its "negation" (the antithesis), and the post–revolutionary period is the synthesis of the two preceding steps.

Before a revolution, the common man takes no part in politics but mistrusts the government. During the revolution he himself becomes a politician. After the revolution he again drops politics but fully trusts the new government.

Before a revolution, therefore, "peace" prevails. During the revolution, the method of political action is open revolt. But afterwards, when the activity of the masses declines, conspiracy replaces revolt. It is safe to say that uprisings against the government have been rendered impossible in Russia for a good many years to come, and that any drastic political changes, *if* any, in the foreseeable future will be brought about by conspiracy not rebellion.

Before the revolution, a hazy patriotism was intermingled with defeatism. The people's attitude toward the Japanese and the German wars gave the measure of this odd state of mind. The revolution proceeded under the banner of growing internationalism. But now we can already observe an extremely strong and vehement nationalism spreading among the widest masses. At one time or other in the past five years every party and every class has contributed to the national defense effort. As a result, the defense of the fatherland has ceased to be the fearful bugaboo it once was. National patriotism, patriotic nationalism, utter indifference to the fate of other peoples "as long as we have it good"—all the prerequisites of an egoistic, aggressive policy already exist in the popular mind.

In addition, there is a new attitude toward all things

Russian. Slavophilism again prevails over Westernism, though as yet in covert form: the sun rises in the East, Moscow is the chosen seat of the Third International. But when the revolutionary storm will have passed, dyed-in-the-wool Slavophilism will again rise to the surface: we shall have studies of "the Russian way of life," "Russian music," and so on, perhaps even of "Russian faith." These elements of Russian romanticism are the more likely to revive the farther the pendulum of history swings toward counter-revolution.

Along with nationalism, there grows in every Russian heart a new love of the military, formerly unknown in our country. Neither the tsar's army, nor Kerensky's army, which suffered defeat upon defeat, was able to win a similar devotion. The rejection of the army that at times approached rejection in principle of discipline, "fraternization," etc., is now beginning to turn into its opposite. From a motley horde, the Red Army is beginning to develop into a true fighting force. It is carrying off marked successes. It is already unifying Russia. And when it will have defeated the Siberian and southern foes, when the result of its victories will be felt in Great Russia in the guise of more consumer goods, it will have its hour of glory. It will be sheathed in glamor, revered, its leaders credited with genius. Belonging to it will become a source of pride to the average man. For now it is *"Russland, Russland über alles, über alles in der Welt."*

The past year has been marked by a rapidly waning interest in civic affairs and social issues. More than that, there is a growing reaction, characteristic of the new spirit, against conferences, conventions, public meetings, unions, committees, commissions, and resolutions of any kind. The coming life will be a calm, peaceful, slightly debauched but on the whole sluggish life, unable to fathom how the words of Gorky's "Stormy Petrel" could ever have quickened anyone's heartbeat—a provincial life, of the kind that Chekhov described in Russia and, Maupassant in France. "My dinner," "my cigar," "my coffee." As to unions and organizations—"Oh, how tired we are of them!"

Almost all trade unions and cooperatives will doubtless

disappear from the scene. The trade unions have already become compulsory state organizations, with members' interests reduced to zero. And as soon as the government, in the new orientation of its internal policy, stops requiring all workers to participate in these organizations, they will collapse like a house of cards. Only a few lucky ones, having defended their independence from the government longer than most, will be able to survive.

The same fate awaits the cooperatives. While the cost of living is rising the usefulness of consumers' unions increases. They provide a modicum of goods and an escape from the inflated prices charged by speculators. But when the economy returns to normal, when prices not only cease to rise but actually fall, when goods are no longer difficult to obtain, cooperatives lose much of their point. In the matter of supply they can hardly compete with private enterprise motivated by profit. If people even now feel no particular loyalty and affection for their "own cooperative," these organizations will fade into the background more and more when they cease to be virtually the only sources of legally purchased goods.

The atomization of the popular masses, the dissolution of their organizations, the transformation of "tight ranks" into "pulverized humanity" will complete the remodelling of the facade of the new social edifice.

An apolitical trend, i.e. indifference to social issues, is gaining ground under our eyes. It will become the rule for all save professional politicians. And its inevitable concomitants are the decay of democracy in all its forms and the dominance of an authoritarian government.

The gradual deterioration of democracy is of tremendous import. It is already going on in the most pronounced form: the executive organs are turning into legislative ones. The local soviets—elected bodies, organs of the peculiar Soviet brand of democracy—are dying out. They no longer meet; there are hardly ever any new elections. Most important of all, the reason they fail to meet is not that the party in power may fear them; and the reason there are no elections is not that the Communists may be defeated. This is not the case. People have simply lost interest in them, and so their members have lost the desire to meet. When they do meet once in a long while, they accept without much debate and without reservations or corrections all the proposals of their executive committees. The same is happening on a national scale: the Central Executive Committee meets only rarely, in gala sessions; it has no part in actual politics. Its Presidium issues laws and performs judiciary functions. At the top is the Sovnarkom, again combining the legislative and the executive. For "the legislative arm must be subordinated to the executive arm" is the motto of the era in which an authoritarian regime supersedes democracy.

In politics, in the national economy, in education, everywhere the social organizations are disintegrating, and in their stead function the numerous "presidiums," which should do no more than preside at general meetings and see that their decisions are carried out. Presidiums instead of associations and unions; *Ispolkoms* instead of soviets; the Sovnarkom instead of the Central Executive Committee; dictatorship instead of democracy. The form of government (dictatorship) will not change simply because of its changing social content and because the dictatorship of the proletariat will become a dictatorship of the "haves."

Autocracy, democracy, Bonapartism: another Hegelian triad. Autocracy was opposed by the whole people; democracy is the rule of the people; Bonapartism is autocracy with the passive approval of the people.

(Translated by Gertrude Vakar)

[1919]

THE SOVIET REVOLUTION: SHATTERED HOPES

I THE FATEFUL YEAR

A turning point in the history of Russia as well as of the whole of Europe came in 1917. The great changes that took place in Petrograd early in March of that year occurred in the midst of a world war which had already taken millions of lives and to which no end was yet in sight. The German coalition was in a favorable position, with its armies in France and deep in Russia. The United States had not yet entered the war. One of the reasons for this American reluctance was the distaste of many Americans for joining unpopular and autocratic Russia as a full-fledged ally.

The tsarist system fell within a few days. The centuries-old, seemingly indestructible throne crumbled beneath the onslaught of popular indignation. Nobody rushed to its rescue—not a single regiment of the army, not a single political party, not even die-hard monarchists from a far-off province of the vast empire. The upheaval was almost bloodless. A Provisional Government took over.

Democracy was the goal of the new regime as well as of almost all of the active Russian political groups. Their attitude towards "the West" was immensely favorable at the time, and a democratic republic on the French or American pattern, with free elections and a free press, law and order, and personal security, was what the great majority of the politically articulate part of the Russian population envisioned. The Provisional Government, for all its shortcomings, was the most democratic regime Russia has ever had, either before or after the revolution.

But in addition to the politically-educated sector in the backward country, there were strata of the population with no knowledge of political realities. Silent and passive under the old system, they began to emerge from below in the midst of the popular excitement that swept the nation. The revolt was like a typhoon that agitates the ocean to its depths. The human mass now coming to the fore was susceptible to extremism of any kind; during the revolutionary years it became fertile soil for anti-democratic communism, then called bolshevism.

Vladimir Lenin returned from exile early in April of 1917 and assumed leadership over the still very small group of Russian Bolsheviks, released from prisons and exile. Soon after, he was joined by Leon Trotsky, who arrived from the United States. The two men, both able, clever and unscrupulous, seeking power and prepared to use any means in their fight against the democratic regime, were successful. After eight months, the fledgling democratic republic was strangled, and a Soviet regime, with Lenin as its leader, emerged in November, 1917.

II SOLEMN VOWS AND REALITY

At that time problems of war and peace were paramount in everyone's mind, and "Peace at any Price" was the great slogan of the Bolshevik movement. Russia had suffered badly in the two and one half years of fighting, but she was bound by inter-Allied treaties not to conclude a separate peace. While demanding "immediate peace," Lenin and Trotsky at first denied that they wanted a separate solution of the war issue; their proclaimed program was a revolution in Germany against the Kaiser. They urged the Russian armies at the front to "fraternize" with the Germans, to distribute revolutionary leaflets among the German soldiers, and to stir up the enemy's revolutionary spirit. What they achieved, however, was only the demoralization of the Russian troops; the morale of the Germans remained unshaken. The Russian army disintegrated, hundreds of thousands deserted, and Russian resistance crumbled even before the Soviet upheaval in November. No sooner had they taken over than Lenin and Trotsky started peace negotiations with Germany; within a few months the separate peace treaty of Brest–Litovsk was concluded. Russia quit the war, and Germany, now free to throw all its armed forces against the West, remained in control of a vast part of Russia.

The Bolshevik hope of at least bringing the terrible bloodshed to an end proved to be a delusion, too: the foreign war was followed by a civil war in which the atrocities and casualties far exceeded those suffered in the war with Germany.

Among the most successful slogans of 1917 was that of "peace without annexations." Lenin maintained that both sides were waging a predatory "imperialist" war since both intended and were preparing to "grab" territories of other nations. Democratic governments, Lenin maintained, must refuse to take part in such unjust wars. He clearly and correctly defined territorial annexation:

> Annexation or seizure of foreign territory . . . means the incorporation of a small and weak nationality by a large and powerful state without a clear, definite and voluntary expression of agreement and desire by the weak nationality.[1]

Lenin and Trotsky violently opposed the "designs of Russian imperialism" for conquering the Dardanelle Straits and annexing Austrian and German lands. Succeeding Soviet governments, however, did not remain faithful to this tenet of Lenin's. They abandoned it as soon as they had

---

[1] V. I. Lenin, *Sochineniya* (Works), 4th ed., XXVI, 218. Lenin's report on peace to the second All–Russian Congress of Soviets, November 8, (October 26), 1917.

accumulated more power and achieved a position of strength. Stalin annexed the vast territory of Eastern Poland in 1939 without the "desire of the weak nationality" (a fraudulent ballot was taken *post factum*); the next year he annexed the Baltic States, Bessarabia, and Northern Bukovina in a similar way; at the end of the second World War he incorporated in the Soviet Union Finnish and German territories, as well as the southern part of Sakhalin and the Kuril Islands. The moral indignation against the annexation of alien peoples and foreign lands had evaporated. Soviet annexations in the six years between 1939 and 1945 constituted a vast empire, one of the largest ever annexed by any "imperialist" power.

Another slogan of Lenin's 1917 bolshevism—"peace without indemnities"—suffered a similar fate. The world still remembered the huge indemnity that France had to pay to Germany after the war of 1870–71. Payment of indemnities by a defeated nation, Lenin and Trotsky had maintained before they came to power, is unjust and impermissible. Since indemnity is a component part of "predatory wars," it is "piracy on a gigantic scale."

This principle, too, was forgotten when the war with Germany ended in 1945. The Soviet government demanded an indemnity that far exceeded the financial ability of the defeated nation to pay. In his negotiations with his wartime allies, Stalin insisted on the payment to Russia of twenty billion dollars by Germany and started to levy this indemnity without the consent of his allies. (Later, however, he reduced it.) For several years thereafter the spectacle of the gigantic dismantling of German industry and the shipping of the machinery to the east served as a striking illustration of the new Soviet attitude toward the question of war indemnities.

In the promise of an entirely new political system to be established in Russia—a new type of a democratic state, nobler than all the democracies that had hitherto existed— we see the Lenin of 1917 as not only a great demagogue but also a utopian leader who really believed in his ability to achieve an unprecedented degree of liberty, equality, and well-being in the new state. In his very first statement

II Solemn Vows and Reality

upon arriving in Petrograd, Lenin promised that the "police, army and officialdom will be abolished." This pet idea of Lenin's was bound to appeal to a nation that for more than a century had endured the omnipotence of the police and the whims and injustices of an archaic bureaucracy. In order to abolish the standing army, Lenin demanded, the whole people must be armed, and the armed people would replace the police as well as the old army. "The substitution of a national militia for the police," Lenin wrote, "is a transformation that follows from the entire course of the revolution . . . there is only one way to prevent the re-establishment of the old police: to organize a national militia, to fuse it with the army. . . . The militia should comprise all citizens of both sexes between the ages of fifteen and sixty-five."[2]

No sooner had Lenin achieved power than he was forced to betray his own hopes and promises. A few weeks after the Soviet upheaval, the embryo of a new secret police, in the form of the notorious Extraordinary Commission, the so-called Cheka, was created. It was not long before the Cheka grew to be one of the most powerful agencies of the new regime. Its network covered the whole country. The secret police had the right not only to arrest people and keep them in concentration camps, but to execute criminals and political adversaries without trial, and of this right it availed itself abundantly. The Cheka was reorganized several times. Its successors—the GPU, NKVD, MVD, MGB, KGB—made the police system of Soviet Russia one of the most stable and characteristic features of the new regime.

In the matter of the army, the Soviet leaders likewise proved themselves unable or unwilling to fulfill their promises. The abolition of the old army, the disintegration of the Russian military force, Lenin's slogan of "arming the whole people," then the creation of a new army and its growth to unprecedented proportions in Russia is a major chapter in Soviet history and one of the greatest issues in the international situation today.

[2] *Ibid.*, XXIV, 49. "The Task of the Proletariat in Our Revolution," (April 10, 1917).

Lenin's opposition to a standing army "divorced from the people" was formulated long before the revolution. "A standing army ... is trained to shoot down the people. ... A standing army is not in the least necessary to protect the country from an attack of the enemy; a people's militia is sufficient. If every citizen is armed, Russia need fear no enemy."[3]

The army, then, had to be reorganized. In 1917 Lenin's party advised its adherents in the army to initiate the selection and removal of officers by majority vote. (This method of selecting and removing army officers was to be—on paper—a feature of the future "People's Army.") "Not only must the army officers be elected," Lenin said, "but every step of every officer and general must be supervised by persons specially elected for this purpose by the soldiers. ... Arbitrary removal of their superiors by the soldiers is desirable and essential in *every respect*. The soldiers will obey and respect only elected authorities."[4] Lenin was not unaware that such a reorganization of the army in wartime might be dangerous. But to him and his Party the Russian revolution was more important than the winning of the war against Germany.

Early in 1918, however, when Lenin's regime was more stable, the Russian people were called upon to create a new armed force—a million-strong standing army. Trotsky, to whom this task was assigned, became People's Commissar of War; his new army was officially called the Red Army. While withdrawing their slogan of a "popular militia" and reverting to the old pattern of a standing army, Lenin and Trotsky promised that the army would be different from and better than all previous armies; in particular, equality would reign in the ranks: "The Army of the Russian Republic henceforth consists of free and equal citizens bearing the honorable rank of soldier of the revolutionary army," and therefore "all privileges connected with former ranks and titles, as well as all external

---

[3] *Ibid.*, VI, 363. "To the Poor Peasants. Explanation to Peasants of What Social-Democrats Want," (March, 1903).

[4] *Ibid.*, XXIV, 76. "Political Parties in Russia and Tasks of the Proletariat," (April, 1917).

distinctions [insignia of rank, epaulettes, decorations] are abolished.... All ranks and titles in the army, starting with that of corporal and ending with that of general, are abolished."[5]

The size and power of the new army proved sufficient to defeat the weak White armies: but after the termination of the Civil War, the Red Army continued not only to exist but to assume more and more traits of the old Russian army. There was no longer any talk of "arming the people." On the contrary, heavy penalties were introduced for carrying arms without permit, and in fact thousands of persons were arrested and many shot when arms were found in their possession. The military ranks in the Red Army were likewise done away with as time went on. In the '30's, grading of officers and generals was reintroduced; shoulder–straps were restored; the uniforms of military chiefs equaled in splendor those of the tsarist army; rules pertaining to subordination and iron discipline returned. Finally, the term "Red Army" was also abolished, and the neutral name "Soviet Army" was substituted. Today the Soviet standing army is the largest of national armies. The Soviet military force has shaken off the utopian vestiges of its early years and of pre–revolutionary bolshevism.

Another important demand in 1917 had been the call for "early convocation of the Constituent Assembly." A Constituent Assembly was viewed as the natural and only means to establish the new Russian republic, promulgate a democratic constitution, and elect a popular government. As part of his wily strategy, Lenin accepted the slogan of "early elections to the Constituent Assembly"; indeed, he accused the Provisional Government of being too slow and reluctant in the matter. The elections took place on November 12 (25), 1917. Of the approximately thirty–six million voters, only nine million, or twenty–five per cent, cast their votes for the Bolshevik Party; the great majority voted for democratic candidates. The first (and last) meeting of the Assembly, in which the majority was anti–Leninist, was held on January 5 (18), 1918. Within a

[5] Decree of December 29 (16), 1917.

few hours it was dissolved by the Soviet government and dispersed by military force.

Another favorite idea of Lenin's, and an important point in his program, was abolition of the professional class of government employees—the state bureaucracy, with its contempt for the common man and with its multitude of privileges. Lenin really believed that he would be able to construct a state machine without the traditional Russian *chinovnik*. Underestimating the skill and knowledge required of government employees, Lenin repeatedly stated that in his and his Party's view, every cook would learn how to govern the state.

The new state machine, that Lenin's government started to erect after his seizure of power, proved a disappointment to all who believed in a "state without bureaucracy." Within a few years the new class of state employees reached unprecedented size. It grew and grew, as the state itself did, to become a new leviathan, the all-embracing apparatus. From about one million on the eve of the revolution the number of state employees grew to about ten million before the second World War, and to about twenty million at the present time. The sacred promise that the new bureaucracy would not acquire new privileges was not kept. In a world of poverty and constant shortages of goods, the Soviet bureaucracy today enjoys rights and titles that make it the upper class of the new society; it stands high above the still very poor, unhappy and voiceless "common man."

Turning its propaganda toward the peasantry, the Bolshevik Party said, in 1917: You, unhappy pariahs of old Russia, take and divide the landed estates, and don't wait for permission from the government for new laws and regulations; do it yourself and without delay! "The party of the proletariat," wrote Lenin in May, 1917, "advocates the immediate seizure of the land by the peasants." Partially before, but mainly after the Soviet upheaval, the peasantry followed Lenin's advice. The large estates disappeared; the holdings of the peasants increased accordingly.

A mere decade or so later, the peasants were deprived of most of their land; between 1929 and 1933 they were forcibly organized into collectives, the so-called *kolkhozes*. Not one of the Communist leaders had uttered so much as a word about these future plans when they appealed for the peasants' support in 1917. On the contrary, Lenin said, and repeated: "No socialism in Russia in the foreseeable future." In May, 1917, he wrote: "The proletariat of Russia, operating in one of the most backward countries of Europe, amidst a vast population of small peasants, cannot aim at immediate Socialist transformation."[6]

Within a few years, Lenin's government embarked upon a series of "Socialist transformations"; a decade later Stalin boasted that his regime had "established socialism" in Russia. Stalin's "socialism" was a system of economy regimented in the highest degree, in no way consonant with the rosy picture Lenin had painted in 1917.

In the new Russia, without a privileged bureaucracy, Lenin promised equality would prevail: "The reduction of pay for all, not excluding government leaders, to the regular wage scale of the worker" was one of the points in his far-reaching program. With this idea in mind, new wage scales were introduced after the November revolution; the large discrepancies in wages and salaries were rectified. Moreover, the grain stores of well-to-do peasants were confiscated, bank vaults were opened and gold, silver and jewelry were taken over by the government. In 1918-20 the great slogan was "equality." Fortunes disappeared, millionaires fled abroad, landed estates were divided, income was equalized.

It was only a few years until a reaction set in against egalitarianism, as the bureaucracy began to widen its power and privileges. Early in the 1930's a new slogan—of inequality—was launched. Egalitarianism became a derisive word. The trend against equality, becoming official policy, was strengthened by the power of the Soviet state. In the '20's and '30's, when attempts were made in a number of industrial plants to introduce equal pay for all workers and employees, the regime considered this a

[6] V. I. Lenin, *Sochineniya* (Works), 4th ed., XXIV, 278. Resolution on the Present Situation, adopted at the Seventh All-Russian Conference of the RSDRP(b), on May 12 (April 29), 1917.

harmful move; it clamped down and destroyed the last sprouts of egalitarianism on Russian soil.

The nationality problem has been one of the most important and difficult issues for every Russian government; it is still so today. The political liberty attained in the first months of the revolution, prior to the advent of the Soviet regime, encouraged the national minorities of Russia in their drive toward greater autonomy; some of them demanded independence and separation from Russia. In some parts of Russia, particularly in Finland and the Polish provinces, secession became the program; similar trends developed in the Ukraine, in the Caucasus, and in Central Asia. These movements created difficulties for the Provisional Government since they carried not only the threat of Russia's disintegration, but the more ominous threat of disintegration of the multi-national army at the German fronts.

Essentially, Lenin and his Party were in favor of a united and highly centralized nation with a powerful government. No privileges were to be granted to any of the component nationalities that might defeat or weaken the regime. But this pattern of a strictly disciplined nation was to be applied only in a future Soviet state; in regard to the short-lived pre-Soviet democratic government, national separatist movements were to be supported. "If Finland, if Poland, if the Ukraine break away from Russia, it is nothing terrible. Wherein is it bad? One who says so is a chauvinist. One must be insane to continue the policy of Tsar Nicholas. Norway has separated from Sweden."[7] Concealing its scheme of a strong centralized revolutionary government, the Conference of the Bolshevik Party proclaimed, in May, 1917: "The Party demands wide regional autonomy, abolition of surveillance from above, abolition of a compulsory official language, and definition of the boundaries of self-governing and autonomous regions."[8]

As far as Poland, the Ukraine and Finland were concerned, Lenin told the same conference of his party: "No

[7] *Ibid.*, p. 267. Speech, May 12 (April 29), 1917.
[8] *Ibid.*, p. 270. Resolution on the National Question, May 12 (April 29), 1917.

one has oppressed the Poles as much as have the Russian people. The Russian people have served in the hands of the tsars as the executioner of Polish freedom. No one hates Russia so intensely as do the Poles. . . .

"Why should we, Great Russians, who have been oppressing a greater number of nations than any other people, why should we deny the right of separation to Poland, the Ukraine, Finland?"[9] In accordance with this political line some Ukrainian Bolsheviks, for instance, supported Ukrainian nationalists in their national policies; a kind of anti-Russian bloc of nationalists and Communists emerged.

No sooner was the new Soviet government in power than the attitude toward national minorities changed. The Ukraine was re-annexed as soon as the Germans retreated. In May, 1919 Trotsky came to Kiev, capital of the Ukraine, disbanded the Ukrainian armed forces, merged them with his Red Army, and abolished a number of other Ukrainian governmental agencies, putting Moscow in actual control. Turkestan was reincorporated after a bloody civil war. The former Russian vassal states of Bukhara and Khiva, in Central Asia, were annexed outright and made components of the Soviet Union; Georgia, in the Caucasus, was reconquered by military force in violation of a peace treaty signed by Lenin and of his solemn recognition of her independence.

Under Stalin, the suppression of all trends toward national autonomy became a consistent Soviet policy. Communists who favored even a degree of autonomy for the national minorities were purged, jailed or executed. In the Ukraine, whose history may serve as an illustration, over forty Communist leaders are known to have been executed in the '30's; their only crime was participation in programs for national autonomy within the framework of the Soviet Union. Among the executed were high-ranking Communist leaders such as Vlas Chubar', Prime Minister of the Ukraine from 1923 to 1933, and Stanislav Kossior,

---

[9] *Ibid.*, pp. 264-65. Speech on the National Question, May 12 (April 29), 1917.

the party's supreme leader for more than a decade.[10] Others committed suicide, among them Nikolai Skrypnik, a friend of Lenin, and Panas Lyubchenko, Prime Minister of the Ukraine in 1937.

III STALIN AND AFTER

Looking back at the history of the Russian revolution, one is stunned by this accumulation of shattered hopes, betrayed ideals and gigantic disappointments, and also by the successful demagogy, the skill applied in the use and misuse of popular passions for the aims of a ruling party. This divergence between slogans and reality, and this failure to fulfill solemn promises, lay at the root of the disintegration in the ranks of the Soviet leadership, the "deviations" and the purges, trials and mass executions in which the flower of Russian communism perished.

It was not all failure, of course. There have certainly also been some great victories and successes. But the victories and successes were in other fields: in war, in the development of modern weapons and industry, in territorial expansion. The ideas and ideals that animated the Russian people at the time of their mighty uprising have remained unfulfilled.

Joseph Stalin was the man chosen by history to carry out, over a period of almost three decades, this retreat from old ideological positions, and to replace the ideas of 1917 with the slogans and achievements appropriate to a Great Power. His harsh terroristic rule over the nation achieved world-wide notoriety. It is important, however, to realize that Stalin, a close associate of Lenin, actually continued his work and embodied, in a changed situation, the spirit and strategy of bolshevism.

Today we are told by Moscow that Stalin was immoral, a perfidious leader, a traitor to his friends, a ruthless torturer and killer; we are invited to erase his memory. We refuse to forget him. All movements and parties have

---

[10] Both have been rehabilitated posthumously.

the leaders they deserve; it is no accident that history chose Lloyd George and Churchill to embody the British spirit, or Franklin D. Roosevelt and Dwight D. Eisenhower to represent America; and it was no accident that the Nazi spirit was embodied in one Adolf Hitler. Stalin rose to power and remained in power because he embodied precisely those traits of the Russian Bolshevik–Communist movement that his successors now want us to view as his personal, non–Communist traits—especially his amorality, ruthlessness, aggressiveness and cruelty. You cannot divorce communism from Stalin.

By his numerous enemies Stalin was sometimes compared to Genghis Khan, the thirteenth century Mongol conqueror. "Ghenghis Khan with a telephone," Stalin was nicknamed—meaning that he combined the main traits of the ruthless barbarian with modern techniques. This image is a correct one.

The so-called "heavy industry" on which emphasis is still being placed in Russia in fact represents a tremendous development of those sectors of the national economy that serve the needs of war and a neglect of those industrial and agricultural enterprises that serve the needs of the population. The Russian emphasis on armies, aviation and especially nuclear weapons is a great menace to all other nations. The strictly centralized state system, which allows no leeway for political opposition or political criticism, makes Russia a formidable war machine. At the same time Moscow frankly acknowledges its backwardness in regard to one of the most important goals of the revolution—the raising of the living standards of the people. For all the miracles Russian industrialization has performed, the standard of living in the Soviet Union is still one of the lowest in Europe—lower than in Rumania or Poland, lower than in Japan. Among the seven or eight great nations that have made world history in the last hundred years, the Russian people still live on the lowest level, and Moscow does not deny this. We must bear this in mind when we try to assess the good and the bad aspects of the Soviet revolution.

The Soviet state at present is a peculiar combination of

old and new features. From Imperial Russia it has inherited the antagonism toward the West, the police system, forcible expansionism, emphasis on power in both domestic and foreign policies. On the other hand, it has acquired techniques indispensable in the twentieth century—literacy, atomic science, aviation, television, "peace" slogans. Modern arms and modern economy cannot be based, as nomad armies were in their time, on muscle and horses, bows and arrows. A better education is required; new intellectual strata are needed—thousands of engineers, economists, teachers and doctors.

Therefore, a new generation of intellectuals is now growing up in Russia, a generation that is dissatisfied with the poor crumbs of "ideology" served them as the official dish; they ask for something more and something better. This is the essence of the new criticism and of the new ideological trends in Russia's universities and among her men of arts and letters. The Soviet educated "intelligentsia" is the arena in which the old and the new trends will be fought out. The yearning for liberty—liberty to live, to think, and to create—grows stronger and threatens to become a formidable force in the nation.

This return to the basic ideas of the pre–Soviet democratic revolution of 1917 is perhaps the most important development in present-day Russia. Although it will not make itself felt immediately in Soviet policies, it augurs well for the future, and it gives rise to the hope that after so many years of disappointment and bloodshed the rays of liberty and a better life will begin to brighten this land of tormented people.

[1957]

SOCIAL CHANGE AND SOVIET FOREIGN POLICY

I THE EASTWARD PATH OF SOCIAL REVOLUTION

The early Socialist thinkers, those whom Marx and Engels called "utopians," had expected that the good will of national rulers would help to establish the new society and that the transition would not involve a political upheaval. According to their thinking, any country—especially England or France—could be the first to achieve the Great Transformation. But in the nineteenth century there emerged the notion of the Socialist movement as a political struggle; the transition was viewed now as a social revolution of the greatest depth and dimensions.

If a revolution were the only way to set up the perfect society, who could rival France as the country most likely to be the first to reach such a goal? France was the classic land of revolution—1789, 1830, 1848, 1870. Nowhere else had revolutionary passion reached such heights; nowhere else had revolutionary skill attained such perfection. That violent revolutionary of the 1790's, Gracchus Babeuf, had been the first exponent of the new trend; his Society of Equals had carried the revolutionary message far and wide. Socialist voices had been loud in the developments of 1848, when the moderate Louis Blanc was the new Socialist political leader. Then came Louis Auguste Blanqui, the conspirator, and his followers in the Paris Commune. France was far ahead in the competition for first place among the countries to achieve the social revolution when Marx's First International was founded.

But ever since the middle of the nineteenth century, France's eastern neighbor, Prussia–Germany, had been rising to a challenging position. There a crop of outstanding revolutionists, devoted Socialists, was growing up. Though they were ferociously at odds, the response to their appeal was impressive. Karl Marx, Friedrich Engels, Ferdinand Lassalle, and especially the young leaders August Bebel and Wilhelm Liebknecht, combined revolutionary passion with German *Gründlichkeit*, and their efforts to create a mass movement, in contrast to a conspiracy, turned all Socialist eyes on their country. Was it possible that socialism would enter through the German gate? Yes, said Marx; France was perhaps destined to ignite the first spark, but Germany would carry the torch.

"I am firmly convinced," Marx wrote Engels in 1870, "that though the first impulse will come from France, Germany is much more ripe for a social movement and will leave the French far behind. It is a serious mistake and self-deception on the part of the latter still to consider themselves a chosen people."[1]

A few months after this letter was written, revolution broke out in Paris, and the Commune was set up. For a while it seemed that France had won in the Socialist contest with Germany. But the Commune did not last, and in the subsequent decades French socialism retreated, disintegrating into groups and factions and losing much of its force and passion, while Germany marched ahead as the leading country of Marxism and revolutionary zeal.

The significance of this transfer of grace from France to Germany lay in the fact that at the time—more than a century ago—France was considered to be generally far ahead of Germany along the path of human progress. In poetry and *belles lettres*, in political institutions, in breadth

[1] K. Marx and F. Engels, *Sochineniya* (Works) (Moscow: State Social–Economic Publishing House, 1931), XXIV, Part 3, p 291.

I The Eastward Path of Social Revolution

of historical horizon, and in economic standards of living France was a "developed" country compared to the tiny nations across the Rhine with their vestiges of the Middle Ages and their petty kings and princes. France, the capital of human civilization, could, it appeared, have only one rival—England; but in terms of being the torch-bearer of a Socialist revolution, England was far behind.

Thus, the Socialist star began to move to the East, halting first over the land of Bismarck and Bebel.

"The French will start, the Germans will finish," was the way Lenin interpreted Marx's views. Lenin and his party became the ablest and most obedient pupils of the teachers and leaders of German socialism. The adoration of the Russian leaders for German Marxism was boundless. Karl Kautsky became the supreme authority, philosopher, scientist, and prophet. Congresses of German Socialists were hailed, attended, and applauded by the Russians. The French Socialists, with their un-Marxist ("petit bourgeois") factions, were unimportant in the eyes of Russian Marxists.

It was during this time that the Russian Marxists acquired their excellent knowledge of German. Emigré Russian leaders in France and Switzerland spoke German, followed the German press, studied German economics, and found in German statistics abundant confirmation of their concepts of capitalist centralization, capitalist pauperization of the masses, and of revolutionary trends. The generation of Lenin, which is now rapidly disappearing, was of this old pro-German breed; they bequeathed their sentiments and thoughts to their younger followers and to the new crop of leaders.

Russia was the least likely pretender to the role of leader of the world revolution. How could poor, backward Russia, this—in Lenin's words—"serfdom-ridden, hibernating, patriarchal, pious, and submissive Russia" challenge the advanced nations? In April, 1917, departing from Switzerland for Russia, Lenin said in a "Farewell Letter to the Swiss Workers": "The idea that the Russian proletariat is the chosen revolutionary proletariat among the workers of the world is absolutely alien to us." No one was more surprised than Lenin, the engineer of the November revolution, that Russia was winning out in the competition, and he believed that if Russia alone won the revolution it would be only to lose it again, that Russian socialism would be only a historical symbol, like the Paris Commune.

Time passed and the "Socialist revolution" was carried out. Lenin still doubted the ability of his country to head the world movement. Russia, he believed, would soon have to relinquish the leading role to a more advanced country. During the remaining years of his life he was never able to reconcile his theories with the unexpected fact of Russia's having been the first to achieve the revolution.

II THE STAR OVER THE KREMLIN OR OVER PEKING?

Thus the star of revolution had moved farther to the East to shine over the Kremlin. Lenin's heirs now abandoned their teacher's humiliating philosophy of Russia's unworthiness and claimed for Russia the right to lead. Under Stalin, the question was definitely settled: the star was there to stay; Russia was worthy, and any who questioned this must be punished.

> The whole world now admits—wrote Stalin in 1930—that the center of the revolutionary movement has shifted from Western Europe to Russia. The revolutionaries of all countries look with hope to the U.S.S.R. as the center of the liberation struggle of the working people throughout the world and recognise it as their only Motherland. In all countries the revolutionary workers unanimously applaud the Soviet working class, and first and foremost the *Russian* working class, the vanguard of the Soviet workers, as their recognised leader that is carrying out the most revolutionary and active policy ever dreamed of by the proletariat of other countries.[2]

This Soviet claim, accepted almost universally by the

[2] J. V. Stalin, "Letter to Demyan Bedny," December 12, 1930. *Works* (Moscow: Foreign Languages Publishing House, 1955), XIII, 25–26.

Communists of the world, was the ideological basis of Russia's supremacy in the Communist movement.

But was this supremacy definitely and firmly established? In the 1950's another eastern nation, poor, backward, even more "underdeveloped" than Russia, advanced to challenge the Soviet pattern of communism and dispute Moscow's superiority. That nation was China. Was the Soviet system of differential wages consistent with the ideals of communism? Could not the Soviet system of economically graded *kolkhozes*, with their private trade and the abyss created between city and village, be converted into an agricultural program with a more Communist countenance? Was the Soviet slogan of "coexistence" with the West not actually a kind of appeasement of capitalism? In posing these challenges, Chinese communism was proclaiming that China must and would be free of these lamentable remnants of the old unjust world, that its system would be a nobler and more equitable one than Russia's. The star that in a period of a hundred years had moved eastward from France through Germany to Russia must continue on the eastward path; it must shine over a country and a people that were marching faster than the standard–bearing Russians along the road to progress. That country and people would soon overtake Britain and, ever accelerating, overtake not only the United States but Russia itself, and finally assume a place worthy of the most populous and ablest people in the world. "China is moving," said *Jenmin Jihpao*, "with lightning speed. Recently, fifty–year old peasants were worried whether they would live to see the wonderful age of communism. Now even eighty and ninety–year–olds are sure that they will be able to enjoy the good fortune of communism."[3]

III THE SEMI-INTELLECTUALS

Western literature has more than once pointed out the disparity between Marxian theory and Communist practice.

[3] Quoted in *Politische Studien (Monatschrift der Hochschule für Politische Wissenschaften*, Munich, 1959), No. 116, p. 807.

In theory it is the advanced industrial and capitalist nations of the West that have created the prerequisites of socialism. In practice, however, it has been the less developed countries—Russia, China—that have provided the most fertile soil, while the advanced nations, after some outbursts, have proved barren. If revolutionary Marxism is a working class movement, as is claimed, how did it happen that China, with little more than three per cent of her population in the ranks of industrial labor, became a fortress of communism, while England, with sixty to seventy per cent of her people in the ranks of labor, and the United States, remained impervious to Communist revolution? Why do millions in Indonesia flock to Communist meetings and vote Communist, while in all of Scandinavia a bare few thousand show any sympathy for this movement?

It is an error to identify a political movement such as communism, democracy, anti–communism, or fascism with an economic group or "social class." Too many politicians and writers in the West have accepted the comfortable philosophy that communism is a working class movement. As a matter of fact, communism is not a labor movement, nor is it a peasant movement, a farmer–labor movement, or a movement of any other economic class. Despite the efforts of the Communist movement to reconcile theory by identifying the party with the class, workers do not constitute the main element of the powerful Communist movement.

At the roots of modern communism lies the great phenomenon of our times—the huge cultural revolution that has taken place in all corners of the world, the emergence of millions of benighted human beings into the light of science and knowledge. At the beginning of this century ninety per cent of India's population were illiterate; in Egypt ninety–two per cent were illiterate, in Serbia eighty–six per cent, in European Russia seventy per cent. In only a minority of the countries of the world—the Western countries—was literacy more or less general. Since the end of the nineteenth century, and especially during the last sixty years, there has been a rapid rise in literacy in the hitherto culturally backward countries. The increase in literacy, the growth of the daily press, and the advent of radio and television have helped to turn over human virgin soil in many countries. This development, which still continues, has created new social strata that are of special significance.

The new strata, when they emerged, were only half-educated; students were poorly prepared, and intellectuals were only semi-intellectuals. Colleges and universities, while growing rapidly, were sites of universal semi-knowledge. The Russians were the first to apply to this large stratum of half-educated people the term "semi-intelligentsia," which carries a derisive overtone. The scorn, however, is not appropriate. There is no other way to raise the backward majority of mankind to new levels without going through the various stages of education; there can be no skipping.

It is the semi-intelligentsia of the initial stages that constitutes the main element of Communist movements in the East and South. Revolutionary Marxism in its extreme, Leninist interpretation is well suited to the quest of the semi-intellectual for the perfect philosophy which has the answers to all questions—the source of evil, war and poverty, the road to the perfect society, and the new *Jihad*, the holy war to exterminate the enemies of paradise on earth.

In stating that Marxism in its primitive interpretation is well suited to the initial spiritual needs of young men and women receiving the ABC's of education in backward countries, we do not mean to convey that the entire stratum will join the extreme revolutionary movement in their country. The great majority go about their own business and remain outside political fights; they are the "non-voters" of their time. It is always a minority among the new intellectuals, usually a small one, that embraces the new faith, but it is this vocal and colorful minority that is characteristic of its era.

In the West a stratum of real intellectuals had been forming gradually since the Renaissance. It was already in existence in the nineteenth century, when the rapid growth of education expanded in the West. The spiritual soil of the Western countries already contained a kind of antidote to primitive philosophies. This is why the experiments in France failed in 1870–71, and it is why German Marxism faded in the first decades of the twentieth century.

The general psychological differential between the initial and the higher stages of cultural growth is the presence of *doubt* at the higher stages in the thinking of man. The ability to swallow entire ideologies, philosophies, political theories and programs without question is a birthmark of the initial stage. As the new generations in the underdeveloped countries grow and mature, the poison of criticism—that trademark of civilization—begins to erode the rapidly embraced and rapidly assimilated new faith. Questions are asked. The overwhelming dynamism that is the product of an uncritical state of mind begins to weaken. When this process reaches a certain stage a high-level intellectual crust forms that is endowed with both knowledge and skepticism, and when this new crust becomes large enough the primitive *Weltanschauung* enters its period of decline.

And this is why the star of revolution had to travel farther to the East to find fertile ground. While there existed in Russia, in the fifty years before the revolution, a stratum of high-level intellectuals, they were neither able nor inclined to try to stop the growth of new philosophies; besides, because of the extremes of autocracy in Russia, many outstanding leaders of Russian thought themselves embraced Marxian philosophy.

Recollections of our own experience may help to illustrate this process of spiritual evolution. During the last decades before the upheaval of 1917 in Russia, revolutionary movements were growing and engaging the interest of very young men and women. Underground "groups" and "circles" served as a kind of preparatory school. Among the youthful members were university students, technical school students, students in the higher grades of high school, and young salesmen, sometimes workers or craftsmen. Often these young people came from families in which

III The Semi-Intellectuals

the parents had had little or no education. The "circle" was not a "party cell," nor was it in general a political organization; it was, rather, a school for future revolutionists and was viewed as such by the party (Social–Democratic or Social–Revolutionary) that sent its "lecturers" to guide the particular groups. Meetings were secret and were usually held in private apartments. There were from ten to fifteen persons in a "circle."

I belonged to Marxist "circles" in St. Petersburg and Vilno, having first joined at the age of about seventeen. All of us were impatient to learn. Instruction was rapid; it had to be comprehensive enough to solve all our problems at once. The political air was electric; revolution was on the order of the day, and we were anxious to be given something that would replace religion, monarchy, capitalism, and family, and that would tell us explicitly what we had to do to achieve the Millenium.

We had two textbooks. One was a Russian translation of Julius Lippert's *History of Culture*, which, in somewhat oversimplified evolutionary terms, described the steps in the progress of humanity from the hoary past to modern times; it was also a kind of refutation of all religious philosophies. The other was *Political Economy*, by two Russian Marxists, A. Bogdanov and I. Stepanov, which contained the main theses of "scientific socialism." We were taught the non–deistic origin of the universe, Darwin's theory of the evolution of species, "utopian" and "scientific" socialism. There were jokes about the all–embracing program of our "circles"—they stretched, it was said, "from the stars through the apes to socialism."

The theories expounded in our textbooks and the speeches delivered by our "lecturers" fell on eager ears. It would be wrong to say that we were "indoctrinated." Rather, we craved doctrine and were, perhaps more eager to get it than our teachers were to teach it. After the courses we felt ourselves to be—and our young "lecturers" agreed with us—knowledgeable and educated men now able to carry the torch forward. We were materialists in philosophy, Darwinians in science, Marxists in sociology. What we knew or presumed to know was definite and certain. Our stratum was the culture medium for revolutionism—primitive, strong, and uncompromising.

It took many years before the worm of doubt began to attack our tree of knowledge and we began to realize how little we really knew. But as our extreme dynamism evaporated, new waves of "beginners" came in to replenish the numbers and the power of the semi–intellectuals.

A similar process, it appears, was taking place while Chinese communism was putting on flesh and muscle. In Yenan, headquarters of Mao Tse–tung during the civil wars, a number of schools for Chinese youth were organized —the institutes of Youth Cadres, a Women's University, and a number of other *sui generis* high schools. The youth flocked to Yenan through the barriers of the war fronts to get revolutionary Marxist wisdom directly from the mouth of the high priest. The difference between China and prerevolutionary Russia was only that in Yenan education could take place openly and without the need to divide the operation into small "circles." Mao Tse–tung has more than once confirmed how great has been the significance of the "revolutionary youth" to his movement, how important it was in forming the cadres of his future government and his armies. Although details of this educational operation are lacking, it is evident that among the young students in Yenan there were few, if any, Chinese workers; the great majority were of "petit bourgeois" origin, mainly from families of city merchants, peasants, and government officials; Mao himself came of a family of Chinese officials.

Chinese communism has been a classic party of the semi–intelligentsia. Mao Tse–tung has never admitted this state of affairs; an orthodox Marxist, he has regarded his party as a labor party and has offered the sophisticated interpretation that it "represents the interests" of the "Chinese proletariat"; whether or not the "Chinese proletariat" was in agreement with this thesis was a secondary matter.

Lenin and his successors faced the same problem. Lenin realized—and said so in writing—that the light of revolutionary socialism in Russia had been kindled in the

III The Semi-Intellectuals

main by non–workers; in fact, his "cadres" were often recruited from among members of the gentry or well–to–do capitalist families; a number of his most trusted lieutenants and fighters came from these social groups. But he insisted that his party was a workers' party, not one among others, but *the* workers' party *par excellence.* Lenin's Central Committees, elected in 1905, 1912, and 1917, were composed of intellectuals, almost without any workers. The qualifications for the great task of leading the movement included prowess, devotion and at least a minimum of knowledge necessary for the task, and workers with these qualifications were not available. For propaganda purposes, however, Lenin displayed another kind of leader —the "pure proletarian." Such, for instance, were the Bolshevik members of the Duma (the pre–revolutionary assembly), whose personalities, speeches, and political attitudes were widely discussed. From abroad, Lenin gave instructions, during the electoral campaign, to nominate workers and to see to it that the Bolshevik faction in the Duma presented a strong image of a workers' party. In rejecting non–workers as candidates, Lenin was depriving his future faction in the Duma of better leadership, but so important did the great symbol of a workers' party appear to him that he took this in stride.

The issue of creating "cadres" of an allegedly workers' party continued to bother the Soviet leadership for a long time after the Soviet revolution of 1917. Strenuous efforts were made to increase the percentage of workers in the party's membership; special recruitment drives were carried out in which only "workers from the bench" were accepted into the party. And then, regularly, the worker element dropped as workers who had joined the party advanced to posts in the administration and lost their proletarian status. So hopeless had the situation become in the early 1930's that Stalin ceased to publish statistics on the social composition of his party in order to conceal the fact that it was becoming a middle class political organization.

IV THE NEW MIDDLE CLASS IN RUSSIA

Thus, in the course of a few decades, a new social

stratum has emerged in Russia, a new middle class whose role has been determined not as much by its size—it probably numbers twenty million today—but mainly by the weight it exerts politically, which is greatly out of proportion to its numbers. When united in its sentiments, the middle class is a powerful force. Its real significance is often hidden under such standard phrases as "workers' interests," "toilers' movements," "popular enthusiasm."

The Soviet middle class embraces practically everybody of importance in Soviet society. The scientists, inventors of Sputniks, generals and marshals, members of government from Khrushchev down to the last "acting second assistant," ballerinas, singers, painters, and editors are segments of a single milieu. Their problems are comparable; they understand one another; they spend their leisure time together, study together, intermarry, and live the life of neighbors in every sense. Not all are members of the Communist Party, although most of the "elite" are. Dependence on Party orders is not always to their liking, but all submit. In Stalin's time this class could say of itself what Abbé Sieyès said on the eve of the revolution: "What is the Third Estate? Everything. What has it been hitherto in the political order? Nothing. What does it desire? To be something." Today the Soviet middle class is already "something"; under Khrushchev it has advanced.

The shortening of working hours has given them a shorter office day. Old–age and veteran pensions have aided them substantially. The refrigerators, television sets, and automobiles which they so eagerly desire are given priority in production over some more vital needs of the workers and *kolkhoz* peasants. The new apartment buildings serve primarily the housing needs of this class (this is one reason why the government does not release statistics on the social composition of the privileged new tenants).

With the passing of the decades the Soviet middle class has risen to a somewhat higher level of education and intelligence. A quarter of a century ago Stalin and his circle could tell the nation that nearly all of its Communist leaders had been foreign spies who had "sold out" to foreign secret services, and many of the middle class

IV The New Middle Class in Russia

believed it. They were told that the culprits—the Zinovievs, Bukharins, Rykovs, and others—had confessed, and they believed it. They were told that old Russian professors had turned to wrecking, poisoning cattle, flooding coal mines, and taking measures to augment famine; they believed it. Stalinism would have been impossible without this unique readiness of the middle class to accept uncritically what they were told.

As the new middle class began to assert itself, the spiritual level rose. Criticism was tolerated, although freedom of thought was limited to certain fields of knowledge—engineering, physics, and some other sectors of science; it did not, of course, extend to history and political affairs, fields strictly controlled by the Party. It became impossible to forbid travel to and contacts with the West; it became impossible to tell student audiences that Trotsky had been a German–British spy; it became impossible to maintain the theory that war is "inevitable," and that violent revolutions are the only way to progress. These myths could now find acceptance in China, but not among the new generations in the Soviet Union.

Some historians and observers apply the term "bourgeoisie" to the millions-strong class that the Communist governments and leadership consider their "intelligentsia." Whether or not the term "bourgeoisie" is appropriate,[4] the evolution of this group over the decades—in Russia over more than forty years—and its growing influence mark one of the most important and basic developments in the history of the countries of the East.

The changes that have taken place in the Soviet Union have brought a modicum of improvement; it might appear that this improvement will be reflected in Russia's international relations. It might appear that a better climate in Soviet–American relations may be expected to develop

[4] To our mind, "bourgeoisie," a term derived from Marxian ideology, is associated with private property, competition, class war, "big business," etc. But the large stratum of government employees, technicians, teachers, policemen, artists, scientists, and students is a new phenomenon, and it seems preferable to call it a "middle class" rather than a "bourgeoisie."

in the new era, that the cold war may soon end and normal relations begin to prevail.

This will not necessarily be the case. To understand the attitude of the new middle class in Russia toward foreign-political issues we must consider its relation to Party politics, its Great Power sentiments, and its ambition to achieve superiority. Although bent on material well-being and a "no-war" course for Russia, it is too weak and too divided within itself to oppose the course of the "strong men" at the helm and paralyze their tremendous offensive dynamism.

[1960]

A REVOLUTION TRANSFORMED

The Russian revolution was an eruption of forces unprecedented in history. It was as if not one but hundreds of extinct volcanoes beneath the soil of Russia, becoming active after ages of dormancy, had begun to pour hot lava on the cities, hamlets, and fields of that vast country. A whole continent was propelled toward a great transformation, in the course of which tradition and heritage were to give way to a new social order. Old Russia—the Russia of inertia, corruption, and the proverbial *chinovnik* (official, called "the man of the 20th" because the 20th of the month was pay–day), the Russia of splendor at the top and starvation at the bottom, the Russia of traditional obedience—was to give way to a "new Russia," the contours of which were vague but beautiful. Old Russia and New Russia: for a long time the contrast between them was the subject of speeches, programs and manifestoes.

Dynamism was rampant. The destruction of the old was carried out radically and cruelly; the construction of the new was an exciting series of experiments, failures, new endeavors, and grand plans following one upon the other. The highest degree of dynamism was embodied in the party that achieved power in November, 1917. It was as if the Bolshevik Party had to suck up from Russia's fields and forests the dormant hatred and militant spirit that had accumulated over the ages, and hurl them into the faces of the old powers and the new claimants to power. No doubts or scruples tempered the fighting spirit of its leadership. The ruling party was of course a minority, even a small minority, at the time, but in times of revolution simple membership statistics do not indicate where real power is centered; party members are to be weighed rather than counted. Passion, ruthlessness, and capacity for self–sacrifice are weighty factors on the scales of history.

For a long time the emphasis was on internal affairs. Revolution was seen as the first phase of a rapid and radical transformation of the country's political, economic, social, and cultural institutions and way of life. Foreign policy was at best a nuisance, an obstacle. The first Soviet Foreign Minister, Leon Trotsky, later recalled that he agreed to take this post only because it would leave him free time for other work. "What diplomatic work are we apt to have? . . . I will issue a few revolutionary proclamations to the peoples of the world, and then shut up shop." Trotsky did not want to appoint more than two reliable Old Bolsheviks to posts in the *Narkomindel:* "You are too valuable," he told them, "for such a job." "What foreign affairs will we have now?" Lenin wondered.[1]

Along with their pre–revolutionary philosophy the Soviet leaders had a suspicious, negative attitude toward foreign policy in general. To them, foreign policy was the embodiment of predatory operations, conquering of weak nations, and exploiting of underdeveloped nations; diplomats were brigands and gangsters. What Lenin wanted during this early era was to get rid of "their" foreign policy; he was inclined to accept President Wilson's and Ambassador Bullitt's offers not only in order to stop military operations, but in general to gain a "breathing spell" from preoccupation with foreign policy. Let the imperialists fight one another; we will have time and energy for our revolution: "When thieves fall out, the honest man gains."

[1] Leon Trotsky, *My Life*, (New York: Grosset & Dunlap, Inc., 1960), p. 341, and *Proletarskaya Revolyutsiya* (Proletarian Revolution), Moscow, No. 10, 1922, p. 99.

A Revolution Transformed

Although the grandiose scheme of world revolution was of course in his mind, the first draft of the organization of the Comintern was not part of "foreign policy" but rather a part of his party's activity.

Revolution meant upheaval in the present and for a long time to come: the tsar and his family were executed, the old state institutions were disbanded, state agencies were revamped, banks and industry were nationalized, freedoms were abolished, the Bolshevik Party was purged, a Soviet state was created. Revolution meant a civil war of unprecedented nature and proportions on all fronts, a civil war in which armies and guerillas would perish from bullets, cold, and starvation, and thousands of corpses would be stacked in long rows along the highways. Revolution meant the *Kombedy* (Committees of Poor Peasants) and terrible violence against the well-to-do; it meant, a decade later, Stalin's *kolkhoz* operations, during which "kulaks" and their families were deported to die by starvation or exposure. It meant the emergence of new industry and the rapid growth of old and new cities all over Russia. Finally, it meant a wholesale liquidation of doubters and deviationists.

This hurricane of revolution lasted about two decades. In the course of those two decades there had of course emerged plenty of foreign policy problems, some of major importance, which had to be solved. In the long run, however, priority was given to issues of the internal transformation, the "building of socialism," in the Soviet Union. Lenin did not once go abroad after November, 1917, and Stalin did not leave Russia once during the first twenty-six years of the Soviet era, until he went to Teheran and Potsdam to meet his temporary allies in the last phases of the second World War.

After two decades the edifice of Stalin's "socialism" was declared ready. The pace of social transformation had slowed down, revolutionary dash had degenerated into a senseless, disgusting purge operation. A great war was looming. Issues of defense, alliances, acquisition of new areas, and aggrandizement of the Soviet Union began to come to the fore.

Foreign policy moved into focus. It was logical that issues

of foreign policy should be the center of attention during a war, but as the fighting approached its end, the great international problems, rather than declining in importance, occupied the scene more and more until, after Stalin's death, foreign policy gained priority over all other Soviet preoccupations.

The great dynamism of the revolutionary party that had come to power in 1917 had not all been spent in the internal upheaval. The stability of the new system had, contrary to all predictions, helped to educate a generation of assured, opinionated leaders with an exaggerated notion of their power, which grew into an exaggerated belief in the impact of the Soviet Union on the world, a generation that is still imbued with hostility and militancy toward all kinds of adversaries. This generation, having fought in Russia's most terrible war, has become convinced of the Soviet's invincibility and "inevitable" growth. The old stream of power dynamism has found a new bed.

It was as if a mighty transformer had been at work at the revolution's power generator converting the old energy into another kind of energy, as though rivers had been diverted to other courses, as if the thousands of volcanoes that had been active under Russia's soil since 1917 had moved to the frontiers to erupt in new ways.

Inside Russia the revolution had ended and a new system had been, at least for a time, firmly established. Russia had become more calm and quiet than the Western nations; for a number of years no mass meetings of dissidents had taken place, no spontaneous street demonstrations or riots had occurred, workers' strikes and peasant revolts had been extremely rare. Today Soviet cities present a picture of a measured way of life, with class distinctions in evidence, with property sternly protected, with the police in full power. No revolution or vestige of a revolution is in evidence. But the dynamism of the revolution is still alive, still rampant, still looking for outlets.

Having moved into the area of foreign affairs, the revolution has produced a dynamism without parallel in Russian history and with only few parallels in the history of other countries. The revolutionary origin of this dynamism is evident in its furious aggression, its limitless aspirations, its expansionism. Foreign policy, spurned by Lenin and Trotsky, now occupies first place among the preoccupations of the Khrushchev government. Whereas Lenin, Trotsky, and Stalin did not travel abroad in peace time to participate in international conferences, summit meetings, or sessions of the League of Nations, Khrushchev's prolonged trips abroad have provoked protests from other Soviet leaders. On his numerous travels, Khrushchev has met with the most "imperialist" heads of state. Since the summit conference of 1955 he has accelerated his pace; within the space of a few years he has visited Paris, Berlin, Vienna, and the United States, in addition to Finland, the satellites, and Southeast Asia. When he returned to Moscow from one such trip that he made with Bulganin, the Supreme Soviet, in a rebuff to the opposition, adopted a resolution which read: "The Supreme Soviet considers that the visit of Comrades N.A. Bulganin and N.S. Khrushchev has demonstrated the great importance of personal contact between statesmen for the promotion of mutual understanding, establishment of confidence between states, and development of international cooperation."

A visit by a foreign diplomat to Stalin before the war was a rarity; even after 1945 it did not occur frequently. Khrushchev, on the contrary, has mixed happily with foreign diplomats; he has visited diplomatic receptions and knows by name the major diplomatic figures in Moscow. His mind has obviously been preoccupied with problems of international relations. For no apparent urgent reason, he personally headed the Soviet delegation to the General Assembly of the United Nations in 1960, remaining in New York for twenty–five days, from September 19 to October 13.

A parallel to this transformation of a revolution's dynamic force from internal upheavals to the area of international relations—a parallel that helps us to understand Russian developments—appeared during a crucial period in the history of France, 1789–1815. The French Revolution was at first entirely preoccupied with internal problems—political and social upheaval, the dethronement and execution of the king, the partitioning of landed estates, the fight against the internal enemies of the republic. But energies gradually turned in new directions; wars followed wars, and while Paris was quieting down, the revolutionary Jacobin, *le petit Corporal* Napoleon Bonaparte, carried the revolutionary storm beyond the frontiers of France. Within a decade he was master of an empire in Europe, surrounded by a number of dependent governments that today we would call satellites—Naples, Spain, the Netherlands, the Kingdom of Italy, the Confederation of the Rhine, Westphalia, the Duchy of Warsaw. Except for Russia, France was the only Great Power on the continent; Napoleon's main enemy, Britain, appeared unable to defeat him and bring about the disintegration of his empire. But he could not stop. Danger lurked everywhere. He had to go forward if he was not to be turned back. He challenged all nations, he menaced all armies. But in the end he fell, and all his acquisitions were lost to France.

The rise and fall of Napoleon's empire, while it is an instructive chapter of history, is not necessarily an obligatory model for Russia. There are no stable laws of history, there are only comparisons, and *comparaison n'est pas raison*. In particular, a great war is not the only possible solution of the world puzzle, nor is it the only way out of an impasse.

[1960]

METHODS OF SOVIET DIPLOMACY

I

There has never been a government foreign office that has worked as feverishly, as diligently, and as productively as the *Minindel* in Moscow. In the sheer size of its performance—the number and length of its statements, notes, memoranda, and communiqués and the diversity of their contents—it has no rival in either the past or the present. Neither the Soviet Premier nor the Foreign Minister can by himself perform the task of initiating, editing, and following up this huge output, even though their names are signed to many of the documents.

In the Soviet view, diplomatic correspondence serves two objectives: it is not only a means of communication and negotiation between governments on business issues, but also an instrument for propagating "campaigns." "Peaceful coexistence," in the Soviet view, extends to all fields, but not to ideology; the preaching of the Good and the denunciation of Evil must continue until the Evil is routed. In this grandiose crusade, foreign policy, and diplomacy in particular, has its peculiar place.

There is a large segment of Soviet international activity that, because it must remain secret, is conducted in the traditional way: confidential conversations with ministers and ambassadors, secret agreements with other states, etc. In these areas of Soviet diplomacy the usual business-like methods are used. In other areas, diplomatic exchanges, statements, and memoranda of the Foreign Office are devised to serve as showpieces and to accord with professed principles of "overt diplomacy" and "no secret treaties."

Moscow issues yearly a *Chronicle of International Events* which contains a list of actions in the foreign field which come within overt diplomacy; enumerated are visits of important personages from other countries, conferences, trade agreements, speeches in the United Nations, and diplomatic notes, exchanges between heads of state, and official TASS statements. The number of foreign–political Soviet actions during a recent period listed in the *Chronicle* was as follows:

July, 1958	77
October, 1958	80
December, 1958	85

The Soviet actions greatly outnumber comparable actions of other governments. In the Soviet view, Soviet diplomatic notes, messages of heads of state, and official communiqués must serve as a means of explaining Soviet policy abroad, not so much to other governments as to the "people." It is from this view of diplomacy that certain of the peculiarities of Soviet exchanges flow. An editorial in a Soviet newspaper, however excellent, is rarely reprinted abroad; its full text remains known to Russian readers only and its impact is limited to the Russian public. The same article, however, if transformed into a diplomatic note and signed by the Soviet Premier or a Soviet minister, has every chance of being widely reported abroad, commented upon, and often reprinted in full in the leading press organs of other countries. The general awe of diplomacy, the aura surrounding some foreign names, and the expectation of possible serious developments attract more attention to a diplomatic document than it might deserve.

The length, form of expression, and use of rhetorical questions and answers that characterize Soviet exchanges make them more like newspaper editorials than documents in matter-of-fact negotiations. If the Soviet notes represented only an effort to discuss and solve a problem, many of them would make no sense at all; as an appeal to the public opinion of another country, however, they make good sense.

As to the length of Soviet diplomatic notes, a few examples will be illuminating:

Messages exchanged between Bulganin and Eden during Suez affair, 1956:

Bulganin to Eden, September 11	1,180 words
Eden to Bulganin, September 16	590 words
Bulganin to Eden, September 28	870 words
Eden to Bulganin, October 6	560 words
Bulganin to Eden, October 23	270 words

(discussion referred to United Nations)

Khrushchev–Adenauer correspondence on Soviet–German relations, August, 1959–January, 1960:

Khrushchev to Adenauer, August 18	3,700 words
Adenauer to Khrushchev, August 27	1,100 words
Khrushchev to Adenauer, October 15	2,700 words
Adenauer to Khrushchev, January 8	2,000 words
Khrushchev to Adenauer, January 28	4,100 words

Exchange of notes between Washington and Moscow, 1958:

Khrushchev to Eisenhower, June 11	3,500 words
Eisenhower to Khrushchev, July 2	800 words
Khrushchev to Eisenhower, July 2	1,800 words
Eisenhower to Khrushchev, July 14	400 words
Khrushchev to Eisenhower, July 9	1,600 words
Eisenhower to Khrushchev, July 22	1,500 words
Khrushchev to Eisenhower, July 23	900 words
Eisenhower to Khrushchev, July 25	650 words
Aide memoire, U.S.S.R. to U.S.A., July 9	620 words
Aide memoire, U.S.A. to U.S.S.R., July 26	500 words
Khrushchev to Eisenhower, July 28	2,200 words
Eisenhower to Khrushchev, August 1	650 words

Exchange of notes between U.S. State Department and Minindel on Berlin question, 1958–1959:

U.S.S.R. note to U.S., November 27	5,700 words
U.S. note to U.S.S.R., December 31	1,800 words
U.S.S.R. note to U.S., January 10	3,450 words
U.S. note to U.S.S.R., February 16	420 words
U.S.S.R. note to U.S., March 2	2,450 words
U.S. note to U.S.S.R., March 26	490 words
U.S.S.R. note to U.S., March 30	330 words

(Soviet Union accepts proposed conference)

Exchange of messages between Macmillan and Khrushchev following abortive Paris summit meeting, 1960:

Macmillan to Khrushchev, July 19	850 words
Khrushchev to Macmillan, August 3	3,650 words

The language of diplomacy (when the diplomacy is overt) is a matter of prime importance. While tact, a polite tone, and understatement may, in the public mind, have made "diplomacy" and "diplomats" the bearers of cant and hypocrisy, nevertheless self–restraint and politeness of tone have tended to create an atmosphere of calm, so important in international negotiations. In his *Diplomacy*, Sir Harold Nicolson, the British author and diplomat, described diplomatic language and its benefits:

> ... if a statesman or a diplomatist informs another government that his own government "cannot remain indifferent to" some international controversy, he is clearly understood to imply that the controversy is one in which his government will certainly intervene. If in this communication or speech he uses some such phrases as "His Majesty's Government view with concern" or "view with grave concern," then it is evident to all that the matter is one in which the British Government intends to adopt a strong line. By cautious gradations such as these a statesman is enabled, without using threatening language, to convey a serious warning to a foreign government. If these warnings pass unheeded he can raise his voice while still remaining courteous and conciliatory. If he says "In such an event His Majesty's Government would feel bound carefully to reconsider their position," he is implying that friendship is about to turn into hostility. If he says "His Majesty's Government feels obliged to formulate express reservations regarding..." he is, in fact,

saying, "His Majesty's Government will not allow...." The expression "in that event, my Government will be obliged to consider their own interests," or "to claim a free hand," indicates that a rupture of relations is being considered. If he warns a foreign government that certain action on their part will be regarded "as an unfriendly act," that government interprets his words as implying a threat of war. If he says that "he must decline to be responsible for the consequences," it means that he is about to provoke an incident which will lead to war. And if he demands, even in terms of exquisite politeness, a reply before "six o'clock on the evening of the 25th," then his communication is rightly regarded as an ultimatum.[1]

In the official three-volume Soviet *History of Diplomacy*, a textbook for students and foreign service aspirants, some remarks are devoted to the literary style of diplomatic exchanges: "In his notes and other diplomatic correspondence the diplomatic representative usually observes the requirements of tact and politeness, avoiding harsh expressions and any kind of attacks that would be insulting to the institutions of state to which he is accredited."[2] This advice to use polite language in Soviet diplomatic exchanges was in accord with traditional diplomacy. But from the very beginnings of the Soviet state, Soviet diplomacy has trod both the path of conventional hypocritical politeness and the path of insult. Lenin, in his exchanges with his adversaries, greatly enjoyed the old aristocratic style of inflicting the worst insult with a polite smile. Years of "coexistence" in one party with the Mensheviks, he said, had taught him the devious uses of diplomacy.

The fighting spirit that pervaded Soviet actions in foreign affairs made it impossible always to follow the rules of courtesy. Revolutionary passions and militancy more often than not won out over reticence; they substituted a

[1] Harold Nicolson, *Diplomacy*, (London: Thornton Butterworth, Ltd., 1939), pp. 227–228.
[2] *Istoriya Diplomatii* (History of Diplomacy), (Moscow: OGIZ, 1945), III, 796.

sincere I–hate–you–and–despise–you tone for the polite diplomatic expressions. Understatement (significantly, there is no Russian equivalent for the term "understatement") frequently gave way to its extreme opposite; as, for example, when Lenin's People's Commissar Georgi Chicherin told President Woodrow Wilson that the United States regime was "the government of anonymous corporations," that "soon" the government system of People's Commissars would become universal, and that the U.S. government was to be blamed for keeping the leftist Eugene Debs in prison.[3]

This alternation of a tongue–in–cheek method with deliberate impertinence continued under Stalin, to whom hypocrisy and deceit were the essence of diplomacy, although the impertinent usually prevailed over the polite. "A diplomat's words," Stalin wrote in January of 1913, "must contradict his deeds—otherwise what sort of a diplomat is he? Words are one thing—deeds something entirely different. Fine words are a mask to cover shady deeds. A sincere diplomat is like dry water or wooden iron."[4]

The two methods of Soviet diplomacy have operated under Khrushchev too, with the impertinent again prevailing over the courteous. Strongly–worded, provocative tones are often considered to have greater impact on the general reader than does the cautious and polite tone. Frequently a Soviet note uses strong aggressive language where such language is entirely uncalled for except for reasons of giving vent to a fighting temper. When a Soviet diplomatic note wishes to indicate that a Western government is exerting pressure, it usually uses the phrase "crude pressure." When, for example, Adenauer's party scored a success in an election, this was due to the "crude intervention of the Western powers in the electoral campaign."[5] The United Nations' discussion of the Hungarian

[3] *Dokumenty Vneshnei Politiki* (Documents on Foreign Policy), (Moscow: Gospolitizdat, 1957), I, 531–539.

[4] J. V. Stalin, *Works*, (Moscow: Foreign Languages Publishing House, 1953), II, 285.

[5] Statement of the Soviet Foreign Ministry, *Pravda*, August 3, 1957.

situation was a "gross violation" of its jurisdiction.[6] Japan's commitment to send troops abroad would be in "crude contradiction" to the interests of peace.[7] With deliberate intent to insult, Khrushchev, in a message to Chancellor Adenauer, compared the political system of West Germany with that under Hitler. "Your hatred toward socialism and communism is obviously preventing you from making a correct evaluation of historical events that occur in your time," Khrushchev wrote Adenauer. "You come out with ridiculous tales."[8]

When Moscow criticizes alliances of weaker nations with the West it says that the alliances are forced upon them.[9] "It is well known" is a phrase used frequently when proof is difficult, as, for example, "It is well known that the [Communist] Chinese–Korean side consistently and strictly complied (after the Korean war) with the terms [of the armistice]."

Threat of the use of military force—in sharp contrast to the precepts of the old diplomacy—occupies a prominent place in Soviet diplomatic exchanges; sometimes the threat is coupled with boasts: "The Soviet Union has rocket techniques of such quantities and on such a level as no other country in the world possesses."[10] In a message to President Eisenhower, Khrushchev wrote: " ... the Soviet Union, too, has atomic and hydrogen bombs, an air force and navy, and in addition ballistic missiles of all types, including intercontinental missiles."[11]

The landing of American forces in Lebanon at the request of the Lebanese government was a "military invasion," Khrushchev wrote Eisenhower on July 19, 1958, and demanded the withdrawal of the "occupying forces." To Prime Minister Macmillan, Khrushchev wrote on the same day that Britain's "unprovoked aggression against

[6] Khrushchev's message to President Eisenhower, June 11, 1958.
[7] Statement of the Soviet Government, *Pravda*, December 3, 1958.
[8] *Pravda*, August 27, 1959 and February 2, 1960.
[9] Soviet note to the Western powers, April 19, 1957.
[10] Khrushchev's message to Adenauer, August 18, 1959.
[11] *New Times*, Moscow, No. 30, (July 25, 1958), Supplement, Documents, p. 7.

Jordan is being crudely covered up by a request of the government" of Jordan; the operation, he told the British Prime Minister, was a "military adventure." The terms "aggression" and "agressors" were repeatedly used.

Threats of military force have now become a regular element of Soviet diplomatic documents, and other governments have become accustomed to accepting them as normal in Soviet international exchanges. Since the emergence of NATO and throughout the years of its growth and the expansion of United States air bases in various countries, the Soviet government has protested vigorously to the respective governments, often adding a threat of armed reaction. In October, 1953, the Soviet government sent a note to Greece protesting against the establishment of United States bases there. In March, 1954, Moscow protested against the setting up of American bases "on Dutch territory"; Holland denied the existence of such bases. Simultaneously a similar protest went to Pakistan ("although, as is well known, no attack threatens Pakistan"). In March, 1957, Premier Bulganin said in his message to Norwegian Premier Einar Gerhardsen: "The Norwegian people, and first of all the working class, to whose fate the Workers' Party headed by you cannot be indifferent, would have to pay dearly for the bases built in Norway with foreign money, should the plans of the NATO strategists materialize."[12]

The list of similar notes could be prolonged. Recent developments enriched this catalogue of diplomatic peculiarities by adding United States naval bases abroad to the roster of topics taken up in Soviet diplomatic correspondence, and, after the U–2 incident of May, 1960, by informing Turkey, Pakistan, and Norway that Soviet armed forces would in future destroy bases from which unauthorized flights over Soviet territory were initiated. To this systematic building up of a fear hysteria abroad, Khrushchev finally added (although not in a diplomatic note) the most alarming threat by his announcement that a neutral country, Austria, henceforth would be subjected to retaliation in case the Soviet Union were attacked with

[12] *Pravda*, March 27, 1957.

missiles from Italy or from United States bases in Italy that overflew Austria.

The Soviet government was of course aware that these protests against various forms of a Western alliance would be ineffectual and would only arouse protests of the other side against Soviet interference in the internal affairs of the states concerned. But the Soviet notes and messages were primarily intended to influence public opinion in the other country. As has already been indicated, in Soviet practice the demarcation line between a newspaper editorial and a diplomatic message is blurred. Actually, interference in the affairs of other countries has in the last decade grown at the same pace as the power and self-assurance of the Soviet government. Reference to such internal affairs in Soviet messages was often preceded by "We do not intend to interfere in your internal affairs, but...."[13] In July, 1959 Soviet President Kliment Voroshilov sent a wire to the King of Greece asking him to "take measures for the liberation of Manolis Glezas," a Greek Communist leader on trial for espionage. Glezas was sentenced to five-years' imprisonment. In a "declaration" made to Lebanon's Foreign Minister the Soviet envoy informed him that "Evidently the present foreign policy of the Lebanese government does not enjoy the support inside Lebanon that the Lebanese government would have liked to enjoy."[14]

In a Soviet statement addressed to Japan the Tokyo government was told how to guard Japan's interests: "The safety of Japan is best secured by strict observance of the statutes of her own Constitution, which rejects rearming and opens for Japan the possibility of maintaining neutrality."[15]

Just as odd was a Soviet note informing the Greek government that in Greece "large sections of the public are denouncing the [Greek-American] agreement as a gross violation of the national sovereignty and independence and a menace to her security."[16] In this case the Greek govern-

---

[13] For example, Bulganin's message to Guy Mollet, May 17, 1957.
[14] *Pravda*, June 12, 1957.
[15] *Pravda*, December 3, 1958.
[16] Soviet note to Greece, March 20, 1954.

ment protested against "outside attempts to intervene in her internal affairs"; in a number of similar cases the other governments reacted likewise.

II

We have seen how Moscow frequently informs another government concerning the attitude and interests of the latter's own people. This is characteristic Soviet behavior; it extends not only to diplomacy but to the press and to political literature; moreover, it emanates from Soviet ideology, and the stronger the Soviet state grows the more often the thesis is propagated that—in Molotov's words— "the interests of the Soviet Union coincide with the interests of the peoples of other countries."[17] The thesis is based on the axiom that in every country the Communist Party represents the interests of "the people," or at least of the majority of its "toilers"; and since Moscow considers itself the spokesman for all Communist parties it is entitled to claim that it knows better than any other government where the real interests of the latter lie. Thus it happens that these interests are always identical with Soviet policy. Disagreement with or opposition to the Soviet course on the part of any government violates the interests of that country.

"The aim of Soviet diplomacy," says the authoritative *History of Diplomacy,* "is to secure peace for the peoples of the Soviet land and to create such foreign political conditions as are necessary for its constructive work. Such a goal coincides with the interests of the whole of progressive humanity."[18]

This outlook is a basic element of Soviet foreign policy and not only of its diplomatic exchanges. When Italy, for example, signed an agreement on United States aerial bases, the report was headlined in the Soviet press: "Against

[17] Speech by Vyacheslav Molotov at the Fourth Session of the Supreme Soviet, August 31, 1939.
[18] *Istoriya Diplomatii* (History of Diplomacy), (Moscow: OGIZ, 1945), III, 764.

Italy's National Interests."[19] Soviet reaction to a similar agreement by Denmark resulted in a Soviet *aide memoire* in which Moscow said: the Danish action (American troops on Danish soil) "is not in the interests of Denmark herself since it creates a threat to her security and independence.... The overwhelming majority of the Danish people" are opposed to "the granting of Danish territory for American bases."[20]

About United States bases in Greece the Soviet government said, in a memorandum to Athens: "The Greek people emphatically come forward against the creation of atomic and missile bases on its territory."[21]

When Iran joined the Baghdad Pact, the Soviet report was headlined: "Against the Interests of Iran."[22] Similarly, "the population of West Germany rejects the policy of the Bonn militarists."[23] In an interview with Turner Catledge, the *New York Times* correspondent, Khrushchev not only attacked Norway, Denmark, and Holland for their alliances with the West but asserted: " 'A majority of the Norwegians would like to leave that organization [NATO] now.' He said the same was true of Denmark and of the Netherlands."[24]

In his message of July 19, 1958 to Prime Minister Macmillan on the Middle East, Khrushchev did not stress Soviet interests in the area but spoke in the name of all "people" of the Middle East: " ... solutions can and should be found that would accord with the vital interests of the Near and Middle East nations."[25]

On the reunification of Germany, "the position of the German Federative Republic is not in accord with the interests of the German people," said the Soviet note to Germany of August 2, 1957.

---

[19] *Pravda*, April 4, 1959.
[20] Soviet Aide Memoire to Denmark, *Pravda*, January 29, 1953.
[21] *Pravda*, May 14, 1959.
[22] *New Times*, Moscow, No. 43, (October 20, 1955).
[23] *Pravda*, August 22, 1953.
[24] *New York Times*, May 11, 1957.
[25] *New Times*, Moscow, No. 30, (July 25, 1958), Supplement, Documents, p. 11.

In a reply to Soviet Premier Bulganin on October 21, 1956, President Eisenhower resorted to stern language in protesting, among other things, Soviet interference in United States internal affairs and characterizing remarks of Bulganin about the U.S. Secretary of State as "offensive":

> First [wrote President Eisenhower] the sending of your note in the midst of a national election campaign of which you take cognizance, expressing your support of the opinions of "certain prominent public figures in the United States" constitutes an interference by a foreign nation in our internal affairs of a kind, which, if indulged in by an Ambassador, would lead to his being declared *persona non grata* in accordance with long-established custom.
> Second, having delivered a lengthy communication in the Russian language, you have published it before it could be carefully translated and delivered to me. Because of this, and of the necessity of placing the facts accurately before the public, I am compelled to release this reply immediately.
> Third, your statement with respect to the Secretary of State is not only unwarranted, but is personally offensive to me.
> Fourth, you seem to impugn my own sincerity.

Since "the peoples" disagree with their governments when the latter oppose the Soviet course, they try to overthrow their leaders when the opportunity presents itself. The success, for example, of General Dwight D. Eisenhower in the presidential campaign of 1952 was due to President Truman's anti–Communist policy in the Korean war. On this point, Foreign Minister Molotov stated:

> The defeat of the Democrats in the presidential campaign is to be explained not by the fact that theirs was a more moderate foreign policy, but rather by the fact that they were responsible for the war they had unleashed in Korea. On the other hand, the Republicans won the election not because they stood for a more aggressive foreign policy but, on the contrary, because to all intents and purposes they were for a

time a political party that was helping to end the war in Korea and re-establish peace, rather than continue the aggression there.[26]

The resignation of Winston Churchill in 1955 generally was assumed to be for reasons of age; the Soviet side, however, knew the real reason: Churchill was guilty of a pro–American, anti–Soviet course, contrary to the wishes of his people:

> Churchill's foreign policy has been a complete failure inasmuch as he ignored the demands of the English people, who insisted on taking effective measures to eliminate the causes of international tension ... he openly put the demands of United States ruling circles above the will of his own people ... his notorious statement of October last about his intention at the end of World War II to use German–Fascist armies and their armament against the Soviet army [undermined his standing].[27]

The fact that Richard M. Nixon, the Republican candidate, failed to win the presidential election of 1960 was due to his party's rejection of a "peace policy" according to the Soviet interpretation:

> ... the majority of the voters disagreed with the present policy of the United States Republican government, which to them did not accord with the national interests of the American people, the interests of preserving peace....
> The American people saw this and drew their conclusions; by rejecting Nixon they have also rejected the notorious policy of strength, the policy of aggression and provocations.[28]

The special aims of Soviet diplomacy are also reflected in the widely publicized Soviet appeals to other countries to follow Soviet moves. When the Soviet armed forces were reduced in 1958 by 1,840,000 (they had been greatly

---

[26] *New Times*, Moscow, No. 7, (February 12, 1955), Supplement, Documents, pp. 28–9.
[27] *Pravda*, April 7, 1955.
[28] *Pravda*, November 10, 1960.

increased in 1950–1955), Andrei Gromyko called upon the other powers to make similar reductions in their armed forces. When the Soviet government, unilaterally and without granting the other countries the right of checking and inspection, announced that it would halt further nuclear tests, Moscow invited the Western powers to follow the Soviet example.[29] The stress on Soviet initiative in beneficial international developments is a constant element of Soviet diplomatic documents and exchanges. In January, 1958, for example, President Eisenhower proposed in a letter to Premier Bulganin to "study together" the ways of "preventing surprise attacks" and, to this end, to appoint "technical groups." The proposal was repeated in his letters to Premier Khrushchev (Bulganin had been removed) of April 8 and April 28. Khrushchev accepted the idea on July 2, but in a subsequent Soviet note it was presented as a Soviet suggestion:

> It is the Soviet Government's opinion that it would be useful if in the nearest future the appropriate representatives including those of defense ministers of both parties, for instance on the level of experts appointed by the Governments of the U.S.S.R., the United States and possibly of some other states, met to study jointly the practical aspects of this problem and within a definite time limit drafted recommendations on measures to prevent the possibility of surprise attack.[30]

The manner of making public the answers of other governments to Soviet messages is also part of the peculiar specific methods of Soviet treatment of international issues. Many facts and arguments contained in foreign notes and memoranda are not revealed to the Soviet

---

[29] Khrushchev's message to President Eisenhower, April 5, 1958.
In December 1948, while in the process of withdrawing its forces from North Korea, the Soviet government appealed to the United States to take similar action in South Korea. The United States complied with the suggestion and withdrew its forces in the spring of 1949. This was followed by an attack from North Korea on the South. It is possible that the Korean war might have been avoided had American forces in Korea been maintained in full strength.

[30] *Pravda*, July 4, 1958.

reader. Should the Soviet government help to create a pro–Western atmosphere in Russia by a complete reporting of foreign arguments that might prove to be convincing, merely because a document carries the signature of a minister and is transmitted by an envoy? The answer is no. In reporting to its own people the Soviet government does not make a distinction between diplomatic documents and general newspaper reports.

When a note of a foreign government reaches Moscow, no announcement whatever is made of it, at least not until the Soviet government has dispatched its reply, which is usually a few weeks, and sometimes a few months later; the Soviet reader must never know the arguments of a foreign government without simultaneously being given the antidote. And then, depending on the contents, the foreign note is either published along with the full text of the Soviet answer, or it is merely mentioned that a note dealing with such and such a subject was received on such and such a date and that the Soviet government has dispatched its reply, which is printed in full. When the text of a foreign note is given, it is often presented in such greatly condensed form that the reader is not able to understand its real meaning.

On October 8, 1960 the contents of a United States reply to a Soviet note on the rearmament of Germany were reported in Russia as follows: " ... the United States note of August 8 ignores the growing concerns and alarm of the European peoples and attempts to justify a policy that may endanger the cause of peace and the security of peoples. As is obvious from the text of the note, the government of the United States does not intend to cease its activities directed toward rearming the West German army with nuclear–rockets armament."[31]

A German note of August 17, 1960 on rearmament was summarized in an unintelligible way:

> On the 17th of August, 1960, the Embassy of the Federative Republic of Germany in Moscow transmitted to the Ministry of Foreign Affairs of the

[31] *Pravda*, October 8, 1960

U.S.S.R. a note of the FRG government, containing a reply to the note of the Soviet government of July 19, 1960 [the Soviet note was published on July 21].

In the note of August 17 the FRG government passes by in silence the question of the arming of the Bundeswehr with "Polaris" rockets, a question which was raised by the Soviet government on July 19.

It claims the need of unlimited armament for the FRG and tries to base this claim on the absence of an agreement on a general controlled disarmament in which it allegedly is interested.

The government of the FRG raises again the question about the so-called right of the Germans to self-determination; the Soviet government is allegedly obstructing it.

The government of the FRG alleges also that it does not see in the Soviet note "the spirit of peaceable disposition and readiness for mutual understanding," which the Soviet government has affirmed many times.[32]

In a note of March 15, 1959 the Iranian government protested against eighty-one cases of violation of Iran's air space by Soviet aviation between November, 1958 and February, 1959. Receiving no answer, Iran sent a second note on April 25 citing new cases of such violation. The Soviet Ministry of Foreign Affairs replied in two notes (May 2 and May 31, published in *Pravda* June 4, 1959) denying the justice of all the complaints; the Soviet press, however, printed only the texts of the Soviet notes.

On April 28, 1959, the Soviet government protested to Italy against that country's permitting NATO missile bases on its territory. Italy replied on May 10. On June 10 Moscow again attacked Italy in a sharp-worded note of 800 words. The Italian note was condensed to 130 words, so that the real meaning of its contents was obscure.

These techniques have long been applied. Condensation of texts of foreign notes is evidently made in the Soviet Ministry of Foreign Affairs and the resulting product serves as a model for the entire press of the Soviet Union.

Finally, the Soviet Ministry of Foreign Affairs does not

[32] *Pravda*, September 4, 1960.

Methods of Soviet Diplomacy 211

always observe the custom of not making public its notes to other governments before the recipient government can acquaint itself with the contents; this Soviet practice, too, is in accord with Moscow's view of diplomatic messages as vehicles for appeals for popular support rather than as instruments of negotiation. In 1958, for example, the Soviet Premier sent twelve letters to President Eisenhower. "Each time Radio Moscow was broadcasting the texts in forty–seven languages before one official translation had been made in Washington. This was an excited, demagogic appeal to sway emotions in the international field, easy to do and more likely to exacerbate relations than accomplish the reverse."[33]

III

Karl Marx said there must prevail in international relations the same simple rules of honesty and ethics that prevail in relations between men. Soviet literature has more than once quoted these words with approval. In 1917–18 Trotsky was convinced that "simple rules" of morality would prevail under his party's regime; he disavowed secret diplomacy, made public the secret diplomatic documents of the old Russian governments, and promised in the future to conduct only open diplomacy. The people of Soviet Russia, he said, were entitled to know anything that alien governments and people learned about the Soviet.

This principle would be hard for any government to maintain, but Soviet Russia of 1917–18 was the least propitious field for diplomacy of this kind. Less than a year after the Lenin–Trotsky government seized power it concluded secret agreements with Germany directed against the Western *entente*. Lenin, more cynical and realistic than Trotsky, had never promised to adhere strictly to the new principles of secret or overt diplomacy. Stalin was even less inclined to follow Marx's principles or Trotsky's ideas

[33] George V. Allen, Director of the United States Information Agency, *New York Times*, February 18, 1959.

and promises. Under Stalin the new system was elaborated that, perfected by his successors, is in force to this day: what is to the advantage of the Soviet Union is ethical and honest; a Communist government may do whatever is of benefit to its cause.

Niccolo Machiavelli, whose name and writings are well known in Russia, described a policy more suitable to the dynamic, aggressive, and bellicose Stalinist course than the "simple rules of ethics." A government, Machiavelli wrote, must "combine the qualities of a lion and a fox—possess the great art of lie and hypocrisy, eliminate adversaries with the help of poison and dagger, take the law into its own hands in regard to unruly subjects, because a good aim justifies bad means."

The old generation of Soviet diplomats, with so many Trotskyites and other oppositionists in its midst, was radically purged on the eve of World War II, and the new crop, educated in the '40's and '50's, has imbibed the Machiavellian principles with the milk of their *alma mater*. They have learned the half-jest, half-truth of a British diplomat that a diplomat is an honest man who is sent abroad to lie for the good of his country. The spirit of purposefulness, of the "good of my country," of "achieving goals by any means" permeates the atmosphere of Soviet diplomacy. The specific methods that have been described here provide an excellent tool for the government, a tool well-adapted to that government's far-reaching aims in world affairs. The Western powers have not found an effective means of reacting to these unique methods in foreign-political negotiation. Although the written and unwritten codes of diplomatic intercourse provide them with a number of possible remedies, they cling to the traditional rules of diplomacy in their effort to maintain an atmosphere of calm and avoid any increase of tension.
[1960]

SOVIET RUSSIA AS A WORLD POWER

War produces not only deadly guns and poison gases, but also golden dreams and illusions. The greater the war, the more fantastic the illusions. In one recurring illusion each war is the "last war"; in another, "swords" are turned into "plough–shares"; in a third, the world is made "safe for democracy." Democracy as the path to a perfect world of peace and plenty has been a focal slogan of our age.

All men are free and equal, the masters of their fate: is not this the essence of modern democracy? If the fate of any given country is decided by its majority, one might conclude that the fate of the world is similarly decided by the majority of mankind. Thus the future belongs to ideas and ideals that are accepted by the majority of the human race. Of the world's about three billion human beings, over one billion—those within the Soviet bloc—follow a Communist set of programs and ideas; half a billion or more side with the West; the rest are uncommitted. Is it not obvious, especially to believers in democracy, which way history is leading us?

At the root of this approach lies the primitive method of counting noses in all the countries of the world, a method in which Bushmen and British, Congolese and Frenchmen are each given an equal voice and equal role in world history. This is of course a crude over-simplification, but this mode of thinking is part of an ideology and plays a role in the philosophical and political discussions of our days. According to this ideology, Moscow rides the wave of the future. Like Lenin and Stalin, Khrushchev has often pointed to the numerical strength of his "camp," and his followers have abundantly repeated it.

In his speech of November 6, 1957, commemorating the fortieth anniversary of the November revolution, Khrushchev said: "Today hundreds of millions are marching under the banner of Marxism–Leninism. Tomorrow additional tens and hundreds of millions of working people will place themselves under that victorious banner."

Other Communists, especially in China, have gone even further, to conclude that the governments in the Soviet bloc represent not only the population of their own countries but also the "interests" of "toilers" everywhere; since toilers constitute the great majority among all nations, the "Socialist commonwealth" can actually profess to speak for ninety per cent of the world's population.

Another widespread illusion counts nations as units rather than their population: does not the majority of the world's 120 to 150 states determine the course of history? And does it not follow that the twelve or so nations of the Soviet bloc are bound to have as great an impact on world affairs as the fifteen nations in NATO? This theory takes for granted that a government represents its people. More realistic than the first one, it nonetheless builds on a substantial fiction: it views Italy as equal to Chad, France as equal to the Cameroons. Moscow has at times promoted this approach as a basis for its far-reaching claims and its general notion of Soviet influence on current history.

As in the UN's forerunner, the League of Nations, the "one state—one vote" principle is a pillar of the United Nations General Assembly. The United Nations proceeds from the "sovereign equality" of its members. Since 1945, the number of members of the United Nations has more than doubled. Large and small nations, strong and weak ones, are equal before the world assembly.

This principle, however, is not carried out consistently:

the UN's most important agency, the Security Council, contains a corrective that violates the thesis of the "sovereign equality" of nations. Five Great Powers have permanent seats in the Security Council and the right of veto—the United States, the Soviet Union, Great Britain, France, and China (the latter having been given the veto power partly for sentimental reasons). The powers defeated in the second World War—Germany, Italy, and Japan—were at first left out of the United Nations; Italy and Japan were later admitted, but without becoming permanent members of the Security Council. Reflecting the political alignment of 1945, the structure of the Security Council has become increasingly obsolete.

The introduction of Great Power privileges into the structure of the United Nations punctured the democratic principle of the equality of nations; but the privileges were indispensable if the United Nations was to come into being. No Great Power would have joined if it had to comply with decisions that were against its own interests. It was President Roosevelt who proposed the right of veto in December, 1944; Churchill and Stalin concurred as a matter of course. The Soviet Union has made abundant use of its veto power—a fact that has produced much unnecessary irritation in the West. There is much in Soviet world policy and conduct to be indignant about, but, having once agreed to admit the Soviet Union to the United Nations, we cannot expect it to act in any different way. When they have found themselves in a minority, other permanent members of the Security Council have likewise used the veto.

The veto privilege as a modification of "equality" takes us from the world of dreams to the harsh reality of international affairs. Neither size of population nor sheer numbers of sovereign states, nor majorities of either, are decisive in world affairs. It is as unpopular today to stress the ultimately decisive role played by the Great Powers as it is considered indecent to talk about certain ugly facts of life. In this respect we are still, all of us, in a primary grade. Yet the fact remains that the Great Powers—with their alliances, competition, and quarrels—remain decisive in the shaping of history.

What are the distinguishing traits of a Great Power? Certainly not the size of its territory. The fact that Europe rather than Asia has been the breeding ground of the modern Great Powers proves this point. Nor is it size of population: the two most populous countries of the world, China and India, have not in recent centuries been among the world's Great Powers, while Britain took the lead among the powers at a time when her population was below ten millions. Nor is the degree of economic or even industrial development decisive in itself: Russia was a Great Power in the eighteenth and nineteenth centuries despite the fact that it was least developed industrially and was in fact a backward state. Scientific progress and general education are also poor yardsticks for measuring Great Power status: Russia's past record once again establishes the point. Nor is political homogeneity a necessary attribute of a Great Power: it is enough to point to France since the end of the nineteenth century. And while peculiarities and specific traits of "national character" may be one element in the total configuration, they are an element of vague significance rather than determinants of a nation's growth to Great Power status.

The fabric of which a Great Power is woven is complex and hard to analyze. The main characteristic of a Great Power is stability over a long period of time. Neither war nor defeat, earthquake, floods, nor epidemic can remove such a nation permanently from the concert of powers. The ability of a Great Power to recover and often rise to new heights after a catastrophe is a trait that distinguishes it from other nations; rehabilitation, of course, implies rehabilitation of military power.

This is not to say that a group of chosen nations has a corner on Great Power status for eternity. History has recorded the passing of great empires—in the Near East, the Mediterranean basin, and elsewhere, including ancient Greece and Rome. More recent centuries have seen the fall of the Ottoman Empire, of Sweden, and Spain, and the destruction of Poland. Yet other powers have proved to be more durable and have lasted for centuries.

Paradoxically, the total destruction of a Great Power in a large-scale war creates a longing for its resurrection on the part of its destroyers. The vacuum it leaves, like the gaping hole left by removing a keystone from an edifice, cries out for restoration, and in their own interests the victorious powers seek to bring it about. In international affairs, too, *natura abhorret vacuum*.

Attempts to deprive a defeated Great Power of its military capacity have regularly failed; more often than not it has been its former enemies who have helped the nation to rearm.

Napoleon's France, definitely beaten in 1815 after a long series of wars in which she was the aggressor, was left impotent and subject to military occupation by an allied force of 150,000. Within a few years France re-emerged as a Great Power of the continent, with Russia, one of the engineers of her defeat, helping her to resume her traditional role.

After the first World War Germany was deprived of her right to maintain an army of over 100,000 men. But long before the Nazis came to power, she was permitted to build a new navy. From 1933 on, the Nazi government disregarded all restrictions and rapidly rearmed the country; this was possible because Britain was not prepared to use force to stop the process.

Russian history presents an exciting record of the rise and fall of a Great Power. In 1918 Russia was defeated and practically disarmed. She was encircled and isolated from the West. From 1922-23 on, Germany, in need of Russia's support against the West, embarked on clandestine military cooperation with her, while the Western powers, for their part, welcomed Russia's return to a modicum of economic normalcy. Russia then gradually proceeded to rebuild a substantial military establishment; her military industrialization in the 1930's, achieved at a tremendous cost in money and human lives, was another indication of her permanence as a Great Power, albeit of the Asiatic type.

In the second World War Russia was again one of the Great Powers in Europe.

The efforts of the victorious powers aimed at militarily denuding a defeated state are natural, logical, and doubtless necessary; however, they can be effective for only a limited time. When applied to a Great Power, the efforts always end in failure. Perhaps the most striking case in point is the policy applied by the Allies toward Japan in 1945–47. The Potsdam Declaration—signed by the United States, Britain, and the Soviet Union—called for the total destruction of Japan's military and naval power. In addition, the American occupation forces put pressure on Japan to adopt a constitution that prohibited the maintenance of men under arms. The new Japanese government and Diet were happy to make their country the first to adopt this most exemplary progressive law—a law that, it appeared certain, would soon be imitated by all other nations.

"Aspiring sincerely to an international peace based on justice and order, the Japanese people"—read Chapter II, Article 9 of the Constitution which came into force on May 3, 1947—"forever renounce war as a sovereign right of the nation and the threat or use of force as a means of settling international disputes.

"In order to accomplish the aim of the preceding paragraph, land, sea, and air forces, as well as other war potential, will never be maintained. The right of belligerency of the state will not be recognized."

General Douglas MacArthur told the Allied Council for Japan on April 4, 1946, that Japan was not only renouncing war, but also surrendering "the sovereign right of resort to arms in the international sphere. Japan hereby proclaims her faith in a society of nations governed by just, tolerant and effective rules of universal social and political morality, and entrusts its national integrity thereto. . . . There can be no doubt that both the progress and survival of civilization is dependent . . . upon the realization by all nations of the utter futility of force as an arbiter of international issues. . . . I therefore commend Japan's proposal for the renunciation of war to the thoughtful consideration of all of the peoples of the world. It points the way, and the only way."[1]

General MacArthur predicted that the renunciation of war would be adopted by other countries, which would peacefully "federate together" in the same manner as the states comprising the United States. This was the same MacArthur who barred Soviet troops from the territory of Japan and opposed Soviet efforts to gain influence in Japanese affairs.

It did not take long before the American authorities had to change their mind. By agreement with the United States, after Japan had been completely demilitarized, a new Japanese "national security force" was initiated in 1947–48. This force was gradually expanded, although the constitutional provision renouncing war provided a barrier and gave the pro–Soviet elements and naive pacifists in Japan strong means, including court proceedings, to oppose the rehabilitation of their country as a major military power.

Allied policy in Germany after the second World War was motivated by the same outlook as in Japan. The conviction prevailed in the West that the main task was to weaken Germany permanently; to accomplish this it was found necessary not only to demilitarize the country but also to lower its economic standards by making it a non–industrial nation. Stalin had never accepted these theories literally; his real long range aim pointed in another direction. For his own reasons, however—in order to strangle all nuclei of anti–Sovietism, among them the potential strength of an independent Germany—he supported the efforts of his allies.

Among the originators of the most fanciful illusions about Germany were a number of highly placed Americans whose views contrasted with those of the more realistic British leaders around Winston Churchill. The Morgenthau Plan, which almost became the program of the United States government, provided for the permanent "pastoralization" of Germany after the war. The Potsdam Conference of 1945 prescribed (Par. 13) that "In organizing the German

[1] *Vital Speeches of the Day*, (New York: City News Publishing Co.), April 15, 1946, XII, No. 13, p. 390.

economy, primary emphasis shall be given to the development of agriculture and peaceful domestic industries." It went almost without saying that a permanent prohibition against the maintenance of armed forces would be imposed. Paragraph 11 of the Potsdam Declaration read: "In order to eliminate Germany's war potential, the production of arms, ammunition and implements of war as well as all types of aircraft and sea–going ships shall be prohibited and prevented." And Paragraph 3 (b) stated: "The maintenance and productions of all aircraft and all arms, ammunition and implements of war shall be prevented."

There was some uncertainty as to whether Germany as a sovereign state should be permitted to exist at all. While Churchill and Stalin did envisage a future German state (each had a different Germany in view), the French wanted to go beyond the Potsdam restrictions to demand permanent partition and the separation of certain territories from Germany. On behalf of the United States, Secretary of State James F. Byrnes submitted to the Allies the draft of a treaty providing for the demilitarization of Germany for a period of twenty–five years. The Soviet government dissented: Molotov demanded forty years. On the other hand, Molotov rejected the French program of separating the Ruhr, Rhine, and Saar areas; he also rejected all "pastoralization" plans and insisted on the establishment of a united German government. While exaggerating the revolutionary potential of Germany, Moscow was in general more realistic than some of the Western Allies about the future re–emergence of Germany as a Great Power.

Germany, sustained by the victors in the first postwar years, became a strong power by the end of the 1940's. A West and an East Germany were created, each of which laid claims to govern a united country. Each was helped by its Great Power allies, and each was rearmed with their help. At first the process of rearmament was opposed, particularly by Moscow. Finally, about 1955, even the Soviet government acquiesced.

In the eighteenth and nineteenth centuries, when Russia was expanding toward the West, there existed in the heart of Europe a large state whose historic function was to serve as a buffer and to cushion drives from the East. This was the Hapsburg empire. More than other states, Austria–Hungary combined under one dynasty a number of national minorities—Slavs, Germans, and Hungarians; the territories of these nationalities had been repeatedly either invaded by the Mongols and Turks or threatened by them. Austria–Hungary (and its predecessor the Austrian Empire), which had earlier served as Europe's bulwark against the East, maintained this role in the nineteenth century; now, however, the enemy was not Turkey, but Russia.

The dissolution of the Austro–Hungarian Empire in 1918–19 brought the structure of Europe tottering. But before long two new big military powers had re-emerged—Germany and the Soviet Union. By swallowing Austria and her neighboring lands, Hitler's Germany arrogated to itself Austria's former role of European bulwark. When the small successor states of Austria–Hungary re-emerged from the holocaust in 1944–45, they were unable singly to resist the big Eastern power; their continued separation from one another was jealously watched over by the new master of Central Europe.

Winston Churchill considered "the complete break-up of the Austro–Hungarian Empire" as a "cardinal tragedy." The Empire, he said, had afforded security "to a large number of peoples, none of whom in our own time had the strength or vitality to stand by themselves in the face of pressure from a revivified Germany or Russia. . . . There is not one of the peoples or provinces that constituted the Empire of the Hapsburgs to whom gaining their independence has not brought the tortures which ancient poets and theologians had reserved for the damned."[2] When Austria–Hungary disintegrated, Europe's masters of the time—France and England—did not recognize the dangers inherent in this process. Both Russia and Germany were impotent in the Versailles and Trianon era, and no one apparently foresaw their early re-emergence in the role of

---

[2] Winston S. Churchill, *The Gathering Storm*, (Boston: Houghton Mifflin Company, 1948), p. 10.

great conquerors. The world paid dearly for this destruction of one of the pillars of Europe's stability.

European stability cannot be restored until a new power is created in Central and Eastern Europe, though on a more modern basis. This implies that lasting peace cannot be achieved until the Soviet empire is dissolved and its western parts combine in some modern form of federation, confederation, or series of alliances.

Unlike the several fallacious theories of international relations discussed earlier in this study, another standard—that of Great Powers as the driving forces and agents of history—will lead to different and more realistic conclusions. In the last one hundred years eight Great Powers have predominated in world affairs: Great Britain, France, Germany, Russia, Italy, and Austria–Hungary, in Europe; the United States; and Japan. After the division of Austria–Hungary (1918) and the defeat of Germany, Italy, and Japan (1945), four powers remained. Overwhelmingly stronger than the nations with which she has alliances or pacts, the Soviet Union alone thus faces the three other Great Powers.

In recent times Russia has rapidly acquired military capability. It has surrounded itself with a number of loyal and almost–loyal satellites; it has created an international system of which it is the undisputed head. This accretion of power and influence is not enough: Russia's isolation cannot be overcome by alliances with the satellites because there is no substitute for firm cooperation with another Great Power in international affairs.

This situation is not simply a matter of a numerical relationship of one against three. Each of the three Western powers, with its inevitable shortcomings, compensates for the weaknesses of the others; each has its special assets—geographical, economic, military. France, it is true, has lost much of her standing since 1940; Britain is usually inclined to flexible policies; the United States is reluctant to plunge deep into European waters. Yet, the three Western powers conjointly constitute such a formidable force that Moscow must draw conclusions from the existence of this force. In particular, the Soviet government must:

(1) Prevent, or at least delay, the complete adherence of France to the bloc of great Western powers, specifically her realignment with West Germany and a close alliance with the United States. From this vantage point, Moscow welcomed France's colonial involvements, which obliged France to keep large forces outside of Europe and to expend large sums and efforts overseas. To the Soviet government, Europe is by far the most important arena of international activity. Up to now it has been happy to have only a feeble France as an adversary on the continent. From the Soviet point of view, the situation has become considerably more complex once the Algerian problem was "solved."

(2) Prevent, or at least delay, the rehabilitation of Western Germany. Germany is a logical candidate for Great Power; its growing role in world affairs cannot be impaired for long by propaganda or diplomatic gestures; it can be paralyzed only by a war, the outcome of which is, however, uncertain. Consequently, Moscow has no effective means of preventing West Germany from attaining the stature of a strong power in addition to the Big Four.

(3) Try to divide the Western coalition, for instance, by splitting Japan and Germany from their Western Allies. A return to the wartime alignment of powers, which made it possible for the Soviet government to extend its control over a number of countries in the West and the East, would be most advantageous for the Soviet Union. But the prospects for such a turn are slim.

(4) Prevent or delay any rapprochement among the countries of Eastern and Central Europe that would be independent of the Soviet Union, no matter what socio–economic system prevailed in these areas. Even Communist governments, adhering to what they view as a Socialist economy, would be dangerous for Moscow once they undertook to play their own role in European affairs. The most menacing kind of rapprochement, certainly, would be a federation or confederation of former Soviet satellites.

(5) Emphasize the tactics of bilateral dealings between

the two super-powers—the United States and the Soviet Union—which between them could solve most outstanding problems. In this club of two super-powers Moscow would not be faced with the unfavorable ratio of one-to-three or one-to-five. Moscow would be glad to enter into a bilateral pact if only the United States dropped her allies: ". . . the entire international situation is to a certain degree dependent on the state of Soviet-American relations. . . . If two such mighty powers as the U.S.S.R. and the U.S.A. would base their relations on the principle of coexistence, this would be to nobody's detriment, while the cause of preserving peace would definitely gain."[3]

Accordingly, the Soviet side tends to minimize the strength and role of Britain and France. "On what ground [Khrushchev asked at a rally in Moscow on his return from the United Nations] can England now be considered a Great Power while India cannot?. . . . Why is France considered a Great Power and Indonesia not? Why are India and Indonesia put in another category at the United Nations than England and France, and why are they not, for example, permanent members of the Security Council?"[4]

In its search for alliances to exploit and manipulate, the leadership of the Soviet Union turns out to consist of peculiarly unrealistic men—who believed only recently that they could, as in earlier years, combine empire-building with Great Power "amity." But blandishments to the West cannot succeed so long as a single state is permitted to wield predominant power over Europe. In the long run, this predominance, achieved by arms, threats, and encroachments, cannot endure.

[1960]

---

[3] *Pravda*, November 10, 1960.
[4] *Pravda*, October 21, 1960.

COMPETITION AND CONFLICT

There is a simple way to extend communism throughout the world, and the Soviet leadership is well aware of it. In the summer of 1957, Khrushchev told his listeners—and the world: "I must warn the capitalist gentlemen that we have a very strong weapon in our arsenal, and this is neither the atomic nor the hydrogen bomb—it is something far stronger. The agriculture of our country is now showing a marked increase; industry is developing rapidly; better living conditions are being created to satisfy the demands of the people. When we give the working class, the peasants and all the working people of our country still more good houses and create an abundance of food and other consumer goods and an even better system of public education, then our ideas will acquire even more invincible force.

"The ideas of Marxism–Leninism are in themselves a great force. But they acquire even greater influence, even greater attraction, when reinforced by an abundance of butter, milk, meat and other products. Then these ideas will penetrate the consciousness of the people of all countries even more profoundly, surmounting any 'iron curtain.' "[1]

The weapon described by Khrushchev is indeed a better one than atomic or hydrogen bombs, ICBM's or submarines.

[1] *Pravda*, June 13, 1957.

Why then does the West, despite Khrushchev's claims, persist in rejecting communism as an economic system? Soviet school children are taught that the bad "capitalists," millionaires and billionaires, though constituting not more than one per cent of their countries' population, are so strong that they constrain their nations to maintain them in their wealth and privileges despite the advantages of communism. Soviet teen-agers may believe this. They cannot be expected to know with what firmness trade unions in the West, and American labor in particular, operate at crucial moments and how little respect they show for capitalist employers when the situation calls for an increase in workers' wages. They know nothing about the protracted strikes conducted with the help of millions of dollars in funds accumulated for this purpose, or about the extent to which the standard of living of Western labor has risen in the last few decades.

There is a simple way open to Khrushchev if he really wanted to convince his audience of the advantages of communism. He would need only to invite labor leaders, professors of economics, and newspaper reporters from the capitalist countries to make a study tour of Russia—not a few days' caviar-and-vodka excursion with laudatory speeches, but a study tour lasting several months. If the conditions he claims for Russia have really been attained, the truth would filter out to the world, and country after country might follow the Soviet example. Large foundations would surely make funds available for such a study, and the United Nations could be included in one way or another. Does Khrushchev claim that such a study would be humiliating to Soviet sovereignty? He could be told that England, America, and other Western countries would gladly permit similar studies in their countries.

Actual facts do not support Mr. Khrushchev's claims or promises. We remember the similar boasts that Soviet Union spokesmen have been making for over forty years. In his well-prepared reports to the congresses of the Communist Party of the Soviet Union during the 1920's and 1930's Stalin gave precise figures about the rise in the standard of living. In Russia progress, which in other countries is measured in decades, was being measured from year to year. If all Stalin's claims of rising standards of living had been based on facts, the economic condition of the people of Russia would have been excellent indeed. But without much ado and without any admission of erroneous figures, the claims were soon dismissed.

Moscow made new claims after the war. Now it was Georgi Malenkov who began to cite precise statistics after Stalin's death. Before long, however, Khrushchev exposed Malenkov and his statistics as a deception of Russia and the world, an effort to conceal the low level of the Soviet economy during Stalin's last years and after his death.

When Khrushchev came to power, his firm hand, his revelations about his predecessors, his promise to adhere to the facts and to permit "no nonsense," made a favorable impression. Here, finally, was a man—scholars and journalists were saying—who sticks to the facts and does not claim more than has actually been achieved. But in the course of a bitter fight with his Communist opponents, Khrushchev, too, came to boast that in three years the Soviet Union would catch up with American standards in respect to the three crucial "m's": *moloko* (milk), *maslo* (butter), *myaso* (meat). The fight over the "three m's" went on during 1957. Three years later Khrushchev's agencies began to remove from their posts the officials allegedly responsible for the failures of the program. Nobody dared tell Khrushchev to his face that his battle of the "three m's" had been lost and the anti–Party group of Malenkov, Molotov, and Kaganovich had been right in their criticism. If the delegates to the Party congresses knew the truth, none had the courage to utter it. Khrushchev was, of course, well aware of this. Just as in the so–called capitalist countries the accumulation of a fortune is often taken as proof of a man's ability and talents, in the Soviet Union agricultural and industrial successes, real or fictitious, are a measure of an official's dedication, loyalty, and brain–power, and serve as the ladder to advancement. Because the system of rewards for successes is universal in the Soviet economy, this method cannot be abolished altogether.

This is why there can be no confidence in Soviet figures and statistics. Stalin's methods of falsifying statistical yearbooks have been discarded, but there is a new product of the Khrushchev era—the 890–page volume, *The National Economy of the Soviet Union in 1959*. In this scholarly volume there are some figures on real wages in the Soviet Union: compared with real wages in pre–revolutionary Russia, real wages in 1959 had risen 3.9 times; taking into consideration the abolition of unemployment, real wages had risen 4.3 times, or, taking into further account the reduction in the working day, 5.7 times. This is all the reader is told about real wages; no other figures, no basis for the calculations are given, not even ruble wages for either the pre–revolutionary era or today; nor is there any indication whether workers' wages include the salaries of officials, millionaire writers, and ballerinas.[2]

This method of releasing figures in statistical yearbooks makes possible preposterous claims and the camouflaging of the real state of affairs.

Khrushchev's claims and arguments have not convinced the West of the advantages of Soviet communism. Not only the "capitalists" but workers, farmers, and intellectuals in the West have rejected communism, as an economic system, as a society with an allegedly higher morality, and as a political state which suppresses the freedom of its people.

But, while rejecting communism for ourselves, are we to fight it beyond our frontiers? Is the United States, as the foremost anti–communist nation in the world, expected to eliminate industrial and agricultural communism in other countries? Long before Nikita Khrushchev made his appearance, and long before his teachers, Lenin and Stalin, were born, the United States engaged in "peaceful co–existence," although it was not referred to in these terms. The United States has coexisted with many people without trying to force them to change their strange ways. It still

[2] *Narodnoe Khozyaistvo SSSR v 1959 godu. Statisticheskii Yezhegodnik* (National Economy of the U.S.S.R. in 1959. A statistical Yearbook), Moscow, 1960, pp. 79–81.

coexists with civilizations practicing primitive religions, and others, even those that until recently practiced slavery.

It was British Prime Minister Lloyd George who, in first proclaiming the Western policy of peaceful coexistence in regard to Soviet Russia, asked: do we not trade with cannibals? Winston Churchill remarked during the war: "We have no special interest in the political regime which prevails in Yugoslavia. Few people in Britain, I imagine, are going to be more cheerful or more downcast because of the future constitution of Yugoslavia."[3]

For one hundred years now the United States has refused to coexist with slavery—in its own country. But it has not taken its armies on missionary crusades beyond its frontiers. As a matter of fact, the United States has not only coexisted with Yugoslavia, but has helped that country militarily and economically. To a lesser degree, the United States has also helped Communist Poland. Economic methods in some countries may not seem sensible to us, and their achievements not impressive, but if some people want to stand on their heads and eat with their feet, why not? Anti-communism may be part of the American people's attitude, but the forcible extermination of communism as such cannot be the foreign policy of the United States.

There is only one aspect of communism—the threat of its military aggression—that determines United States foreign policy to the point of making peaceful coexistence impossible so long as the foreign policy of the major Communist states endangers the security of the United States. Khrushchev repeatedly juxtaposes capitalism and communism, as does, frequently though perhaps thoughtlessly, the Western press. Yet this is an entirely wrong way of looking at the confrontation. It is a fallacy to reduce Soviet-American conflicts to the difference between their economic systems. To define the Soviet system as the economic system of "communism," and the American system as the economic system of capitalism is to miss the main point. A far more important difference is that between

[3] Fitzroy Maclean, *Escape to Adventure*, (Boston: Little, Brown and Company, 1950), p. 414.

their political systems. As far as popular American attitudes toward Russia are concerned, it is of no significance that in Russia food is produced on collective farms, that the national bank belongs to the state, or that shoe factories are controlled by the regional Council of National Economy. American attitudes have been shaped by the record of Stalinism, by the fiction of Soviet "elections," by the tight controls over the Soviet press, by the treatment of men like Boris Pasternak. Here and there, popular sentiments may be influenced by outstanding developments of internal policy, but these do not determine the course of foreign affairs.

Beginning with 1933, popular antagonism toward Hitler's Germany was aroused by the Reichstag fire, by the methods of the Gestapo, and by the pogroms against the Jews, but until 1941, hardly anyone in the United States urged military action against Germany; United States neutrality laws were passed at a time when the Nazi crimes were well known. The accession to power of a military clique in Japan provoked a general outcry in the United States, but there was no demand that Japan's domestic policy or power structure be "corrected" by a military operation on the part of the United States. A similar independence of foreign policy from popular attitudes toward domestic affairs of other nations was exemplified by the relationship between Washington and Moscow during the second World War, and by the attitude of the Great Powers toward Franco Spain.

The nations of the world do not have a standard approach to foreign policy. In this century, American policy abroad is aimed at preventing the emergence of a military power, East or West, that could endanger the United States or prove superior to it. The United States abandoned its neutrality only when Nazi Germany embarked on conquest in Western Europe, when the nightmare of a tremendous German-controlled empire of the Atlantic threatened to become a reality, and when the independence of Britain—America's shield in the East—was in jeopardy. The conquest of France along with the virtual absorption of Denmark, Norway, Belgium, and the Netherlands into

Germany—making the Eastern Atlantic the playground of a power whose arms and military potential were superior to those of any other world power—provided, before Pearl Harbor, the setting of America's inching toward war. The prospect of a Berlin-ruled Europe, as the counterpart of the United States on this side of the Atlantic, was so shocking and so real that the United States had to change its course.

Relations with Japan similarly deteriorated in the late 1930's as the prospect emerged of a military power ruling from Tokyo over all the Western Pacific; eastern China, Indonesia, and the Philippines, as part of an emerging Japanese empire, would become a Japanese outpost unless the United States took a firm stand. It was necessary to prevent the emergence of powers that endangered the security of the Western Hemisphere; war was the only way to achieve this goal.

Certain American experts and commentators on recent history have sought to show that for the United States war was not inevitable, that only the allegedly misguided policy of its President pushed this country into war. As an answer to this view it suffices to imagine how the world would have looked in 1945 if the United States had remained on the sidelines: the victorious Axis Powers would have made an attempt to subdue America from both sides and—as Tokyo had promised—to dictate a peace in Washington. A war would then have erupted—more terrible, more bloody, and more dangerous than the campaigns of 1941–45; and whether such a war could have been won by the United States is not at all certain.

The same doctrines that in the 1930's governed the foreign policy of the United States toward the growing menace of German and Japanese military power have determined United States policy toward the Soviet Union since the late 1940's. Once again an overwhelming power was emerging that could before long, it seemed, subdue Germany, France, and smaller nations of Western Europe; that would set foot on the Chinese shores of the Pacific; that would control the highly developed armament industry of a number of nations, West and East; that could create a great navy and air force with the help of nations that only a short time before had proven their superior military skills.

Was it necessary to stop Stalin's drive to the West? Would he not have refrained from extending his rule in the direction of the Atlantic? The demarcation lines that we call the Iron Curtain are almost identical with those of the Soviet empire as it emerged in 1945: from Stettin on the Baltic to Trieste on the Adriatic. If it had been true that Soviet ambitions did not go beyond this line, then a lasting peace between West and East would be possible today, on the basis of the recognition, once and for all, of Eastern Europe as part of the Soviet orbit.

Actually Stalin's ambitions went much farther than these geographic lines. He expected to see a number of other territories join his "Socialist sphere" before long. There was Austria, which, while a small country, was of great importance to Stalin because of its geographical configuration and its location next to other strategic territories. It was a disappointment to Moscow when developments in Austria made it impossible to establish a pro-Soviet regime there. Then, an uprising in Greece encouraged in Moscow hopes that the Soviet orbit might be extended to the Aegean. In 1945-46 France and Italy seemed ripe for a Soviet-type transformation. Moscow expected that the Communist members of the Paris and Rome governments would expel their "bourgeois" colleagues from the government. The reverse actually happened, and the leaders of the French and Italian Communist parties, Palmiro Togliatti and Jacques Duclos, were severely reprimanded in the official statements of the first conference of the Cominform in September, 1947.

There was disappointment on both sides. The West was impatient to change the state of affairs behind the Iron Curtain and it did not want the new military power of Russia to expand over Central Europe. The Soviet government for its part, was disappointed to have its postwar expansion limited to the less developed parts of Europe and its political drive stopped long before it had reached the shores of the Atlantic. When Stalin tried to resume this drive with the blockade of West Berlin in 1948–49, he was stopped by the American airlift.

The role of the United States in the Berlin operation, and its decisive military power in Europe during these years, revealed the peculiar mission of the United States in postwar history: to prevent the further growth of the new great military empire. No more and no less. No less, for if the American air force had not saved West Berlin, if American armies had not been stationed in Germany, if American help had not saved Greece during the postwar crisis there, the other powers could not have done it alone. France was still recuperating from military and economic defeats; Germany was a shambles; England, never a great continental power, could do nothing against the immense accumulation of Soviet military might. Had it not been for United States policy and potential, the Soviet Union would have extended its power over Western Europe.

Indignant voices from Moscow and the satellite capitals have urged America to withdraw and leave Europe to its own fate. On the other hand, political leaders in Western Europe and spokesmen of anti–Communist movements in the East European satellites have castigated America's passivity and its acquiescent attitude toward Russian communism; they have expressed the hope that a new administration in Washington might embark upon a more consistent policy toward Russia and Russian expansionism. And in this country we hear many demands for a more active—or less active—a more energetic—or less energetic —policy toward Russia. Real peace, it is claimed, would be possible immediately if this country acquiesced in Russia's gains and acceded to some of Moscow's demands in other parts of the world. From the history of the years since the war we must draw the conclusion—perhaps obvious even before that—that the United States has set itself a difficult but limited task in world affairs. It will neither fight a *Weltanschauung* propagated from Moscow, nor will it start a crusade to revamp the map of Europe. But it will stop, by military means if necessary, any new attempt to extend the Soviet sphere. It will not resort to arms to spread the Western way of life. George F. Kennan, one of the ideologists of American foreign policy, recommended to the United States a policy aimed at "containing" the Soviet Union. Containment does not mean a fight for the independence of "subjugated nations," or self–determination and unification of Germany. It means only maintenance of the *status quo*.

America's long–range program for Europe might seem to be identical with that of Soviet Russia. The American long–range objective includes, in the first place, the withdrawal from the old continent of United States armies, with their varied facilities, equipment, and personnel. Along with the withdrawal of armies, American air and naval bases, infested by spies from East Germany, the satellites, and Russia, would be given up. U.S. nuclear military installations would be abandoned, as would middle–range and long–range missiles and their launching sites. Finally, the reduction in the military budget and in federal taxes, must also be considered.

These were precisely the demands which Moscow for a number of years has been urging on the United States and on America's allies in Western Europe. As enunciated by Moscow, the program professes to secure the "independence" and self–government of Europe: what business has a power from another continent to interfere in European affairs? "Yankee go home!" is the slogan launched from the front pages of Soviet and satellite newspapers.

The most significant difference between the Washington and Moscow program for American withdrawal from Europe is the question of timing. Moscow wants the United States to pull out now, without delays, without conditions, without commitments for the future. Had it followed Moscow's wishes, the United States would have returned all of its military and most of its civilian forces to its own shores long ago. The United States, however, will not withdraw from Europe until a new balance of power is established on the old continent—that is, not until Western Europe has reached an economic and military level that will enable it to neutralize any other force that might attempt to revamp the balances and borders of the Old World. For centuries Europe was able itself to repel incursions from Asia, to settle its own disputes, in peace or in war, without invoking the help of an external force. The developments of the twentieth century, however, made American intervention in Europe imperative—an intervention that cannot be terminated until Europe has again the capability to solve her problems by herself. This is the historic mission of the United States in this century— to enable Western and Central Europe to defend themselves against all possible dangers from without.

There are many Americans who, hating the autocratic political system of Spain and Portugal, would be glad to intervene and even, if necessary, give their lives in a fight for the freedom of these countries. There are many Americans who are opposed to the economic order prevailing in some European countries and who are ready to force upon these countries a system of private enterprise. Such convictions will remain a private matter among segments of this country's citizens, but the United States as a nation, and the United States government cannot engage in war to alter the political or economic system of any other country —whether democratic or totalitarian, capitalist or socialist. American commitments in Europe will end when Europe can look after herself, when there is no more danger to the United States from the superior military might of a European power.

To the Soviet government Europe is the area of greatest concern, of primordial tasks—the problem above all other problems. Congo, Laos, Cuba, and India are no doubt of great interest to the Soviet Union, but only in terms of Soviet prestige and long-range goals. A breakthrough in Europe, however, would upset the existing balance of power and give the Soviet Union an advantage greater than any that it could derive from Congo, the mountains of Laos, or the waters of the Pacific. Though little discussed in recent years, a breakthrough in Europe is eagerly and passionately desired by Moscow. The destruction of NATO, the removal of American air bases from Scandinavia to North Africa, the closing down of United States naval bases in Britain, the reduction of atomic stockpiles in

Western Europe, and the alienation from Washington of at least one of these nations to the point of joining the neutralist camp—all these or similar events make sense to Moscow, however, only if they occur very soon. It will not be long before the countries of Western Europe themselves develop into what Moscow will call militarist, imperialist powers. Thinking in terms of decades and generations, Stalin—who had witnessed the resurrection of defeated, dismembered, and impoverished Germany into a first-class military power—understood better than his successors how temporary is the subjection of a great nation, how quickly it recovers its old status after defeat. This was one reason for Stalin's impatience and his eagerness for speedy action after the war. Conditions as favorable to Moscow as those of 1944–50 were exceptional, and they had to be made use of with the greatest urgency. In Stalin's time it took one generation for the transition from the glorious end of the first World War to the start of the second, one generation of twenty-two years. Almost as many years have elapsed since the second World War, and the forces of resurrection and rehabilitation of industrial and military power have been vigorously operating once again. How much time does Moscow have left? Will it not soon be too late for a new drive?

This question is at the root of Soviet nervousness and unflagging activity. The task is to remove American power from Western Europe or reduce it substantially.

The question whether and how much progress Soviet policy has made, particularly as compared with the policy of the United States, has been hotly debated in recent years. On the surface, Russia has made long strides in many parts of the world, while she has seldom retreated from earlier positions. The fact that this progress has been achieved in less than a decade, combined with Russian technical-military superiority in many fields, permits the Soviet Union to claim tremendous achievements in world affairs; in fact, official Soviet publications never cease to stress that "at present the Socialist camp [in the first place, the Soviet Union] is stronger than the capitalist camp."

On the other side of the scale is Western Europe. All Soviet efforts to extend its arms to the West have been in vain. The Soviet Union did not succeed in sharing in the occupation of the Ruhr, which would have meant a foothold in the heart of West Germany; it has not succeeded in expelling the West from West Berlin; it has lost Yugoslavia as a member of its alliance; it has alienated anti-Communist Austria. Now Albania is lost. More important has been the fulfillment of Stalin's prediction that West Germany would be rehabilitated and could again challenge the new frontiers and the new order in Europe.

It is debatable whether or not recent Soviet successes surpass the achievements of the West. What is true is that the contest is being waged on a new level, that its scope is growing from year to year, and that the contending forces continue to increase their preparedness for the inevitable crisis that lies ahead.

[1960]

David J. Dallin's Writings:
BIBLIOGRAPHY

The following bibliography includes all the known and published writings of David J. Dallin. Except for individual articles of particular significance, articles in daily newspapers, letters to the editor, and book reviews have been omitted. The various publications appeared under one of the following names or pseudonyms: David J. Dallin, David Dalin, D. Yu. Dalin, D.D., S.D., S. Dalin, and David Lewin.

The following abbreviations have been used throughout for two periodicals to which he contributed over a considerable period of time:

NL—*The New Leader*, New York
SV—*Sotsialisticheskii Vestnik* (Socialist Courier), Berlin, Paris, New York

Books

Theorie des Existenzminimums. Berlin: Verlag Julius Springer, 1913. 70 pp.

Der Arbeitslohn und die soziale Entwicklung. Berlin: Verlag Julius Springer, 1913. V. 206 pp.

Posle voin i revolyutsii (After Wars and Revolutions). Berlin: "Grani" Publishing House, 1922. 287 pp.

Soviet Foreign Policy 1939–1942. New Haven: Yale University Press, 1942. XX. 452 pp.

Russia and Postwar Europe. New Haven: Yale University Press 1943. X. 230 pp.

The Real Soviet Russia. New Haven: Yale University Press, 1944. VIII. 260 pp.

The Big Three: The United States, Britain, Russia. New Haven: Yale University Press, 1945. VI. 292 pp.

[with Boris I. Nicolaevsky] *Forced Labor in Soviet Russia*. New Haven: Yale University Press, 1947. XV. 331 pp.

Soviet Russia and the Far East. New Haven: Yale University Press, 1948. VII. 398 pp.

The Rise of Russia in Asia. New Haven: Yale University Press, 1949. XI. 293 pp.

The New Soviet Empire. New Haven: Yale University Press, 1951. VIII. 216 pp.

Soviet Espionage. New Haven: Yale University Press, 1955. XIV. 558 pp.

The Changing World of Soviet Russia. New Haven: Yale University Press, 1956. IX. 422 pp.

Facts on Communism. Volume II: *The Soviet Union From Lenin to Khrushchev*. Washington, D.C.: United States Government Printing Office, 1960. IV. XIX. 367 pp.

Soviet Foreign Policy After Stalin. Philadelphia, J.B. Lippincott Company, 1961. XII. 543 pp.

Chapters and Pamphlets

"Narodnoe khozyaistvo i 'sotsialism' " (National Economy and "Socialism"), *Za god; sbornik statei* (For a Year; Collection of Articles). Petrograd–Moscow: "Kniga" Publishing House, 1919, pp. 55–67.

"Bez sovetov" (Without Soviets), *Rossiya i Emigratsiya* (Russia and the Emigration). Paris: Editions Russes, Les Independents, 1947, pp. 23–25.

The Economics of Slave Labor. Chicago: Henry Regnery Company, 1949, 33 pp.

"Verbrechen und Strafrechtssystem," *Handbuch des Weltkommunismus*, edited by Joseph M. Bochenski and Gerhart Niemeyer. Freiburg/München: Karl Alber, 1958, pp. 329–364. Revised edition in English, "Crime and Punishment Under the Soviet Regime," *Handbook on Communism*, edited by Joseph M. Bochenski and Gerhart Niemeyer. New York: Frederick A Praeger, 1962, pp. 315–345.

"Obryvki vospominanii" (From my Memories), *Martov i ego blizkie* (Martov and Those Close to Him). New York: n.p., 1959, pp. 103–118.

Articles

1911

"Nachalo izbiratel'noi bor'by (Pis'mo iz Berlina)" (The Beginning of the Election Campaign [Letter from Berlin]), *Nasha Zarya* (Our Dawn), St. Petersburg, No. 4 (April, 1911), pp. 58-64.

1912

"Rost vooruzhenii v Germanii" (Armament Increase in Germany). *Nevskaya Zvezda* (The Neva Star), St. Petersburg, No. 2, May 3(16), 1912, pp. 32, 33.

1913

"K teorii zarabotnoi platy" (On the Theory of Wages), *Nasha Zarya*, St. Petersburg, No. 7/8, 1913, pp. 25-34.

"Ekonomicheskaya voina" (Economic Warfare), *Novaya Rabochaya Gazeta* (The New Workers' Gazette), St. Petersburg, (September 10, 1913).

1914

"Pervye shagi rabochego dvizheniya" (The First Steps of the Labor Movement), *Nasha Zarya*, St. Petersburg, No. 6, pp. 17-24, No. 7/9, pp. 16-25.

1917

"Finansy novoi Rossii" (Finances of New Russia), *Letopis'* (Annals), Petrograd, No. 2-4, (February-April, 1917), pp. 412-424.

"Izbiratel'nyi zakon v Uchreditel'noe Sobranie" (The Electoral Law Concerning the Constituent Assembly), *Rabochaya Gazeta* (The Workers' Gazette), Petrograd, No. 36, (April 21, 1917).

"Revolyutsiya vo vneshnei politike" (Revolution in Foreign Policy), *Rabochaya Gazeta*, No. 60, (May 19, 1917).

"Kak podgotovlyayutsya 'politicheskie vystupleniya'." (How Political Actions are Staged), *Rabochaya Gazeta*, No. 81, (June 15, 1917).

"Otvet g. Milyukovu" (Reply to Mr. Miliukov), *Rabochaya Gazeta*, No. 105, (July 13, 1917). [Revolution and military defeat.]

"Soznatel'nost i stikhiinost' v rabochem dvizhenii" (Consciousness and Spontaneity in the Labor Movement), *Rabochaya Gazeta*, No. 161, (September 15, 1917).

"Eshche odna rezolyutsiya" (One More Resolution), *Rabochaya Gazeta*, No. 170, (September 26, 1917). [On the railway strike.]

"Zarabotki rabochikh vo vremya voiny" (Workers' Wages in Wartime), *Rabochaya Gazeta*, No. 177, (October 4, 1917).

"V zashchitu revolyutsii" (In Defense of the Revolution), *Rabochaya Gazeta*, No. 187, (October 15, 1917).

"Konferentsiya fabrichno-zavodskikh komitetov" (Conference of Factory Committees), *Rabochaya Gazeta*, No. 189, (October 18, 1917).

"Kak bol'sheviki nakormyat golodnykh" (How the Bolsheviks Are Going to Feed the Hungry), *Rabochaya Gazeta*, No. 197, (October 27, 1917).

"Za Uchreditel'noe Sobranie" (For the Constituent Assembly), *Rabochaya Gazeta*, No. 201, (November 2, 1917).

"Konets bol'shevizma" (The End of Bolshevism), *Rabochaya Gazeta*, No. 203, (November 4, 1917).

"Kuda my idem" (Where We Are Going), *Rabochaya Gazeta*, No. 206, (November 7, 1917).

"Razgon demokraticheskikh organov" (Suppression of Democratic Institutions), *Rabochaya Gazeta*, No. 207, (November 8, 1917).

"Zavoevanie Gosudarstvennogo Banka" (The Conquest of the State Bank), *Rabochaya Gazeta*, No. 208, (November 9, 1917).

"Peremirie ili porazhenie?" (Armistice or Defeat?), *Rabochaya Gazeta*, No. 210, (November 11, 1917).

"Ekonomicheskaya svyaz' soyuznikov s Rossiei" (Economic Ties Between the Allies and Russia), *Klich* (The Call), Petrograd, No. 1, (November 23, 1917).

"Lenin, 'Pravda' i rabochii kontrol' " (Lenin, *Pravda* and Workers Control), *Plamya* (The Flame), Petrograd, No. 1, (November 24, 1917).

"Eshche o rabochem kontrole" (More on Workers' Control), *Molniya* (The Lightning), Petrograd, No. 1, (November 26, 1917).

"Zavoevanie Petrograda" (Conquest of Petrograd), *Novyi Luch* (The New Ray), Petrograd, No. 1, (December 1, 1917). [How the Bolsheviks rigged municipal elections.]

"Finansovye genii Smol'nogo Instituta" (The Financial Wizards of the Smolny Institute), *Novyi Luch*, No. 3, (December 3, 1917).

"Demobilizatsiya Rossii" (The Demobilization of Russia), *Novyi Luch*, No. 5, (December 6, 1917) and No. 22, (December 29, 1917).

"Zakhvat bankov i ego posledstviya" (Seizure of the Banks and Its Consequences), *Novyi Luch*, No. 14, (December 17, 1917).

"Torgovlya s Germaniei" (Trade With Germany), *Novyi Luch*, No. 17, (December 21, 1917).

1919

"Gryadushchaya Epokha" (The Coming Era), *Mysl'* (*Thought*), Khar'kov, No. 11, (May, 1919), pp. 403-410.

"Ekonomicheskie korni Ligi Narodov" (Economic Roots of the League of Nations), *Mysl'*, No. 14, (June, 1919), pp. 605-611.

Bibliography

1921

"Proch' illyuzii!" (Rid of Illusions!), *SV*, (May 20, 1921).

" 'Nullifikatsiya' i 'Naturalizatsiya' " ("Nullification" and "Naturalization"), *SV*, (June 5, 1921). [On abolition of currency in Russia.]

"V chem prichiny neudach?" (What Are the Causes of Failure?), *SV*, (June 19, 1921). [On the economic situation.]

"Golod" (Famine), *SV*, (August 5, 1921).

"Novaya sotsiologiya" (The New Sociology), *SV*, (September 1, 1921). [On Soviet terror against Socialists.]

"Die soziale Gleichheit im kommunistischen Russland," *Der Sozialist*, Berlin, VII, No. 18, pp. 418-422, and No. 19, pp. 443-447.

"Logika veshchei" (The Logic of Events), *SV*, (October 1, 1921). [On the economic situation in Russia.]

"Novaya burzhuaziya" (The New Bourgeoisie), *SV*, (October 15, 1921).

1922

"Finansy 'novogo kursa' " (Finances of the "New Course"), *SV*, (January 1, 1922).

"Butyrskaya golodovka" (The Hunger Strike in the Butyrki Prison), *SV*, (January 19, 1922).

"Kanitel' " (Procrastination), *SV*, (January 19, 1922). [On agreements with the Bolsheviks.]

"Reaktsionery i liberaly" (Reactionaries and Liberals), *SV*, (February 3, 1922). [Among the Communists.]

" 'Novyi kurs' v professional'nom dvizhenii" (The "New Course" in the Trade Union Movement), *SV*, (February 23, 1922).

"Opyat' 'perelom' " (Another "Break"), *SV*, (April 3, 1922). [In the New Economic Policy.]

"Deistvennaya lyubov' i kommunisticheskaya monopoliya" (Effective Love and Communist Monopoly), *SV*, (May 2, 1922). [How to help the famine-stricken regions.]

"Na pol-doroge" (Half-Way), *SV*, (May 16, 1922). [On the agrarian question.]

"Mezhdu Londonom i Moskvoi" (Between London and Moscow), *SV*, (June 18, 1922). [On a united front of the Socialist and Communist Internationals.] (In German trans. as "Zwischen London und Moskau" in *Der Sozialist*, Berlin, 1922, VIII, No. 25/26, pp. 387-391.)

"Krizis NEP'a" (Crisis of the NEP), *SV*, (August 2, 1922).

"K poznaniyu Rossii" (Toward an Understanding of Russia), *SV*, (September 8, 1922).

"Nerodivshayasya dusha" (An Unborn Soul), *SV*, (October 19, 1922). [On the Urquart Concession.]

"Pervyi blin" (The First Attempt), *SV*, (November 21, 1922). [On concessions to foreign capitalists.]

1923

"Denatsionalizatsiya" (Denationalization), *SV*, (January 1, 1923).

"Bezdorozhie" (Impassable Roads), *SV*, (February 21, 1923). [On the economic policy of the Soviets.]

"Trishkin kaftan" (Patchwork), *SV*, (March 16, 1923). [On taxes in kind and the state budget.]

"Fel'dfebel' v Vol'terakh," (A Sergeant Turned Voltaire), *SV*, (May 12, 1923). [On Trotsky's ideas about Soviet economy.]

"Gnusnaya komediya" (A Disgraceful Comedy), *SV*, (May 12, 1923). [On Menshevik renegades.]

"Za bortom" (Beyond the Pale), *SV*, (June 12, 1923). [On the group "Zarya".]

"Gosudarstvennyi kapitalizm" (State Capitalism), *SV*, (July 1, 1923).

"Lovlya muzhika" (Catching the Peasant), *SV*, (July 26, 1923).

"RKP na shestom godu revolyutsii" (The Russian Communist Party in the Sixth Year of the Revolution), *SV*, (August 16 and September 16, 1923).

"Men'shevistskii 'rabkrin' " (The Menshevik "Workers' and Peasants' Inspection"), *SV*, (September 16, 1923). [On the controversy with the Socialist-Revolutionaries.]

"Nado dodumat' do kontsa!" (It Must be Thought Through), *SV*, (October 18, 1923). [On the Communist Opposition group "The Workers' Truth."]

"V sovremennoi derevne" (Today's Village), *SV*, (November 3, 1923).

1924

"Rassloenie novoi derevni" (Stratification of the Peasantry), *SV*, (January 10, 1924).

"Ekonomicheskie zigzagi" (Zigzags in the Economic Policy), *SV*, (January 25, 1924).

"Novaya valyuta" (The New Currency), *SV*, (February 25, 1924).

"Troyanskii kon' " (The Trojan Horse), *SV*, (March 8, 1924). [On the new enrollment in the Communist Party.]

"Dva aresta. (Otryvki iz vospominanii)." (Two Arrests. [Fragments of Reminiscences]), *SV*, (April 4, 1924). [On J. Martov.]

"Nazad!" (Back!), *SV*, (May 10, 1924). [On steps toward the abolition of the NEP.]

'XIII syezd R.K.P." (The 13th Congress of the Russian Communist Party), *SV*, (June 20, 1924).

"Ekonomicheskaya Platforma RSDRP" (The Economic Platform of the Russian Social-Democratic Party), *SV*, (July 6, 1924).

"Reparatsionnoe soglashenie" (The Reparations Agreement), *SV*, (August 16, 1924). [The London Conference and the Dawes Plan.]

"Derevnya" (The Village), *SV*, (October 22, December 1 and December 20, 1924).

"Kavkazskoe lechenie" (The Caucasian Cure), *SV*, (December 20, 1924). [On Trotsky's "deportation" to the Caucasus.]

1925

"To, o chem molchit kazennaya pechat' " (What the Official Soviet Press Does Not Report), *SV*, (February 18, 1925). [On the new currency and the economic situation in Russia.]

"Vokrug muzhika" (About the Peasant), *SV*, (March 5, 1925).

"Sotsialdemokratiya i novoe krest'yanskoe dvizhenie" (Social-Democracy and the New Peasant Movement), *SV*, (March 19, 1925).

"Iz vospominanii" (Reminiscences), *SV*, (April 4, 1925). [On J. Martov and on the foundation of the Socialist Courier.]

"IKKI" (The Executive Committee of the Communist International), *SV*, (April 25, 1925). [On the enlarged Plenum.]

"S kem?" (With whom?), *SV*, (May 14, 1925). [On peasant policy.]

"Nenavistnaya demokratiya" (Hateful Democracy), *SV*, (June 20, 1925). [On a speech by G. Zinoviev.]

"Puti diktatury" (Paths of Dictatorship), *SV*, (July 25, 1925).

"Pod'em, urozhai i politicheskii krizis" (The Boom, the Harvest and the Political Crisis), *SV*, (September 28, 1925).

"Pod znakom restavratsii" (Restoration), *SV*, (November 14, 1925). [On the Russian emigration.]

1926

"Ot 'burnogo rosta' k promyshlennomu krizisu" (From "Stormy Growth" to an Industrial Crisis), *SV*, (March 31, 1926).

"Dr. L. Jurowsky: Die Währungsprobleme Sowjetrusslands," *Die Gesellschaft*, Berlin, No. 5, (May, 1926), pp. 487-488.

"Krest'yanstvo i diktatura" (The Peasantry and the Dictatorship), *SV*, (April 25, May 12 and May 22, 1926).

"Gromadnyi progress" (Immense Progress), *SV*, (June 11, 1926). [On espionage in Soviet Russia.]

"Linyayut starye znamena" (The Old Banners Are Fading), *SV*, (June 26, 1926). [On concessions to the bourgeoisie in Soviet Russia.]

"O russkoi emigratsii" (On the Russian Emigration), *SV*, (July 10, 1926).

"Na drugoi den' " (The Day After), *SV*, (August 25, 1926). [On the political crisis of the Soviet regime and its possible aftermath.]

"Zarodyshi novogo imperializma" (Sprouts of a New Imperialism), *SV*, (October 2, 1926).

"Der Staat, das Recht und die Wirtschaft des Bolschewismus," *Die Gesellschaft*, No. 10, (October, 1926), pp. 376–378.

"Na mertvoi tochke" (At the Dead Point), *SV*, (December 6, 1926). [On the economic situation in Russia.]

"Zagranichnye shataniya" (Waverings Abroad), *SV*, (December 20, 1926). [On Russian emigrants.]

1927

"Zavershenie revolyutsii" (The Completion of the Revolution), *SV*, (January 15, 1927).

" 'Industrializatsiya'bez inostrannogo kapitala" ("Industrialization" Without Foreign Capital), *SV*, (February 5, 1927).

"Prokhvost" (A Scoundrel), *SV*, (February 26, 1927). [On Molotov's statement that the Social-Democrats and Socialist-Revolutionaries are paid agents of the bourgeoisie.]

"Mnogo shumu" (Much Ado), *SV*, (April 23, 1927). [On industrialization.]

"Tyazhelye rody" (A Painful Birth), *SV*, (May 21, 1927). [On the discussion within the Communist Party on the attitude toward peasantry.]

" 'Edinstvo emigratsii' " ("Unity Among the Emigrés"), *SV*, (June 20, 1927).

"Problema sosushchestvovaniya" (The Problem of Coexistence), *SV*, (July 2, 1927).

"Raspad Anglo-Russkogo Komiteta" (The Collapse of the Anglo-Russian Committee), *SV*, (July 18, 1927).

"Oborona i 'neizbezhnaya voina' " (Defense and the "Inevitable War"), *SV*, (August 1, 1927).

"Vampuka" (A Farce), *SV*, (September 22, 1927). [On the industrialization.]

"O Termidore" (On Thermidor), *SV*, (December 1, 1927).

"Zheneva, Kanton, Moskva" (Geneva, Canton, Moscow), *SV*, (December 21, 1927).

1928

"Budni" (Routine Life), *SV*, (February 6, 1928). [The Soviet regime is a degenerated form of a revolutionary dictatorship.]

"O sushchnosti rezhima" (On the Essence of the Regime), *SV*, (March 6, 1928).

"Kraplenye karty" (Marked Cards), *SV*, (March 21, 1928). [On the alleged conspiracy in Donbass.]

"Bol'shevizm i revolyutsiya" (Bolshevism and Revolution), *SV*, (May 18, 1928).

" 'Eti lyudi . . . ' " ("These People . . . "), *SV*, (June 23, 1928). [On Stalin and the Right Opposition.]

"Na tom zhe meste" (At the Same Spot), *SV*, (July 23, 1928). [On the policy toward the peasantry.]

"Intelligentsiya, byurokratiya i diktatura" (The Intelligentsia, the Bureaucracy, and the Dictatorship), *SV*, (September 5, 1928).

"Ob ekonomicheskikh pobedakh i nashem porazhenii" (On the Economic Victories and Our Defeat). *SV*, (October 13, 1928). [On the economic situation in Russia.]

"Pravyi uklon v VKP" (The Rightist Deviation in the All-Union Communist Party), *SV*, (November 14, 1928).

"Zametki" (Notes), *SV*, (December 5, 1928). [On embezzlers in Russia.]

"Shtrikhi k'pravomu uklonu' " (Features of the "Rightist Deviation."), *SV*, (December 19, 1928).

1929

"Tovarnyi golod" (Shortage of Goods), *SV*, (January 9, 1929).

"Trotsky i Trotskizm" (Trotsky and Trotskyism), *SV*, (January 24, 1929).

"Trotsky v Turtsii" (Trotsky in Turkey), *SV*, (February 22, 1929).

"NEP i antinep" (NEP and Anti-NEP), *SV*, (March 8, 1929).

"Razoruzhenie i Liga Natsii" (Disarmament and the League of Nations), *SV*, (May 4, 1929).

"Itogi" (The Balance Sheet), *SV*, (May 25, 1929). [On the NEP and the shifts in the Communist Party.]

"Kloaka" (A Sewer), *SV*, (July 15, 1929). [On the forgery of documents by Russian refugees.]

"Dal'ne-vostochnyi konflikt" (The Far-Eastern Conflict), *SV*, (September 11, 1929).

"Sotsial'nyi zakaz" (Social Command), *SV*, (September 27, 1929). [On the conspiracies allegedly uncovered by the GPU.]

"Goni prirodu v dver' " (Chase Nature Out the Door), *SV*, (October 10, 1929). [Clashes in the trade union of metal workers.]

" 'Shapkami zakidaem' " ("We Can Win Hands Down"), *SV*, (October 24, 1929). [On a Sino-Soviet dispute.]

"Shuitsa i desnitsa 'pravoi oppositsii' " (Right and Left in the "Rightist Opposition"), *SV*, (November 21, 1929).

"Krest'yanskaya emigratsiya" (Peasant Emigration), *SV*, (December 5, 1929). [The home-bound German settlers in Russia.]

"Posle pobedy" (After Victory), *SV*, (December 21, 1929). [The Communist Party after the rout of the Rightist and Leftist Opposition.]

1930

"Zametki" (Notes), *SV*, (January 11, 1930). [On the repentence of Zinoviev, Kamenev, Bukharin, and Shlyapnikov.]

"Neurezannyi kommunizm" (Unabridged Communism). *SV*, (January 25, 1930).

"Bezzabotnost' . . . " (Heedlessness), *SV*, (February 8, 1930). [*Pravda's* attack on the Mensheviks.]

"Sotsial'nye chudesa" (Social Miracles), *SV*, (February 25, 1930). [On farm collectivization.]

"Bor'ba s religiei" (The Struggle Against Religion), *SV*, (March 15, 1930).

"Perspektivy kollektivizatsii" (Perspectives of Collectivization), *SV*, (April 12, 1930).

"Ataki na dvukh frontakh" (Assaults on Two Fronts), *SV*, May 17, 1930). [Criticism of the Socialist International by Communists and Russian Democrats.]

"Politicheskie sud'by krest'yanstva" (The Political Fate of the Peasantry), *SV*, (May 17, 1930).

"Nashi tempy" (Our Tempo), *SV*, (May 31, 1930). [On Soviet industrial development amidst the poverty of the population.]

"Indiya i angliiskoe rabochee pravitel'stvo" (India and the British Labor Government), *SV*, (June 14, 1930).

"Korrektivy iz Rossii" (Corrections From Russia), *SV*, (June 26, 1930). [On the emigré group "Peasants' Russia."]

"Propaganda kapitalizma" (Propaganda of Capitalism), *SV*, (July 12, 1930). [On special stores in Russia which sell only for foreign currency.]

"Vokrug natsional'nogo voprosa" (On the National Question), *SV*, (July 26, 1930).

"Vse soglasny" (All Agree), *SV*, (August 12, 1930). [On the Congress of the All-Union Communist Party.]

"Vozvrashchenie k krepostnomu pravu" (Return to Serfdom), *SV*, (October 11, 1930). [On measures against the mobility of labor.]

"Ser'eznyi krizis" (A Serious Crisis), *SV*, (November 8, 1930). [On the Nazi advance in Germany.]

"Dushevno-bol'noi prokuror" (The Mentally Deranged Prosecutor), *SV*, (November 22, 1930). [Krylenko in a forthcoming show trial.]

1931

"Fashistskaya volna" (The Fascist Wave), *SV*, (January 9, 24, and February 28, 1931).

"Inostrannye rabochie" (Foreign Workers [in Russia]), *SV*, (February 9, 1931).

"Poslednie otkliki" (Latest Comments), *SV*, (April 25, 1931). [Trotsky and Gorky on the Menshevik trial in Moscow.]

"Vokrug pyatiletki" (The Five-Year-Plan), *SV*, (June 13, 1931).

" 'Ne-Svoboda ne meshaet' ... " ("Lack of Freedom Is No Hindrance"), *SV*, (July 2, 1931). [On the new intelligentsia.]

"Poiski novykh putei" (Looking for New Roads), *SV*, (August 22, 1931). [On Soviet economic difficulties.]

"Komissiya po razoruzheniyu" (The Disarmament Commission [of the Socialist International]), *SV*, (September 12, 1931).

"Ne vozvrashchenchestvo, a amnistiya" (Not Mere Home-Coming but Amnesty), *SV*, (September 26, 1931). [On the right of refugees to return to Russia.]

"Reformy Stalina" (Stalin's Reforms), *SV*, (October 24, 1931). [Reforms in the economic field.]

"Eshche o reformakh Stalina" (More on Stalin's Reforms), *SV*, (November 28, 1931).

"Izolyatsiya" (Isolation), *SV*, (December 12, 1931). [Soviet Russia's isolation in international relations.]

"Zimnyaya putina" (The Winter Trail), *SV*, (December 30, 1931). [On the preparations to the Communist Party Conference: denunciations, exposure, repentence.]

1932

"O reparatsiyakh, dolgakh i svyashchennykh obyazatel'stvakh" (On Indemnities, Debts, and Sacred Commitments), *SV*, (February 13, 1932).

"Pyatnadtsat' let" (Fifteen Years), *SV*, (March 12, 1932). [Since the Russian Revolution.]

"Preodolenie kapitalizma v SSSR?" (Is Capitalism Being Overcome in the U.S.S.R.?), *SV*, (April 30, 1932).

"Surrogat NEP'a" (Substitute for NEP), *SV*, (June 11, 1932).

"Zakonnost' v tsarstve proizvola" (Legality in the Realm of Arbitrariness), *SV*, (July 9, 1932). [On the decree on "Revolutionary Legality."]
"Svyashchennaya sobstvennost' " (Sacred Property), *SV*, (August 27, 1932). [On the decree on the safeguarding of public property.]
"Zametki" (Notes), *SV*, (August 27, 1932). [On the food problem.]
"Novye vybory v Germanii" (New Elections in Germany), *SV*, (September 26, 1932).
"Yubilei" (An Anniversary), *SV*, (November 12, 1932). [Fifteen years after the November Revolution.]
"Novaya Programma RDO" (The New Program of the Russian Democratic Union), *SV*, (December 10, 1932).
"Pechal'nye simptomy" (Sad Symptoms), *SV*, (December 24, 1932). [On the Franco-Soviet Pact and the die-hards of the Russian emigration.]

1933

"Samyi vazhnyi yubilei" (The Most Important Anniversary), *SV*, (January 27, 1933). [The anniversary of the GPU.]

1940

"Razrushennye legendy" (Shattered Legends), *SV*, (March 5, 1940). [The prestige of Moscow is falling.]
"Zametki" (Notes), *SV*, (March 24, 1940). [On the annexation of Karelia; on the protection of frontiers.]
"K voprosu o kolkhozakh" (The Kolkhoz Problem), *SV*, (April 25, 1940).
"Pervye itogi" (The First Results), *SV*, (December 5, 1940). [On the war.]

1941

"Sdvig Ameriki" (The United States Shifts), *SV*, (January 19, 1941).
"I neitral'nost' soblyusti i kapital priobresti" (How to Acquire Capital While Staying Neutral), *SV*, (February 10, 1941). [On Soviet foreign policy.]
"Reorganizatsiya Krasnoi Armii" (The Reorganization of the Red Army), *SV*, (February 25, 1941).
"O samom glavnom" (The Crucial Question), *SV*, (March 11, 1941). [On the Russian Revolution and the position of the Mensheviks.]
"Soviet Conference was Warned on Bureaucracy But Efficiency of GPU as Example was Ignored," *NL*, (March 15, 1941).
"Metla da sobach'ya golova" (The Broom and the Dog's Head), *SV*, (March 26, 1941). [On the rehabilitation of Ivan the Terrible in Soviet literature.]

"Zametki" (Notes), *SV*, (April 12, 1941). [On the U.S.S.R., Japan, Washington.]
"Zametki" (Notes), *SV*, (April 26, 1941). [On Soviet-German relations.]
"Zametki" (Notes), *SV*, (May 22, 1941). [Different aspects of Soviet life.]
"New Nazi-Soviet Pact Partitions Near East," *NL*, (May 31, 1941).
"Zhestokii ekzamen" (A Cruel Ordeal), *SV*, (July 17, 1941). [The war a severe trial for Stalin and the Communist Party.]
"Zametki" (Notes), *SV*, (August 4, 1941). [On terror in the USSR; on the Comintern; on the American Communists.]
"A Distorted Mirror," *NL*, (August 30, 1941). [On Max Werner's *Battle for the World*.]
"Kak Gitler i Stalin gotovilis' k voine" (How Hitler and Stalin Prepared for the War), *SV*, (September 20, 1941).
"Svoboda religii v SSSR" (Freedom of Religion in the USSR), *SV*, (October 15, 1941).
" 'Vtoroi' front i kommunisty" (The "Second" Front and the Communists), *SV*, (October 31, 1941).

1942

"Berlin's Three-Year See-Saw on Main Enemy Angers Japs, Lays Basis for Future Split of Axis Partners," *NL*, (January 10, 1942).
"Komintern v voine" (The Communist International in the War), *Novyi Zhurnal (New Review)*, New York, I, 1942, pp. 247-259.
"Staroe v novom" (The Old in the New), *SV*, (March 14, 1942). [On the evolution of communism.]
"Yaponskaya imperiya" (The Japanese Empire), *SV*, (April 12, 1942).
"Soviet Soldiers," *NL*, (December 12, 1942).

1943

"Tainoe oruzhie" (The Secret Weapon), *SV*, (February 5, 1943). [On the war, Stalin's policy, the Red Army, hopes of the Russian people for a democratization of the regime.]
"Politika Martova v pol'sko-sovetskoi voine" (Martov's Attitude Toward the Polish-Soviet War), *SV*, (April 7, 1943).
"Krasnaya Armiya" (The Red Army), *Novyi Zhurnal*, IV, 1943, pp. 273-293.
"Bor'ba s Gitlerom i 'revolyutsionnaya gimnastika' " (The Struggle Against Hitler and "Revolutionary Acrobatics"), *SV*, (June 7, 1943). [Moscow sparks partisan warfare.]

"Permanentnyi konflikt" (Permanent Conflict), *SV*, (July 8, 1943). [Stalin's policy toward Poland.]

"Vlast' i armiya" (The Regime and the Army), *SV*, (September 8, 1943).

"Russia's Aim in Europe," *The American Mercury*, New York, (October 1943), pp. 391-402.

"V osvobozhdennoi Evrope" (In Liberated Europe), *SV*, (October 9, 1943).

"Sovetskaya sfera bezopasnosti" (The Soviet Security Sphere), *Novyi Zhurnal*, VI, 1943, pp. 258-273.

"Kak zarozhdaetsya novaya reaktsiya" (How New Reactionary Trends Emerge), *SV*, (November 8, 1943). [Activity of Communists in Eastern Europe and the Balkans generates reaction.]

"Blizhaishaya reforma—tabel' o rangakh" (The Next Reform—A New Table of Ranks), *SV*, (December 10, 1943).

1944

"Bez belil i rumyan" (Without Make-Up), *SV*, (January 10, 1944). [On Soviet concentration camps.]

"Sanitarnyi kordon" (Cordon Sanitaire), *SV*, (February 11, 1944). [Stalin intends to build a *cordon sanitaire* after the war.]

"An Honest Report on Russia," *NL*, (March 18, 1944). [On the Russian army.]

"O gromkikh slovakh i o zhivykh lyudyakh" (On Loud Words and Live People), *SV*, (May 15, 1944). [On Soviet foreign policy.]

"Vsio okazalos' v poryadke" (Everything Is in Order), *SV*, (June 20, 1944). [On Soviet foreign policy and on Kerensky's position.]

"Will Russia Join a World League?" *NL*, (June 24, 1944).

"Henry Wallace Speaks Russian," *NL*, (July 8, 1944).

"The New League—Is It Premature?" *NL*, (August 12, 1944).

"Political Rise of Red Army," *NL*, (September 9, 1944).

"Thorny Passes Through the Oaks. Does the Dumbarton Oaks Conference Promise Collective Security?" *NL*, (September 16, 1944).

"Russia's Plan for Germany," *The American Mercury*, (October, 1944), pp. 440-447.

"The Soviet Postwar Plans," *The Sign*, Union City, N.J., (October, 1944), pp. 117-120.

"Moscow to Baghdad. Iran—Cockpit of the New Oil Diplomacy," *NL*, (November 18, 1944).

"Shadow on the Greek Conflict. The Role of British-Russian Rivalries," *NL*, (December 23, 1944).

1945

"Politics and World-Economy in the Great Depression of 1929-1934." *The Review of Politics*, Notre Dame, Indiana, (January, 1945), pp. 15-28.

"Comments on [Current] Soviet Policy," *NL*, (February 24, 1945).

"Chem kumushek schitat' truditsya . . ." ("A Mote in the Eye"), *SV*, (March 28, 1945). [Polemics with the group "Novyi Put'."]

"Comments on [Current] Soviet Policy," *NL*, (March 31, 1945).

"Na Dal'nem Vostoke" (In the Far East), *SV*, (April 28, 1945).

"Future of the Big Three," *The Sign*, (May, 1945), pp. 523-526.

"Soviet Strategy in San Francisco. Moscow Has No Faith in Dumbarton Oaks—Aims to Expand," *NL*, (May 5, 1945).

"Germaniya posle voiny" (Germany After the War), *SV*, (May 29, 1945).

"Between War and Peace," *NL*, (June 9, 1945).

"What Russia Wants in the Far East," *The American Mercury*, (July, 1945), pp. 26-34.

"Vooruzhennyi mir," (Armed Peace), *SV*, (July 3, 1945). [On Soviet Russia's postwar policy.]

"The Armed Truce—The Big Three in the Postwar Period," *NL*, (July 21, 1945).

"Konsolidatsiya sovetskoi sfery v Evrope" (Consolidation of the Soviet Sphere in Europe), *SV*, (August 8, 1945).

"The European Cockpit—Showdown Nears on Soviet Puppet Regimes," *NL*, (August 25, 1945).

"Stalin Signs Six Treaties. Agreements Between Russia and China Give no Assurance of Peace," *NL*, (September 1, 1945).

"Sovetskaya Rossiya i Kitai" (Soviet Russia and China), *SV*, (September 6, 1945).

"Otvet kritiku. (Ob ekonomicheskom vosstanovlenii Rossii i o politike Stalina.)" (Reply to a Critic. [On the Economic Rehabilitation of Russia and on Stalin's Policy]), *SV*, (September 6, 1945).

"The Growing Crises in Europe. Communist 'Wave of the Future' Is Subsiding," *NL*, (September 15, 1945).

"The London Conference. An Imaginary Report from Molotov to Stalin," *NL*, (September 29, 1945).

"Stalin nepogreshimyi" (Stalin the Infallible), *SV*, (October 10, 1945).

"Trends in International Affairs. New Resistance Movements Arise in Europe," *NL*, (October 13, 1945).

"Molotov Speaks for Stalin," *NL*, (November 10, 1945).

"Molotov vmesto Stalina" (Molotov Instead of Stalin), *SV*, (November 10, 1945).
"Bolshevism and Nationalism. Can the Ideologies of Communism and Russian Nationalism be Reconciled?" *NL*, (November 24, 1945).
"Kak pishetsya istoriya" (How History is Written), *SV*, (December 10, 1945). [On Soviet Far-Eastern policy.]
"Cooperation or Capitulation?" *NL*, (December 15, 1945).
"Germany Between War and Peace," *NL*, (December 22, 1945), Section II, pp. 2–12.

1946

"Consistency of Stalin," *The American Mercury*, (January, 1946), pp. 7–15.
"Ne po puti" (No Common Path), *SV*, (January 18, 1946). [On Socialist-Communist cooperation in postwar Europe.]
"United Nations Organization. Birth-Pangs or Death Rattle?" *NL*, (January 26, 1946).
"Opyat' kovarnyi Al'bion" (Once More Perfidious Albion), *SV*, (February 15, 1946). [On Soviet postwar policy toward Britain.]
"Behind the Fascist Scenes," *NL*, (February 16, 1946).
"Stalin Has Spoken. Atomic Bombs Instead of Meat and Bread Are Promised," *NL*, (February 23, 1946).
"The Abyss That Cannot be Bridged. In False Unity There is Not Strength But Weakness," *NL*, (March 9, 1946).
"Golovokruzhenie ot uspekhov" (Dizziness From Success), *SV*, (March 15, 1946). [On Soviet foreign policy.]
"Between Indignation and Appeasement," *NL*, (March 30, 1946).
"The Aims of Soviet Russia," *The Sign*, (April, 1946), pp. 16–18.
"Latvian Fascists in Germany. Anti-Democratic Elements Active in British and American Zones," *NL*, (April 4, 1946).
"Zametki" (Notes), *SV*, (April 18, 1946). [On Stalin-Hitler Relations.]
"Zametki" (Notes), *SV*, (June 21, 1946). [On Soviet foreign policy.]
"The Drive to the Mediterranean. Russia, Turkey, and Britain," *NL*, (May 4, 1946), Section II, pp. 2–12.
"The French People Are Still Devoted to Liberty and Democracy. An Open Letter to Leon Blum," *NL*, (May 11, 1946).
"Collective Action Against Aggression," *NL*, (May 18, 1946).
"Two Worlds. Differing Concepts of Peace Bar Understanding and Collaboration," *NL*, (June 1, 1946).
"Zametki" (Notes), *SV*, (June 21, 1946). [On Soviet foreign policy.]
"Russia and the Baruch Plan," *NL*, (June 22, 1946).

"Kak Rossiya oboronyalas' " (How Russia Defended Itself), *Novyi Zhurnal*, XIV, 1946, pp. 213-231.

"Poland Remains The Acid Test. American Policy Toward the Soviet Satellite is Confused and Weak," *NL*, (July 13, 1946).

"Henry Wallace on a Guided Tour," *NL*, (August 10, 1946).

"General Vlasov, Eve Curie, and Frederick Schuman," *NL*, (August 10, 1946).

"GULAG" (The GULAG), *SV*, (August 20, 1946). [On forced labor in Soviet Russia.]

"Armed Peace or War. Who Will Be Responsible If a Conflict Breaks Out?" *NL*, (August 31, 1946).

"Nazad k polnokrovnomu stalinizmu" (Back to Fullblooded Stalinism), *SV*, (September 20, 1946).

"Poland and Britain," *NL*, (September 21, 1946).

"The Tragic Dilemma," *NL*, (October 19, 1946). [On Soviet foreign policy.]

"Wallace vs. Roosevelt. FDR's Great Designs Excluded Spheres of Influence and Imperialist Expansion," *NL*, (November 23, 1946).

"Na tekushchie temy" (On Current Topics), *SV*, (November 23, 1946). [On disarmament; Soviet-Nazi relations.]

"The Failure of a Policy," *NL*, (December 7, 1946). [On American-Soviet Relations.]

"International Notes. Back to the Hotel Lux; India's Dilemma; The Socialist International," *NL*, (December 21, 1946).

"Zametki" (Notes), *SV*, (December 27, 1946). [On Stalin and Hitler, a.o.]

1947

"This Troubled Globe. The Moscow Conference on Germany; Students Demonstrate in China; Ten Years of Stalin's Constitution," *NL*, (January 11, 1947).

"Stalin to Thorez," *NL*, (January 25, 1947).

"Zabytyi dogovor" (Forgotten Treaty), *SV*, (February 3, 1947). [The Anglo-Russian Treaty of 1942.]

"Drought- or Man-Made Starvation?" *NL*, (March 1, 1947).

"Tridtsat' let" (Thirty Years), *SV*, (March 12, 1947). [Anniversary of the Revolution of 1917.]

"More Zigzags or Consistency? The Need for a Dynamic Policy for America," *NL*, (March 22, 1947).

"Looking at the World. Pure Coincidence?" *NL*, (April 5, 1947). [On Henry Wallace's speech a.o.]

"Looking at the World. Gromyko Is Right," *NL*, (April 12, 1947). [On Gromyko's speech in the Security Council; on reorientation of Soviet foreign policy."

"Zametki" (Notes), *SV*, (April 15, 1947). [On imperialism, socialism, communism; the UN; a.o.]

"Looking at the World. Irresponsible Leadership; Henry Wallace and the British Tories; a.o." *NL*, (April 19, 1947). [On Greece; U.S. and Britain; a.o.]

"Naive Strategy," *NL*, (April 26, 1947). [On U.S. at the Moscow Conference.]

"Lessons of the Moscow Conference," *NL*, (May 3, 1947).

"France's Intermittent Fever.—The Conference of the Socialist International," *NL*, (May 10, 1947).

"Inner Mongolia.—Between the USA and USSR," *NL*, (May 17, 1947).

"Zametki" (Notes), *SV*, (May 22, 1947). [Drought or politics? On the food situation in Russia; a.o.]

"Pietro Nenni vs. Léon Blum," *NL*, (May 24, 1947).

"Does Sovietization Mean Security? An Open Letter to Harold Laski," *NL*, (May 31, 1947).

" 'Dollar Imperialism' vs. Soviet Imperialism. An Open Letter to Harold Laski," *NL*, (June 7, 1947).

"Tito-Dimitrov-Hoxha.—Stalin and Stassen," *NL*, (June 14, 1947.)

"The Zurich Conference," *NL*, (June 21, 1947). [Conference of Socialist Parties.]

"Amerika, Evropa i Sovetskii Soyuz" (America, Europe, and the Soviet Union), *SV*, (June 25, 1947).

"Outstanding Military Successes," *NL*, (June 28, 1947). [On the forcible repatriations of Russian displaced persons.]

"Too Many Democrats," *NL*, (July 5, 1947). [In Spain and Rumania.]

"His Majesty the Leader," *NL*, (July 12, 1947). [The Supreme Soviet Session and Stalin.]

"Sources of Soviet Conduct," *NL*, (July 19, 1947). [On the policy of "containment."]

"War in Indonesia," *NL*, (July 26, 1947).

"From Behind the Bars," *NL*, (August 9, 1947). [The Socialist International and Socialists from behind the Iron Curtain.]

"Destruction of the German Army is Inadvisible," *NL*, (August 16, 1947). [On the "Free German" organization.]

"Naprolom" (A Breakthrough), *SV*, (August 20, 1947). [On Soviet belligerency.]

"Capitalism in One Country?" *NL*, (August 23, 1947). [On the British-American loan negotiations and Moscow's contention that the West is forming a capitalist coalition.]

"When Stalin is Nice and Pleasant," *NL*, (August 30, 1947). [Stalin, the Nazis, and the Japanese.]

"A Philosopher Condemned," *NL*, (September 6, 1947). [On the removal of G. Alexandrov in Moscow.]

"The Harlots of Budapest," *NL*, (September 13, 1947). [On the satellization of Hungary.]

"Poland as a Puppet," *NL*, (September 20, 1947).

"SSSR, Balkany i Germaniya" (USSR, the Balkans, and Germany), *SV*, (September 23, 1947).

"Schumacher and U.S. Labor," *NL*, (September 27, 1947).

"Last Time I Heard Vyshinsky," *NL*, (October 4, 1947).

"Two Types of Socialists," *NL*, (October 11, 1947).

"A New Russian 'Non-Returner,'" *NL*, (October 18, 1947).

"Zametki" (Notes), *SV*, (October 23, 1947). [Soviet Russia and the Far East; Korea; Iran; spy-mania in Russia.]

"The Trend to the Left." *NL*, (October 26, 1947.) [In the East.]

"Whither Russia?" *The Sign*, (November, 1947), pp. 23-25.

"Bad Habits," *NL*, (November 1, 1947). [Vyshinsky's behavior at the discussion of forced labor in Soviet Russia in a UN Committee.]

"Juliu Maniu's Trial," *NL*, (November 8, 1947).

"Germany and the London Conference," *NL*, (November 15, 1947).

"The Right to 'Warmonger'," *NL*, (November 22, 1947).

"Na temy dnya" (Topics of the Day), *SV*, (November 25, 1947). [On Soviet foreign policy.]

"Prominent New Emigres," *NL*, (November 29, 1947). [Refugees from the satellites.]

"Molotov Gives a Hint," *NL*, (December 6, 1947). [On the German issue.]

"The Decay of the Socialist International," *NL*, (December 13, 1947).

"Moscow Barometer Falling," *NL*, (December 20, 1947).

"Novye formuly" (New Formulas), *SV*, (December 26, 1947). [Stalin's Communism.]

"Peculiar Water Conservation," *NL*, (December 27, 1947). [On non-returnees from Nationalist China and other non-Communist countries.]

1948

"A Great Beginning. AFL and International Affairs," *NL*, (January 3, 1948).

"Why Stalin Votes for Taft," *NL*, (January 10, 1948).

"The Evolution of Stalin's Communism," *NL*, (January 17, 1948).

"A Few Who Went Back," *NL*, (January 24, 1948). [Repentent Russian refugees.]

"Novaya platforma RSDRP" (The New Platform of the Russian Social-Democratic Party), *SV*, (January 26, 1948).

"Tri mesyatsa s novoi emigratsiei" (Three Months With the New Emigrants), *Narodnaya Pravda (People's Truth)*, Paris-New York, No. 1, 1948.

"Stalin and Molotov. In 1939-41 and 1945-48," *NL*, (January 31, 1948).

"Showdown in the World Labor Movement," *NL*, (February 7, 1948).

"A Spurious Alibi," *NL*, (February 14, 1948). [Documents on Soviet-German diplomacy 1939-1941.]

"The Lost Dream," *NL*, (February 21, 1948). [On the publication of Soviet-Nazi documents.]

"The Rape of Czechoslovakia," *NL*, (February 28, 1948).

"Anti-Semitism in Russia," *NL*, (March 6, 1948).

"At Its Face Value," *NL*, (March 13, 1948). [On Soviet-Finnish relations.]

"The Greek Situation," *NL*, (March 20, 1948).

"Too Little But Not Too Late," *NL*, (March 27, 1948). [Communism in Italy.]

"The Acid Test," *NL*, (April 3, 1948). [Repatriation of Armenians to the U.S.S.R.]

"The Marshall Plan in Operation," *NL*, (April 10, 1948).

"Either—Or," *NL*, (April 17, 1948). [On the Berlin situation.]

"Where ERP is Needed Most," *NL*, (April 24, 1948). [The satellites and the Marshall Plan.]

"A Late Awakening," *NL*, (May 1, 1948). [The Conference of East-European Socialists in Paris.]

"The Mundt-Nixon Bill," *NL*, (May 8, 1948).

"The Fruit of the Molotov Plan," *NL*, (May 15, 1948).

"Zametki" (Notes), *SV*, (May 20, 1948). [The USSR and the Marshall Plan; Eastern Socialists; the Kravchenko trial.]

"The Stalin-Wallace Program," *NL*, (May 22, 1948). [On foreign policy.]

"Moscow and Tel Aviv," *NL*, (May 29, 1948).

"The Naked Man in a Silk Hat," *NL*, (June 5, 1948). [On the United Nations.]

"And They Call 'Em Trade Unions ... ," *NL*, (June 12, 1948). [On Soviet trade unions.]

"Poor Prisoner in the Kremlin," *NL*, (June 19, 1948).
"The Ugly Issue," *NL*, (June 26, 1948). [The German Problem.]
"On the Razor's Edge. Between War and Peace, Soviet Russia and the West Still Can Find a Workable Compromise in Shaping Their Foreign Policy," *The Sign*, (July, 1948), pp. 22-24.
"Forced Labor in U.S.S.R.," *The New Statesman and Nation*, London, (July 3, 1948), p. 10.
"Tito: 'Stalin of the Balkans,' " *NL*, (July 3, 1948).
"Purge Without End," *NL*, (July 10, 1948).
"Streamlining for War," *NL*, (July 17, 1948).
"Stalin Wants War," *NL*, (July 24, 1948).
"The Atom Bomb," *NL*, (July 31, 1948).
"The Case of Robert Magidoff," *NL*, (August 7, 1948).
"With Whom and For What?" *NL*, (August 14, 1948). [Goals of foreign policy.]
"Paris After Eight Years," *NL*, (August 21, 1948).
"A Russian Peasant Abroad," *NL*, (August 28, 1948).
"From the German 'Front.' 'We Are Staying Too Long,' " *NL*, (September 11, 1948).
"Stalin's '*Mein Kampf,*' " *NL*, (September 18, 1948).
"Is Nazism Dead?" *NL*, (September 25, 1948).
"Interview with Schumacher," *NL*, (October 2, 1948).
"The 'German' Front. The CP in Two-Part Time," *NL*, (October 9, 1948).
"One Step From the Iron Curtain," *NL*, (October 16, 1948).
"The 'Front' in France. Postwar Foreign Policy," *NL*, (October 23, 1948).
"The Potsdam Policy. The Crisis in Germany," *NL*, (October 30, 1948).
"Inside the Kremlin's Walls. The Stalin Machine in Action," *NL*, (November 6, 1948).
"The UN in Paris. Is There Ground for Hope?" *NL*, (November 13, 1948).
"The Heyday of Hypocrisy," *NL*, (November 20, 1948). [Moscow denounces capital punishment.]
"The Debacle in China," *NL*, (November 27, 1948).
"Nazism Weighed and Measured," *NL*, (December 4, 1948).
"The German 'Front.' The Background of Mistakes," *NL*, (December 11, 1948). [USA supports shady displaced persons in Germany.]
"The German 'Front.' Three Cinderellas in Moscow," *NL*, (December 18, 1948). [German fellow-travelers in Moscow.]

"The European 'Front.' The Politics of Hypocrisy," *NL*, (December 25, 1948). [U.S.S.R., guilty of genocide, decries others for it.]

1949

"The Soviet Victory in China," *NL*, (January 1, 1949).

"An Unfinished Task," *NL*, (January 8, 1949). [On forced labor in the USSR.]

"De-Gaullism, Communism, Socialism," *NL*, (January 15, 1949).

"Peace Hopes Are Premature," *NL*, (January 22, 1949).

"Reward for Bad Policy," *NL*, (January 29, 1949). [In Japan.]

"Stalin unter Zensur," *Der Monat*, Berlin, No. 4, (January, 1949), pp. 96-99.

"Po povodu stat'i N.S. Timasheva" (On the Article by N.S. Timashev), *Novyi Zhurnal*, XXI, 1949, pp. 292-294. [On the number of inmates in the Soviet concentration camps.]

"Russia's Peace Offensive. A New Teheran?" *NL*, (February 5, 1949).

"Norway and the Atlantic Pact," *NL*, (February 12, 1949).

"Tri mesyatsa s novoi emigratsiei." (Three Months With the New Emigrants), II, *Narodnaya Pravda*, No. 2, (February, 1949).

"Three New Blunders," *NL*, (February 26, 1949). [On U.S. foreign policy.]

"Labor in Exile," *NL*, (March 5, 1949). [On the International Center of Free Trade Unionists in Exile, in Paris; on the trade unions in Yugoslavia; on Hungary, a.o.]

"The New Spy Case," *NL*, (March 12, 1949). [The Coplon-Gubichev case.]

"Miss Bucar's Good-Bye," *NL*, (March 19, 1949).

"Atlantic Charter—Atlantic Pact," *NL*, (March 26, 1949).

"Trans-Atlantic Facts," *NL*, (April 2, 1949).

"Utmost Confusion in German Affairs," *NL*, (April 9, 1949).

"Chto izmenilos' " (What Has Changed), *Narodnaya Pravda*, No. 3, (April, 1949). [Soviet developments.]

"Rightist and Leftist Ostriches," *NL*, (April 23, 1949). [In USA.]

"A Chinese Tito?" *NL*, (April 30, 1949).

"A New Policy for China," *NL*, (May 7, 1949).

"Communist Numerical Strength," *NL*, (May 14, 1949).

"Is the Line Changing?" *NL*, (May 21 and May 28, 1949). [An analysis of Russia's latest actions.]

"Ob emigratsii" (On the [Russian] emigration), *Narodnaya Pravda*, No. 4, (June, 1949).

"Germany is America's Problem," *NL*, (June 4, 1949).

"Lattimore on China," *NL*, (June 11, 1949).
"Stalin Pro-American?" *NL*, (June 18, 1949).
"Justice Department Travesty," *NL*, (June 25, 1949). [The case of the legless veteran James Kutcher.]
"Soviet Imperialism," *Air University Quarterly Review*, Montgomery, Ala., (Summer, 1949), IV, No. 1, pp. 88-91.
"Cold War: Act Two," *NL*, (July 2 and 9, 1949).
"Russia's Iron Hoop," *NL*, (July 16, 1949). [On Russian prestige.]
"Go To The Hills," *NL*, (July 23, 1949). [The Hungarian radio broadcasts to the Yugoslav Communists.]
"Albania the Aggressor," *NL*, (July 30, 1949). [Target: Greece].
"Vatican and Kremlin," *NL*, (August 6, 1949).
"No Need for Retribution," *NL*, (August 13, 1949).
"Six Soviet Wars," *NL*, (August 13, 20, and 27, 1949).
"La confession d'un policier soviétique," *Figaro Litteraire*, Paris, August 20, 1949).
"La police soviétique dans la guerre avec les Nazis 1939-1945," *Figaro Litteraire*, (August 27, 1949).
"Facts About Germany," *NL*, (September 3, 1949).
"He Chose Prison," *NL*, (September 10, 1949). [On the redefector Anatol Barsov.]
"A Democratic International?" *NL*, (September 17, 1949).
"By Implication," *NL*, (September 24, 1949). [Foreign Communists to repay Moscow.]
"Red Atom Blasts US Security, But No A-War in Near Future.—UN Control Illusory—Soviets Won't Permit Real Inspection," *NL*, (October 1, 1949).
"Told Behind the Iron Curtain," *The New York Times Magazine*, (October 2, 1949), p. 15.
"Na pravom flange" (At the Right Flank), *Narodnaya Pravda*, No. 5, (October, 1949).
"The Repercussions," *NL*, (October 8, 1949). [The Soviet A-bomb.]
"Free Labor vs. Slavery," *NL*, (October 15, 1949).
"The Navy's Rebellion," *NL*, (October 22, 1949). [US Navy.]
"Exterminate the Russians? 'Diaperologists' Call Them 'Inferior,' Imply We Should," *NL*, (October 29, 1949).
"The Real Power in China," *NL*, (November 5, 1949).
"The Yugoslav Issue," *NL*, (November 12 and 19, 1949).
"The Bridge of Brest-Litovsk," *NL*, (November 26 and December 3, 1949). [How Stalin delivered the German Communists to Hitler.]
"The Black Market in Russia," *The American Mercury*, (December 1949), pp. 676-684.

"Krizis solidarizma" (Crisis of Solidarism), *Narodnaya Pravda*, No. 6, (December, 1949). [Split of a Russian emigré group.]

"The Viceroy of Poland," *NL*, (December 10, 1949). [Marshal Konstantin Rokossovsky.]

"Stalin's Birthday," *NL*, (December 17, 1949).

"In the Dark," *NL*, (December 24, 1949). [US discriminates in favor of rightist Russian refugees.]

"Pax Amicorum?" *NL*, (December 31, 1949). [On the foreign policy program of American Quakers.]

1950

"Heir Presumptive," *NL*, (January 7, 1950). [Georgi Malenkov.]

"Harold Laski on Stalin," *NL*, (January 14, 1950).

"East and West.—A Russian Talks.—The Scoundrel.—FDR as Hitler Ally," *NL*, (January 21, 1950). [A refugee's lecture; Ilya Erenburg; *Pravda* on FDR.]

"Moscow and Peiping," *NL*, (January 28, 1950).

"From Our Special Correspondent," *NL*, (February 4, 1950). [On Ralph Parker's *Conspiracy Against Peace*.]

"David Rousset's Plan," *NL*, (February 11, 1950). [Slave labor in the U.S.S.R.]

"The Two Bombs," *NL*, (February 18, 25 and March 4, 1950).

"Kennan Breeds Overoptimism," *NL*, (March 11, 1950).

"The Soviet 'Elections,' " *NL*, (March 18, 1950).

"A Truman-Stalin Meeting?" *NL*, (March 25 and April 1, 1950).

"Mao and Stalin," *The Sign*, (April, 1950), pp. 27-29.

"The Ex-Communists," *NL*, (April 8, 1950).

"More Harmful Than Spies," *NL*, (April 15, 1950). [On McCarthyism.]

"Soviet Colonizers," *NL*, (April 22, 1950).

"The Baltic Incident," *NL*, (April 29, 1950). [Anti-Americanism.]

"Golubi mira" (Doves of Peace), *Narodnaya Pravda*, No. 7-8, (May, 1950).

"Many Enemies, Much Honor—New Leader Wartime Story," *NL*, (May 6, 1950).

"Writings of Owen Lattimore Reflect Pro-Soviet Views," *NL*, (May 13, 1950).

"An Open Letter to Henry Wallace," *NL*, (May 20, 1950).

"The New Anti-Russians. Hating the Russian People is no Way to Fight Their Oppressors," *NL*, (May 27, 1950).

"U.S.S.R. Building Vast New Bases in Baltic," *NL*, (June 3, 1950).

"U.S.S.R. Weak in Air, Strong on Land," *NL*, (June 10, 1950).

Bibliography

"Why Isn't Formosa Covered by 'Total Diplomacy' Too?" *NL*, (June 17, 1950).

"Recognizing Mao: A Futile Move," *NL*, (June 24, 1950).

"ERP and the Pact: A Balance Sheet," *NL*, (July 1, 1950).

"Unite the Two Koreas," *NL*, (July 8, 1950).

" 'Not Korea, But Japan,' " *NL*, (July 15, 1950). [Stalin's current drive is really aimed at Japan.]

"Korea Is Only the Beginning," *NL*, (July 22, 1950).

"The 23 Laborites Are Not Nehrus," *NL*, (July 29, 1950). [On Korea.]

"Stalin Is the War Criminal—Let's Call a Spade a Spade," *NL*, (August 5, 1950).

"Stalin Speaks Out," *NL*, (August 12, 1950).

"Pyat' let sovetskoi imperii" (Five Years of the Soviet Empire), *Novyi Zhurnal*, XXIII, 1950, pp. 142–159.

"Russia's New Empire," *The Yale Review*, New Haven, Conn., XL, No. 1, (September, 1950), pp. 6–26.

"Stalin Takes a Breather," *NL*, (September 9, 1950).

"New Light on the Comintern," *NL*, (September 16, 1950).

"A Tale of Terror and Treachery," *NL*, (September 23, 1950). [The MVD in the Ukraine.]

"Rearmed Germany and Japan Essential for Western Defense," *NL*, (September 30, 1950).

"Communism Means War," *The American Mercury*, (October, 1950), pp. 400–409.

"Another Victory for Stalin: The Waldorf-Astoria Decisions," *NL*, (October 7, 1950). [On Germany.]

"Truman Doctrine is a Failure," *NL*, (October 14, 1950). [On Korea.]

"Kremlin Planned Korea Atrocities," *NL*, (October 21, 1950).

"Korea Deflates Soviet Prestige," *NL*, (October 30, 1950).

"Nashi oborontsy" (Our Defensists), *Narodnaya Pravda*, No. 11–12, (November, 1950). [Some refugee groups support Soviet "defense" efforts.]

"A United World—The Ultimate Goal," *NL*, (November 6, 1950).

"Soviet Slaves Speak Out," *NL*, (November 13, 1950).

"Why Red China Intervened. The Chinese Communists' Role in the Korean War Was Decided Upon last February—in Moscow," *NL*, (November 20, 1950).

"Asia or Europe?" *NL*, (November 27, 1950). [The next Soviet move.]

"Soviet Slavery Stands Trial," *NL*, (December 11, 1950). [The Rousset trial in Paris.]

"France—the West's Weakest Link," *NL*, (December 18, 1950).
"Stalinism on Trial," *NL*, (December 25, 1950). [In Paris.]

1951

"Soviet Slaves Bear Witness," *NL*, (January 1, 1951). [In the Paris trial.]
"Soviet Blackmail and French Nerves," *NL*, (January 8, 1951).
"The French CP At Ebb Tide," *NL*, (January 15, 1951).
"The McCarran Pro-Communist Law," *NL*, (January 22, 1951).
" 'Kravchenko Trial' in Germany," *NL*, (February 5, 1951).
"The Wrong Russians Again," *NL*, (February 12, 1951). [U.S. intelligence manoeuvers among Russian displaced persons.]
"Germany and the West," *NL*, (February 19, 1951).
"The U.S. Press And Germany," *NL*, (February 26, 1951).
"Hoover and Taft Seen From Europe," *NL*, (March 5, 1951).
"Russian Soldiers Who Hate Stalin," *NL*, (March 12, 1951).
"Jungle Law in Berlin," *NL*, (March 19, 1951). [On kidnapping.]
"Red Germany's Army of Spies," *NL*, (March 26, 1951).
" 'Political Lessons' in the Red Army," *NL*, (April 2, 1951).
"Stalin the Great," *NL*, (April 16, 1951).
"Europe and MacArthur," *NL*, (April 30, 1951). [On MacArthur's dismissal.]
"Europe Looks at MacArthur," *NL*, (May 7, 1951). [Also on Moscow's role in Korea and on Stalin's wartime strategy.]
"New Faces For Big Three," *NL*, (May 14, 1951).
"Cold War Smuggling," *NL*, (May 21, 1951). [Illicit trade between East and West.]
" 'Between Hitler and Stalin,' " *NL*, (May 28, 1951).
"Russia Has Socialized Medicine," *Catholic Digest*, (June, 1951), pp. 93-96.
"Nazi Victims Judge Stalinism," *NL*, (June 4, 1951). [The Brussels trial.]
"Is Slave Labor Profitable?" *NL*, (June 11, 1951).
"A Mistaken 'Peace Offensive,' " *NL*, (June 18, 1951). [On the Korean war.]
"No Cease-Fire At the 38th!" *NL*, (June 25, 1951).
"Letters the 'Nation' Didn't Answer," *NL*, (July 9, 1951).
"Our Forgotten Russian Allies," *NL*, (July 16, 1951). [The Soviet defectors.]
"Neobkhodimoe razyasnenie" (An Essential Explanation), *Golos Naroda*, Munchen, (July 22, 1951). [On political activities of Russian refugees.]

Bibliography

"'Defend Europe on the Elbe.' Interview with Kurt Schumacher," *NL*, (July 23, 1951).

"Germany's Socialists and Rearmament," *NL*, (July 30, 1951).

"Soviet Defectors Speak Up Frankly," *NL*, (August 6, 1951).

"The East German Police State," *NL*, (August 20, 1951).

"Myth of Chinese 'Titoism' Revived," *NL*, (August 27, 1951).

"Counter-espionage in East Germany," *NL*, (September 24, 1951).

"American Labor's Anti-Cominform," *The American Mercury* (October, 1951), pp. 14–23.

"Der Westen und die Zukunft Russlands. Eine Rundfrage zu George F. Kennans Aufsatz," *Der Monat*, No. 37, (October, 1951), pp. 59–62.

"Soviet Kidnappers in Germany," *NL*, (October 1, 1951).

"Report on Europe: 1. 'The West' Doesn't Exist," *NL*, (October 8, 1951).

"The Slave Empire Within the Soviet Empire," *The New York Times Magazine*, (October 14, 1951).

"Report on Europe: 2. France and German Rearmament," *NL*, (October 15, 1951).

"Henry Wallace and Chinese Communism," *NL*, (October 22, 1951).

"Mossadegh's Men On Soviet Payroll," *NL*, (October 29, 1951).

"The Essence of Stalinism: Murder," *NL*, (November 5, 1951).

"Stalin Had His 'Iran' in 1929." *NL*, (November 12, 1951). [On the Soviet-Chinese conflict.]

"The Meaning of Wallace's Trip," *NL*, (November 19, 1951).

"Our Enemy Is Not The Russian People," *NL*, (November 26, 1951).

"Why Europe Won't Fight," *The American Mercury*, (December, 1951), pp. 30–39.

"The Morale of the Soviet Army," *The Sign*, (December, 1951), pp. 9–11.

"The 'Ukrainian Army' Myth," *NL*, (December 3, 1951).

"Europe After Stalin Falls," *NL*, (December 17, 1951).

"The Wrong Kind of Anti-Communism," *NL*, (December 24, 1951).

"Russian Emigré Talks Hit Snag," *NL*, (December 31, 1951). [Russian emigré problems.]

1952

"Counter-measures To Communist Lies," *NL*, (January 14, 1952).

"Lenin-Litvinov, Stalin-Vyshinsky," *NL*, (January 21, 1952).

"New Soviet Arms Plan an Illusion," *NL*, (January 28, 1952).

"An Indictment Written in Blood," *NL*, (February 4, 1952). [The Chinese prisoners of war on Koje island.]

"Republican Foreign Policy," *NL*, (February 11, 1952).
"How to Deal With the Satellites," *NL*, (February 18, 1952).
"Can We Rely on France?" *NL*, (February 25, 1952).
"Jacob Malik on World War III," *NL*, (March 3, 1952).
"Soviet Russia's 'Mozhno' Girls," *NL*, (March 10, 1952).
"Cloak-and-Dagger In Soviet Strategy," *NL*, (March 17, 1952).
"The Farce of Soviet 'Neutrality,' " *NL*, (March 24, 1952).
"Gesammelte und vergessene Werke," *Der Monat*, No. 43, (April, 1952), pp. 79-83. [On Stalin's incomplete "Collected Works."]
"Our Blunder in Greece," *NL*, (April 7, 1952).
"Russia's Secret Weapon ... Every Communist a Spy," *Grafic Magazine*, Chicago, Ill. (April 20, 1952).
"The Repatriation Crime of World War II," *NL*, (April 21, 1952).
"Stalin Can't Let Germany Reunite," *NL*, (April 28, 1952).
"Operation 'Kidnap.' Berlin's Soviet Underworld," *The American Mercury*, (May, 1952), pp. 55-62.
"Is the 'Germ War' Made in Moscow?" *NL*, (May 5, 1952).
"The Soviet 'Germ War,' " *NL*, (May 12, 1952).
"The Faceless Men of Soviet Diplomacy," *NL*, (May 19, 1952).
"German War 'Confession,' " *NL*, (May 26, 1952).
"Why the Germans Distrust America," *NL*, (June 2, 1952).
"Can the European Army Succeed?" *NL*, (June 9, 1952).
"We Must Bar POW Surrender," *NL*, (June 16, 1952).
"Signs of Weakness on Truce Talks," *NL*, (June 23, 1952). [In Western diplomacy.]
"Espionage Agents in Striped Pants," *NL*, (June 30, 1952).
"After the Yalu Bombings," *NL*, (July 7, 1952).
"New Data on U.S.-Soviet Ties," *NL*, (July 14, 1952).
"How FDR Met Soviet Pressures," *NL*, (July 21, 1952).
"New Soviet 'Peace' Fraud," *NL*, (August 4, 1952).
"The Problem of Tito: Should We Accept Undemocratic Allies?" *NL*, (August 11, 1952).
"Policy of Containment," *The Annals of the American Academy of Political and Social Science*, Philadelphia, (September, 1952), pp. 22-30.
"The Race For Stalin's Throne," *NL*, (September 8, 1952).
"Eisenhower Chief Soviet Target," *NL*, (September 15, 1952).
"George Kennan's Mission to Moscow," *NL*, (September 22, 1952).
"Liberation or Containment?" *NL*, (September 29, 1952).
"Zarubin: Soviet Innocent Abroad," *NL*, (October 6, 1952).
"Why We're Losing in Germany," *NL*, (October 13, 1952).

"The Kennan Fiasco," *NL*, (October 20, 1952).
"Moscow Russifies The Satellites," *NL*, (October 27, 1952).
"Exit Politburo: Enter Presidium," *NL*, (November 3, 1952).
"How to Lose Friends in Germany," *NL*, (November 10, 1952).
"Eisenhower Rides Anti-Red Wave," *NL*, (November 17, 1952).
"Shift in the Balance of Power," *NL*, (November 24, 1952).

1953

"The Future of Russian Jewry," *NL*, (January 5, 1953).
"The World Ike Faces," *NL*, (January 19, 1953).
"Are U.S. Authorities Promoting Reaction Among Soviet Defectors?" *NL*, (February 2, 1953).
"Germany Ten Years After Stalingrad," *NL*, (February 16, 1953).
"Why German Socialists Oppose the Treaties," *NL*, (March 2, 1953).
"Kremlin Spies on Trial. One Group has Already Stood Trial in West Germany; Three Others Await the Courts," *NL*, (March 16, 1953).
"Europe's New Anti-Americanism," *NL*, (March 30, 1953).
"New Deal in Moscow?" *NL*, (April 27, 1953).
"Moscow's Strategic Retreat," *NL*, (May 4, 1953).
" 'Half-way' to Moscow is Suicide," *NL*, (May 25, 1953).
"The Strange Case of Lord Jowitt," *NL*, (June 15, 1953). [On the Alger Hiss case.]
"Otvet S. Mel'gunovu," *Kolokol (The Bell)*, Hamburg, (July-August, 1953), pp. 21-22. [Should refugees accept financial aid.]
"Puti i zigzagi revolyutsii." (Ways and Zigzags of the Revolution), *Novyi Zhurnal*, XXXII, 1953, pp. 224-244.
"Communist Innovations," *The Yale Review*, XLII, No. 3, (March, 1953), pp. 343-350.
"The New Russian Intelligentsia," *The Yale Review*, XLIII, No. 2, (December, 1953), pp. 188-203.

1954

"What Malenkov Wants," *NL*, (January 25, 1954).
"How to Win in Indo-China," *NL*, (February 22, 1954).
"DESI [Desinformation] on the New Russia," *NL*, (March 29, 1954).
"Notes on Geneva," *NL*, (April 26, 1954). [Negotiating with the U.S.S.R.]
"The Dulles Dilemma," *NL*, (May 24, 1954).
"Molotov Reports to Malenkov. How the Soviets View Geneva, Indo-China and Europe," *NL*, (June 28, 1954).

"Les débuts de l'espionage soviétique en France," *B.E.I.P.I. Bulletin de l'Association d'Etudes et d'Informations Politiques Internationales*, Paris, (July 1-15, 1954), pp. 8-15.

"Is France Our Ally? NO Says David J. Dallin," *NL*, (July 26, 1954).

"Amerikanskaya politika v Rossii" (U.S. Policy in Russia), *Novyi Zhurnal*, XXXVI, 1954, pp. 273-289.

1955

"What's Peaceful Coexistence?" *The Sign*, (January, 1955), pp. 27-29.

"Europe Comes First," *NL*, (January 3, 1955).

"Who Are the Real Bosses of Red Russia?" *The Wall Street Journal*, New York, (February 10, 1955).

"The Austrian Treaty," *NL*, (April 25, 1955).

"The Meeting at the Summit," *NL*, (May 23, 1955).

"Why Russia Can't Attack Us Now," *NL*, (June 27, 1955).

"Soviet Policy After Stalin. From Offensive to East-West Detente," *NL*, (August 15, 22; September 5, 12, 1955).

"Relations With Red China," *NL*, (October 10, 1955). Reprinted in *Time*, (October 24, 1955), as "Red China Recognition May be Inevitable."

"Soviet Policy in the Middle East," *Middle Eastern Affairs*, New York, (November, 1955), pp. 337-344.

[Henry Kasson, pseud.] "The Zborowski Case," *NL*, (November 21, 1955).

"After Stalin," *The Yale Review*, XLV, No. 2, (December, 1955), pp. 252-266.

1956

"New Wind in Moscow?" *NL*, (February 27, 1956).

"Mark Zborowski, Soviet Agent," *NL*, (March 19 and 26, 1956).

"Whither Soviet Russia," *The Sign*, (June, 1956), pp. 13-15.

"Like a Century Ago," *Mainichi*, Tokyo, (November 22, 1956). [The Hungarian Uprising.]

1957

"The Future of the Sino-Soviet Alliance," *Orbis*, Philadelphia, I, No. 3, (Fall, 1957), pp. 315-325.

"Der harte Kurs in Moskau," *Der europäische Osten*, Munich, No. 10, (October, 1957), pp. 588-592.

1958

"Russia Five Years After Stalin. Foreign Policy," *NL*, (March 24, 1958).

"Soviet Policy and the Summit," *Problems of Communism*, Washington, D.C., VII, No. 3, (May-June, 1958), pp. 1-4.

"Notes on Soviet Power," *NL*, (June 9, 1958). [Disengagement; the Rapacki Plan; the economic race.]

"Stalin, Renner und Tito," *Europa-Archiv*, Frankfurt/M., No. 15/16/17, (August 5/20; September 15, 1958), pp. 11030-11034.

"The Soviet 'Drang nach Süden,'" *Problems of Communism*, VII, No. 5, (September-October. 1958), pp. 50-52.

"The 'New' Communism," *Challenge*, New York, (October, 1958), pp. 80-84.

"Soviet Designs in the Middle East," *NL*, (October 13, 1958).

"Russia: Advanced Nation?" *The Sign*, (December, 1958), pp. 19, 20, 80.

1959

"The Main Traits of Soviet Empire Building," *The Russian Review*, Hannover, N.H., XVIII, No. 1, (January, 1959), pp. 3-13.

"In the Time of Tolstoy an Artistic Dynasty Was Born," *Saturday Review*, New York, (April 4, 1959), pp. 17-18.

"Khrushchev's Berlin Campaign," *NL*, (April 6 and 13, 1959). [The second article has the title "Moscow's Basic Error."]

"Communist Politics in the Western World," *The Annals of the American Academy of Political and Social Science*, (July, 1959), pp. 1-7.

"Camp David Meeting," *NL*, (October 5, 1959).

1960/1961

"The New Class in Russia," *Modern Age*, Chicago, Ill., (Winter, 1960/61), V, No. 1, pp. 5-12.

"Methods of Soviet Diplomacy," *Modern Age*, (Fall, 1961), V, No. 4, pp. 341-351.

1962/1963

"A Revolution Transformed," *Modern Age*, (Spring, 1962), VI, No. 2, pp. 119-122.

"The Kravchenko Case," *Modern Age*, (Summer, 1962), VI, No. 3, pp. 267-276.

"Soviet Russia as a World Power," *Modern Age*, (Winter, 1962/63), VII, No. 1, pp. 17-24.

INDEX

Academy of Sciences, U.S.S.R., 31
Accidents, U.S.S.R., 24, 109; automobile accidents, 44–46, 106; industry accidents, 23–26, 101, 102, 105, 108, 109; railway accidents, 23, 24, 26, 27, 107, 108
Adenauer, Konrad, 197, 200, 201
Adriatic Sea, 232
Aegean Sea, 118, 232
Africa, 235
Albania, 118, 237
Alexander II, 40, 41
Alexander, Harold, 129, 130, 130n
Algeria (Algerian), 223
Alksnis, Y. I., 12
Allen, George, 211n
Allied armies. *See* Western armies
Allied Control Council for Germany, 132
Allied Council for Austria, 132, 133, 137, 139; for Japan, 21
Allied Powers, Allies. *See* Western Alliance
Allies. *See* Western Alliance
Alma-Ata, U.S.S.R., 93n
America (American), 31, 36, 98n, 125, 129, 132, 133, 136, 141, 148, 151–153, 161, 162, 187, 207, 219, 227, 229, 230, 231, 233–235. *See also* United States of America
American army. *See* United States of America, army
Amur, U.S.S.R., 34
Anarchists, 47
Andreev, Andrei, 18
Andreev, Vladimir, 74, 76, 77n
Angriff, Der, Berlin, 73

Anschluss, 120, 121
Anti-Communism (Anti-Communist), 180, 206, 228, 229, 233, 237
"Anti-Soviet Trotskyite Center," 12, 27n
Anti-Stalinism, 5, 56, 68, 70
Anzherka, U.S.S.R., 43
Arbeiterbladet, Copenhagen, 60
Arbeit-Zeitung, Vienna, 122
Airmont, *German engineer*, 76
Armenia, 100
Arnold, Valentin, 79, 88, 106, 110, 114
Asia (Asiatic), 193, 216, 217, 235
Atomic bomb. *See* Nuclear weapons
Austria (Austrian), 49, 61, 117–148, 163, 202, 203, 221, 232, 237; army, 119; Austrian-Soviet Oil Corporation, 132, 133; Burgenland, 125n; Carinthia, 128, 129, 142; emégres, 120, Lower Austria, 125n, 140; Ministry of Internal Affairs, 126, 133, 134, 137; Parliament, 120, 123; Peace Treaty (1955), 131, 138, 141, 142n, 143; police, 126, 133, 137, 138n, 139, 140; political cabinet, 103, 136, 137; Provisional government, 126, 130, 133; *putsch* (uprisings), 135, 138–141; Styria, 125n, 140
Austria-Hungary, 221, 222
Automobile accidents, U.S.S.R. *See* Accidents, U.S.S.R., Automobile accidents
Axis powers, 231
Azerbaidjan: Iranian, 45; Soviet, 45, 100

Babeufm Gracchus (Francois Noel), 175
"Bacteriological warfare," charged at Pyatakov–Radek trial, 30–39
Baghdad Pact, 205
Bakaev, Ivan, 94
Baldwin, Stanley, 78
Balkans, 36, 38, 128, 141
Baltic Sea, 118, 232
Baltic States, 164
Baum, German press attaché, 84
Bavarian Revolution (1919), 153
Bebel, August, 176, 177
B.E.I.P.I. *Bulletin de L'Association D'Etudes et D'Informations Politiques Internationales* (*Est & Ouest*), Paris, 44, 45
Belgium, 230
Belgrade, Yugoslavia, 128, 129
Belinsky, Vissarion, 155
Belvedere Palace, Vienna, 143
Beria, Lavrenti, 13, 42
Berlin, Germany, 41, 50, 60, 72, 73, 76, 83, 90, 91, 93, 103, 117, 193, 237
Berlin, blockade, 233
Berlin Conference of Foreign Ministers. *See* Foreign Ministers Conferences
Berman–Yurin, Konon, 69
Bessarabia, 164
Big Four, 141, 223
Big Three, 128, 129, 131
Bismarck, Otto, 177
Blanc, Louis, 175
Blanqui, Louis Auguste, 176
"Bloc of Rightists and Trotskyites," 13
Blyukher, Vasili, 12
Blyumkin, Yakov, 51, 93n
Bogdanov, Alexander (Malinovski, A.A.), 183
Boguslavski, Mikhail, 53, 54, 77, 78, 88, 100, 101
Bolshevik (Bolshevism), 10, 12, 13, 21, 42, 45, 47, 48, 51, 52, 54, 66, 70, 76, 79, 121, 152, 162–164, 167, 168, 171–173, 185, 189–191. *See also* Communist Party of the Soviet Union.
Bolshevik Party. *See* Communist Party of the Soviet Union.
Bonapartism, 160
Borsig, 39, 89
Boyarshinov, 104
Bremen, Germany, 49
Brest–Litovsk, U.S.S.R., 50, 53
Brest–Litovsk Treaty, 48, 53, 150, 163
Bristol, Hotel. *See* Hotel Bristol
Britain (British), 30, 45, 51, 53, 78, 136, 148, 154, 173, 175, 177, 179, 180, 194, 198, 199, 201, 202, 207, 212, 213, 217–219, 221, 222, 224, 226, 230, 233, 235; army, 117, 125, 128, 129; as a Great Power, 215, 216, 222; intelligence of. *See* Intelligence, British;
—Relations with: Austria, 121, 125, 126, 128, 130, 131, 137; Soviet Union, 201, 202, 224, 229, 233; Yugoslavia, 28–130, 229
Budenny, Semion, 12
Bukhara, 171
Bukharin, Nikolai, 13, 15, 16, 18–20, 46, 47, 84, 90, 94, 111, 116, 187
Bukharin–Rykov trial, 13, 14, 22, 57, 81
Bukhartsev, Dmitri, 91
Bukovina, 164
Bulganin, Nikolai, 193, 197, 202, 206, 208
Bulgaria, 141
Bullitt, William, 190
Bureaucracy, Soviet, 165, 168, 169
Bushmen, 213
Byelorussia, 28
Byrnes, James, 130n, 220
Byulleten' Oppozitsii (*Bolshevikov–Leninitsev*) (Bulletin of the Opposition (Bolshevik–Leninists), Berlin, Paris, New York,

Index

6n, 42n, 51n, 65, 66n, 68, 75n, 92 (n. 95)

Cachin, Marcel, 86, 87
Cameroons, 214
Capitalism (Capitalist), 34–36, 41, 56, 142, 179, 225, 226, 228, 229, 235; "Restoration" in the U.S.S.R., charged at Moscow trials, 12, 35, 36, 75, 80, 86, 87, 96, 99
Catledge, Turner, 205
Caucasus, U.S.S.R., 13, 42, 100, 170, 171
Center. *See* "Parallel Center"
Central Asia, U.S.S.R., 21, 45, 53, 110
Central Executive Committee, 5, 6, 8, 20, 52, 78, 104, 160; Presidium of, 5, 6, 114, 160; Session of January, 1936, 37
Chad, 214
Cheka, 33, 60, 63, 68, 165. *See also* GPU, NKVD, MVD, MGB, KGB
Chekhov, Anton, 158
Chemical Industry, U.S.S.R., 25, 60, 61, 77, 85, 88, 89, 100, 105, 108, 109
Chernyshevsky, Nikolai, 155
Chicherin, Georgi, 200
Chief Prosecutor of the U.S.S.R. *See* Vyshinsky, Andrei
China (Chinese), 31, 36, 179, 180, 184, 187, 201, 215, 216, 231
Christian-Social People's Party of Austria, 125, 126, 134, 135, 139
Chronicle of International Events, Moscow, 196
Chubar, Vlas, 44, 64, 171
Churchill, Winston, 128–130, 130n, 173, 207, 215, 219–221, 229
Civil War in Russia, 21, 23, 48, 51, 53, 54, 66, 140n, 148, 151, 153, 163, 166, 171
Clark, Mark, 132n

Coal Industry, U.S.S.R., 74, 76, 77, 85, 88, 100–103, 105, 106
Coexistence, 179, 195, 199, 224, 228, 229
Collective farms. *See Kolkhoz*
Cominform, 232
Comintern, 8, 39, 50, 60, 158, 191; Executive Committee of, 21, 50
Commissariat of Foreign Affairs. *See* Ministry of Foreign Affairs, U.S.S.R.
Commissariat of Internal Affairs. *See* NKVD
Commission of Security. *See* Communist Party of the Soviet Union, Politburo–Presidium, Security Commission.
Committees of Poor Peasants. *See Kombedy*
Communism (Communist), 11, 17, 36, 37, 39, 56, 60, 86, 93n, 119, 121, 125, 132, 149, 162, 173, 179, 180, 181, 187, 201, 204, 212–214, 223, 225, 228, 229, 233
Communist Information Bureau. *See* Cominform
Communist International. *See* Comintern
Communist Party: of Austria, 119, 120, 124–126, 128, 133–141; of China, 179, 184, 214; of Czechoslovakia, 60; of Denmark, 60, 61; of France, 65, 118, 232; of Germany, 60; of Iran, 45; of Italy, 118, 232
Communist Party of the Soviet Union, 3–8, 18, 20–22, 27, 42, 44, 47, 48, 50, 52–57, 59, 60, 62–64, 75, 76, 80, 86–88, 94, 97, 104, 106–108, 113, 116, 159, 162–165, 167, 168–173, 177–179, 185–192, 211, 226, 233; Bureau of Appointments, 21
—Central Committee, 4, 7, 8, 13, 14, 18, 20, 21, 43, 48, 50, 52, 53, 62–64, 185; Plenums of, 8, 143

Central Control Commission, 8, 21
—Conferences, 46; May, 1917, 170, 171
—Congresses, 226; Fifteenth (1927), 53; Sixteenth (1930), 53; Seventeenth (1934), 21, 53; Twentieth (1956), 6, 10, 14, 43, 44, 63; Twenty-first (1959), 227; Twenty-second (1961), 6n
—Opposition (Oppositionists), 12, 14, 15, 25, 27, 29, 33, 36, 40, 41, 46, 56, 72, 84–86, 89n, 94, 99, 113, 172, 191; Anti-Party Group, 193, 227; Left Opposition, 4, 15, 17, 19, 35, 39, 43, 46, 48, 50–52, 54, 94, 95. *See also* Trotskyism (Trotskyites); "New Opposition." *See* Zinoviev-Kamenev group; Right Opposition, 4, 5, 13, 15, 18–20, 22, 43, 46, 90, 94; Workers' Opposition, 15
Orgburo, 21
—Politburo-Presidium, 4–8, 14, 17, 20, 21, 37, 42, 50, 94; Security Commission, 8, 14, 18, 21
Purges, 3–5, 7, 8, 12–14, 22, 63, 72, 113, 116, 172, 191
[Communist Party of—cont.]
Communist Youth League, U.S.S.R. *See Komsomol*
Concentration camps, U.S.S.R., 6, 10, 12, 56, 165
Confederation of the Rhine, 194
Conference of Three Internationals, 500
"Confessions," U.S.S.R., 9–14, 44, 55, 58, 59, 63, 64, 77n, 78–86, 89, 113, 114, 187
Congo (Congolese), 213, 235
Congress of Soviets, 6; Second (1917), 163n; Seventh (1935), 37
Constituent Assembly, 167, 168
Copenhagen, Denmark, 92n

Council of Labor and Defense, U.S.S.R., 8
Council of National Economy, U.S.S.R., 230
Council of People's Commissars, 8, 160
Council of War, U.S.S.R., 8
Criminal Code of the Russian Soviet Federative Socialist Republic (RSFSR), 75, 88
Cuba, 235
Czechoslovakia (Czech), 60, 117–119, 132

Dallin, Alexander, 29n
Danube countries, 36
Danube Federation, 118
Dardanelle Straits, 163
Darwin, Charles Robert, 183
Dashnaktsutyun Party of Armenia, 100
David, Fritz, 59
Davies, Joseph, 98n, 115
Debs, Eugene, 200
Dehlmann, 103
Demag, 39, 89
Denazification, 136, 137
Denikin, Anton, 54, 148, 152
Denmark (Danish), 60, 61, 205, 230
Denny, Harold, 21n
Department of State. *See* United States of America, Department of State
Displaced persons, 136
"Diversion," accusation of at the Moscow trials, 11–13, 26–28, 43, 72, 74, 77, 87, 88, 90, 91, 105, 109, 116
Dnepropetrovsk, U.S.S.R., 43
Dobretsberger, Josef, 139
Dollfuss, Engelbert, 123
Don, U.S.S.R., 148, 152
Dreitzer, Yefim, 94
Drobnis, Yakov, 54, 74–79, 88, 101, 102
Duclos, Jacques, 114, 232
Duma, Russian, 185
Duranty, Walter, 111, 115

Index

Dutch. *See* Netherlands, The
Dutov, A. I., 148, 152
Dynamo Plant, Moscow, 16

Eastern and Siberian Coal Trust. *See* Coal Industry, U.S.S.R.
East Germany. *See* Germany (Germans), East
Ebert, Friedrich, 120
Echo de Paris, Paris, 114
Eden, Anthony, 78, 117, 197
Egypt, 180
Eikhe, Robert, 42, 63, 64, 77, 101, 103, 106
Eisenhower, Dwight, 173, 197, 201, 206, 208, 208n, 210
Engels, Friedrich, 116, 175, 176
England. *See* Britain (British)
Ere Nouvelle, Paris, 114
"Espionage," accusation of at the Moscow trials, 11–13, 36, 39, 43, 61–64, 73, 75, 87, 88, 109, 187
Est &Ouest, Paris. *See B.E.I.P.I.*
Etienne. *See* Zborowski, Mark
Europe (European), 38, 61, 67, 119, 124, 142, 152–154, 156, 161, 169, 173, 194, 209, 216, 218, 221–224, 231, 233–235, 237; Central, 132, 221–223, 232, 235; Eastern, 117, 222, 223, 232, 233; Western, 89, 153, 178, 230, 231, 233–237
Executive Committee of the Communist International. *See* Comintern, Executive Committee of
Extraordinary Committee. *See* Cheka

Far East, 31, 34, 38
Fascism (Fascist), 17, 33, 37, 72–78, 80, 91, 92, 116, 120–122, 136, 180, 207
Federal Bureau of Investigation, 67
Feuchtwanger, Lion, 86, 115
Finland (Finnish), 106, 148, 164, 170, 171, 193

First International, 176
Fischer, Ernst, 119, 125, 126, 139
Five-Year Plan, 49
Foreign Department of the NKVD. *See* NKVD, Foreign Department
Foreign Ministers Conference: Berlin Conference (January, 1954), 143; Moscow Conference (October, 1953), 118
Fourth International, 68, 69
France, (French), 37, 43, 44, 52, 65, 67, 70, 86, 98n, 114, 118, 148, 154, 158, 161, 162, 164, 175–177, 179, 182, 193, 194, 213–215, 220, 221, 223, 224, 230–233; French–Soviet relations, 37, 233, 224; as a Great Power, 216, 217, 222, 224; Revolution, 175, 193, 194
Franco, Francisco, 230
Frankfurt, Germany, 138n
"Free Austria" radio in Moscow, U.S.S.R., 119
Free Austrian Group, Paris and London, 119
French Revolution. *See* France (French), Revolution
Fröhlich-Knüpfel-Dehlmann, 103
Fürnberg, Friedl, 119, 125

Gagra, U.S.S.R., 90, 99
Gamarnik, Yan, 12n, 57
General Commissar of State Security. *See* Yezhov, Nikolai
Geneva, Switzerland, 98
Genghis Kkan, 173
Georgia, Caucasus. *See* Gruzia, U.S.S.R.
Georgian Communist Party, U.S.S.R., 13
Gerhardson, Einer, 202
Germany (German), 22, 28, 29, 31, 33–39, 49, 50, 53, 54, 59, 60, 72–78, 80–84, 86, 87, 89, 91, 92n, 95–97, 99, 103–105, 108, 109, 111, 115, 117, 118, 120, 121, 127, 128, 131, 132,

135–137, 143, 148, 154, 157, 161–165, 170, 171, 176, 177, 179, 182, 187, 197, 200, 207, 211, 215, 217, 219–223, 230, 231, 233, 234, 236; as a Great Power 217, 222, 223; assets of, 130, 131, 142; East, 118, 220, 221, 234, 236; National Socialist Party. *See* Nazi, Nazism; rearmament of, 207, 209, 210, 217, 219–221, 236; reunification of, 205, 234; Soviet-German relations, history, 36–38, 211; West, 201, 205, 209, 210, 220, 223, 237
Gestapo, 18, 66, 77, 91, 103, 110, 114, 230
Glezas, Manolis, 203
Gloggnitz, Austria, 120, 121, 123
Goltsman, Eduard, 92n, 93n
Gorky, Maxim, 158
Gosplan, 53
Gouzenko, Igor, 30
GPU, 9, 20, 21n, 51, 56, 60, 63, 67, 72, 73, 104, 165. *See also* Cheka, NKVD, MVD, MGB, KGB
Great Britain. *See* Britain (British)
Great Powers, 124, 172, 188, 194, 215–218, 220, 222, 224, 230
Greece (Greek), 202–205, 216, 232, 233
Gromyko, Andrei, 208
Grosskopf, German Consul, 77
Gruber, Karl, 133n, 139–141
Gruziya, U.S.S.R., 13, 100, 171
Guerillas, Soviet, 28, 29

Hammer and Sickle plant, Moscow, 16
Hapsburg monarchy, 118, 221
Hegel, Georg Wilhelm Friedrich, 157, 160
Herzen, Alexander, 51
Hess, Rudolf, 34, 91
Hilger, Gustav, 84n
Hirohito, 31
Hiroshima, S., 32, 107, 108

History of the Communist Party, Short Course, 7n, 40n
Hitler, Adolf, 38, 114, 120, 122, 123, 129, 130n, 173, 201, 221, 230
Hitlerism (Hitlerites), 123, 136
Hönefoss, Norway, 65
Hofbauer, Josef. *See* Khokhlov, Nikolai
Holland. *See* Netherlands, The
Holtzman, Edouard. *See* Goltsman, Eduard
Honner, Franz, 119, 125, 126, 133
Hotel Bristol, Copenhagen, 92, 92n
Hrasche, Ivan, 60, 61, 88, 108, 109
Hull, Cordell, 117
Hungarian Revolution (1919), 153
Hungary (Hungarian), 117, 119, 141, 200, 201

ICBM. *See* Rockets
Indemnities. *See* Reparations
India, 180, 216, 224, 235
Indonesia, 180, 224, 231
Industrial Party, trial of, 24, 87
Intelligence: British, 187; Czech, 109; German, 14, 35, 36, 74, 100, 103–105, 108, 109, 234; Japanese, 14, 32, 35, 36, 107, 108; Soviet, 30, 70, 121, 136, 138n, 234
Intelligentsia, 155, 156, 174, 181, 182, 187
International: First. *See* First International; Second. *See* Socialist International; Third. *See* Comintern; Fourth. *See* Fourth International
International Commission Against Concentration Camp Practices, Paris–Brussels, 3n
International Institute of Social History, Paris, 66, 69
Iran, 45, 205, 210
Iranian Azerbaidjan. *See* Azerbaidjan, Iranian

Index

Iron Curtain, 232
Ispolkoms (Executive Committees of Soviets), 160
Isotoriya Diplomatii, Moscow, 199, 204
Istria, 128
Italy, 118, 141, 194, 203-205, 210, 214-216, 222, 232
Izvestia, Moscow, 9, 17, 19, 42, 83, 84, 91, 98, 111, 129, 130n

Jacobins, The, 194
Japan (Japanese), 3, 33-36, 38, 39, 47, 72, 82, 87, 95-97, 99, 108, 111, 129, 157, 173, 201, 203, 215, 218, 219, 222, 223, 230, 231; army, 31, 219; Constitution, 203, 218, 219; Diet, 218; General Staff, 31; Intelligence. See Intelligence, Japanese; war criminals, trial of, 31
Jemin Jihpao, Peking, 179
Jewish Socialist Party, 54
Jews (Jewish), 53, 131, 230
Jihad (Holy War), 181
Jogiches, Leo. See Tyszka, Jan
Jordan, 202

Kadets (Constitutional Democrats), Russia, 149
Kafka, Gustav, 142n
Kaganovich, Lazar, 18, 37, 42, 43, 101, 107, 108, 227
Kaiser. See Wilhelm II
Kaledin, Alexei, 152
Kalinin, Mikhail, 18, 98n
Kamenev, Lev, 7, 11, 14, 15, 17, 46, 47, 56, 58, 78, 81, 86, 90, 91, 95, 98, 99
Karakhan, Lev, 12
Kautsky, Karl, 177
Kedrov, NKVD official, 57, 79
Kemerovo, U.S.S.R., 25, 26, 43, 72, 74-76, 88, 105
Kemerovo Combined Chemical Works, 25, 88, 105
Kemerovo mines, 25, 72, 74-76, 77n

Kennan, George, 233, 234
Kerensky, Alexander, 50, 149, 150, 158
Kérillis, Henri de, 114
KGB, 165. See also Cheka, GPU, NKVD, MVD, MGB.
Khabarovsk, U.S.S.R., 31
Khalkhyn-Gol, 31
Khar'kov, U.S.S.R., 100, 147n
Khiva, 171
Khokhlov, Nikolai, 138n
Khrushchev, Nikita, 186, 214, 227-229; on advantages of communism, 225, 226, 228; demands executions of Communist leaders, 16, 115, 116; foreign policy, 193, 197, 198, 200-202, 205, 208, 224; secret report of February 24, 1956, 5n, 6n, 10n, 14n, 20n, 44n, 45n, 62n, 63n, 64n, 113n; on Stalin's terrorism, 6, 10, 43, 44, 63, 64, 112, 113
Kiental Conference, 50
Kierulf-Nielsen, 60
Kiev, U.S.S.R., 42, 43, 47, 54, 77, 171
Kiev Soviet, 48
Kirov, Sergei, 5, 6, 11, 41, 43-45, 83
Kirovabad, U.S.S.R., 45
Kjellere airfield, Norway, 92, 93
Klagenfurt, Austria, 128
Knudsen, Konrad, 65
Knyazev, Ivan, 26, 27, 32, 33, 35, 79, 88, 107, 108, 110
Konigsberg (now Kalinigrad, U.S.S.R.), 84
Kolchak, Alexander, 148, 152
Kolkhozy, 41, 62, 94, 96, 169, 179, 186, 191, 230
Kombedy, 191
Kommunist, Geneva (1915), 47
Kommunisticheskii Soyuz Molodezhi (Young Communist League). See Komsomol
Komsomol, 9, 76, 113
Koplenig, Johann, 119, 125, 126
Koptelov, Mikhail, 140, 141

Korea (Korean), 125, 143, 201, 206, 208n
Korean War, 30, 31, 140, 142, 143, 201, 206, 207, 208n
Kornilov, Lavr, 152
Kosarev, Alexander, 44, 64
Kossior, Stanislav, 42, 44, 64, 107, 171
Kovalenko, Ivan, 74, 76, 78
Krakow, Poland, 49
Krasnov, Piotr, 152
Kravchenko, Victor, 71
Kremenchug, U.S.S.R., 53
Kremlin, 17, 46, 152, 156, 178
Krestinsky, Nikolai, 13, 57
Krivitsky, Walter, 6, 9, 22, 70, 80n
Kruglyansky. *See* David, Fritz
Kuban', U.S.S.R., 148
Kulaks, 41, 42, 191
Kumykin, P. N., 132
Kuril Islands, 164
Kurov, Mikhail, 74, 75
Kuzbass, U.S.S.R., 43, 44, 62, 76, 88, 103, 104, 106
Kuznetsk Coal Basin. *See* Kuzbass, U.S.S.R.

Land and Freedom. *See Zemlya i Volya*
Laos, 235
Lashevich, Mikhail, 45
Lassalle, Ferdinand, 176
Lausanne, Switzerland, 70, 72
League of Nations, 38, 139, 214
Lebanon (Lebanese), 201, 203
Leftist Socialist-Revolutionaries. *See* Socialist-Revolutionaries, Leftist
Leipzig, Germany, 49
Lenin, Vladimir, 3, 4, 10, 12, 18, 47–50, 52, 116, 120–122, 150, 151, 162, 163, 168, 172, 181, 184, 185, 191, 214, 228; foreign policy, 190, 193, 199, 200, 211; Testament, 47
—views on: army, 165–167; bureaucracy, 168; Constituent Assembly, 167; expropriation of land, 168, 169; indemnities, 131n, 164; individual terror, 40; national question, 170, 171; police, 165; Russia's readiness for leadership in world revolution, 177, 178
Leningrad, U.S.S.R., 5, 6, 21, 43, 52
"Leningrad Center," 6, 7
Leningrad NKVD, 6, 45
"Leningrad Underground Counter-Revolutionary Group," 7
Leonenko, Nikolai, 74, 76, 78
Liebknecht, Wilhelm, 176
Lippert, Julius, 183
Lithuania, 148
Litvinov, Maxim, 73, 98n
Livshitz, Yakov, 27, 88, 100, 106, 107
Lloyd George, David, 173, 229
Loginov, Vladimir, 42, 100
Lominadze, V. V., 15
London, Britain, 53, 72n, 78, 97, 114, 119, 126, 142
Lund, Sigurd, 60
Luxemburg, Rosa, 49
Lvov, U.S.S.R., 49
Lyashchenko, Ivan, 74, 76
Lyubchenko, Panas, 172

MacArthur, Douglas, 218, 219
Machiavelli, Niccolo, 212
Maclean, Fitzroy, 229n
Macmillan, Harold, 198, 201, 202, 205
Maisky, Ivan, 78
Malenkov, Georgi, 227
Manchuria, 125
Mao Tse-tung, 184
March Revolution. *See* Russian Revolution, March, 1917
Maritime Province of the Far East, U.S.S.R., 34, 96
Marseilles, France, 70
Marshall Plan, 139, 140, 140n
Marx, Karl, 116, 175–177, 179, 187n, 211
Marxism (Marxist), 47, 52, 176,

Index

177, 179, 180–184, 187n
Marxism–Leninism, 214, 225
Maryasin, M., 27
Matulevich, I. O., 87
Maupassant, Guy de, 158
Mavrogordato, Ralph, 29n
Mdivani, Budu, 100
Mediterranean, 216
Medvedev, Sergei, 15
Mensheviks, 11, 100, 149, 199; trial of, 87
Mexico, 69, 98n
Meyer, Alfred, 84n
Meyer-Heydenhagen, 77
MGB (Ministry of State Security), 112n, 165. *See also* Cheka, GPU, NKVD, MVD, KGB
Middle East, 205
Mikhailovsky, Nikolai, 155
Mikoyan, Anastas, 18, 122
Milan, Italy, 118
Milyukov, Pavel, 151
Minindel. *See* Ministry of Foreign Affairs, U.S.S.R.
Ministry of Defense, U.S.S.R., 12n, 21
Ministry of Foreign Affairs, U.S.S.R., 81, 92, 143, 190, 195–197, 200, 209, 210
Ministry of Internal Affairs, U.S.S.R., *See* MVD
Mixed companies, 39
Molinier, Raymond, 65, 68
Mollet, Guy, 203n
Molotov, Vyacheslav, 18, 37, 38, 42–44, 46, 62, 84, 98n, 101, 103, 104, 106, 108, 130, 131, 141, 143, 204, 206, 220, 227
Mongolia, Outer, 31
Mongol (Mongolians), 173, 221
Morgenthau Plan, 219
Moscow, U.S.S.R., 16, 19–21, 38, 43, 44, 51–53, 68, 69, 71–76, 79, 82, 86, 90, 93n, 94, 96, 98n, 101, 103, 108, 113, 115, 116n, 117, 119, 125, 126, 128, 142, 147n, 148, 158, 193, 195, 209, 211, 233

Moscow Academy of Sciences. *See* Academy of Sciences, U.S.S.R.
"Moscow Center," 7
Moscow Conference. *See* Foreign Ministers Conference, Moscow Conference
Moscow Declaration (October, 1943), 117
Moscow Soviet, 51, 54
Moscow trials, 10–14, 22, 38, 40, 41, 56, 59, 60, 63, 64, 66, 71, 72, 113
Moscow underground counter-revolutionary group. *See also* "Moscow Center."
Mosely, Philip, 142n
Moskalev, A. M., 94
Mrachkovsky, Sergei, 94
Munich, Germany, 118
Muralov, Nikolai, 46, 51, 76, 77, 77n, 78, 79, 90, 103, 104
Mussavist Party of Azerbaidjan, 100
Mussolini, Benito, 129, 130n
MVD (Ministry of Internal Affairs), 5, 165. *See also* Cheka, GPU, NKVD, MGB, KGB
Mysl' (The Thought), Khar'kov, U.S.S.R., 147n

Nabokov, Vladimir, 151
Naples, Italy, 194
Napoleon Bonaparte, 194, 217
Naptha Syndicate, U.S.S.R., 53
Narkomindel. *See* Ministry of Foreign Affairs, U.S.S.R.
Narodnaya Volya, 39, 40
Narodniki, 39–41
Narodnoye khozyaistvo SSSR v 1959 godu, Moscow, 228n
Nashe Slovo, Paris, 52
National Economy of the Soviet Union in 1959. *See Marodnoe khozyaistvo SSSR v 1959 godu*, Moscow
National Socialism. *See* Nazi
NATO (North Atlantic Treaty

Organization), 202, 205, 210, 214, 235
Naville, Pierre, 65, 68
Nazi (Nazism), 14, 33, 34, 36, 37, 68, 72, 78, 103, 120, 121, 124, 136, 137, 173, 217, 230
Nazi intelligence. See Intelligence, German
Near East, 30, 205, 216
Nelidov, 57
NEP (New Economic Policy), 94
Netherlands, The, 194, 202, 205, 230
"New Opposition." See Zinoviev-Kamenev group
New Times, Moscow, 136
New York, U.S.A., 10, 66, 67, 106, 115, 193
New York Times, New York, 21n, 71, 115, 205
Nicholas II, 170, 191
Nikolaev, NKVD official, 64
Nikolaev, Leonid, 5, 6
Nicolson, Harold, 198, 199
Ninbo region, China, 31
Nixon, Richard, 207
NKVD (People's Commissariat of Internal Affairs), 6, 8, 9, 11, 13, 14, 17, 20–22, 42, 44, 55–72, 74, 79–83, 85, 87, 92, 94, 97, 105, 109, 112, 113, 165. See also Cheka, GPU, MVD, MGB, KGB; Economic Administration, 61; Foreign Department, 68
Norkin, Boris, 27, 41, 79, 88, 105, 106
North Africa. See Africa
North Atlantic Treaty Organization. See NATO
Norway (Norwegian), 65, 69, 83, 92, 93, 170, 202, 205, 230
Noskov, Ivan, 74, 75, 101, 102
November Revolution. See Russian Revolution, November, 1917
Novosibirsk, U.S.S.R., 43, 72, 73, 77

Novosibirsk trial, 62, 72–79, 101, 105
Nuclear tests, 208
Nuclear weapons, 30, 173, 201, 209, 225, 234, 235

Oberländer, Theodor, 83
Octobrist Party, Russia. See Oktyabristy
Odessa, U.S.S.R., 43
OGPU. See GPU
Oktyabristy, 149
Olberg, Valentin, 54, 60, 69, 72
Old Bolshevik. See Bolshevik
Omsk, U.S.S.R., 43
Ordzhonikidze, Grigori (Sergo), 42–44, 48, 104, 106
Orlov, Alexander, 6, 11, 42n, 57, 61, 66
Oslo, Norway, 83, 91–93
Osteuropa, Stuttgart, 142n
Ottoman empire, 216
Ouralov, Alexandre, 18n
Outer Mongolia. See Mongolia, Outer

Pacific Ocean, 231, 235
Pakistan, 202
"Parallel Center," 33, 43, 49, 82–84, 87, 88, 90, 91, 94, 95, 97, 99, 111. See also "Parallel or Reserve Trotskyite Center"
"Parallel or Reserve Trotskyite Center," 19. See also "Parallel Center"
Paris, France, 52, 65, 67–69, 71, 98, 98n, 118, 119, 176, 193, 194
Paris Commune, 176, 178
Paris summit meeting (1960). See Summit meetings
Partisans, Soviet. See Guerillas, Soviet
Pasternak, Boris, 230
Pearl Harbor, 231
Peking, China, 178
People's Commissar of: Agriculture, 21; Communications, 20; Foreign Affairs, 53, 73, 85, 98, 190, 200; Heavy Industry, 48,

Index

85; Internal Affairs, 20; Transport, 85, 88, 107; War, 166
People's Commissariat of: Communications, 54; Finance, 53; Foreign Affairs. See Ministry of Foreign Affairs, U.S.S.R.; Internal Affairs. See NKVD; Transport 52; War. See Ministry of Defense, U.S.S.R.
People's democracies, 128, 134, 135, 138, 142. See also Soviet bloc and Soviet sphere
People's Will. See Narodnaya Volya
Perm'-Urals Railroad, 26, 88, 108
Peshekhonov, Ivan, 74, 75, 77n
Petrograd. See St. Petersburg, U.S.S.R.
Philippines, 231
Piesch, Hans, 128
Pisarev, Dmitri, 155
Pishevari, S., 45, 46
Piyade, Mosha, 128n
Poland (Polish), 49, 67, 117, 118, 135, 136, 164, 170, 171, 173, 217, 229
Polaris missiles, 210. See also Rockets
Polish Socialists, 49
Politiken, Copenhagen, 60
Politische Studien, Munich, 179n
Poltava, U.S.S.R., 52
Populists. See Narodniki
Portugal, 235
Postyshev, Pavel, 42, 44, 107
Potsdam, Germany, 131, 191, 220
Potsdam Conference (1945), 129-131, 219
Potsdam Declaration (1945), 218, 220
Pravda, Moscow, 9, 16, 17, 52, 74, 77, 78, 86, 114, 210
Preobrazhensky, Yevgeni, 17, 46
President of the Austrian Republic. See Schärf, Adolf
President of the Supreme Court, U.S.S.R. See Ulrikh, Vasili

Presidium of the All-Russian Central Executive Committee. See Central Executive Committee, Presidium of
Prokop'evsk, U.S.S.R., 25, 43, 104
Proletarskaya Revolyutsiya, Moscow, 190n
Prorvich, A., 28n
Provisional Government of Austria. See Austria, (Austrian) provisional Government
Provisional Government of Russia, 161, 162, 167, 170
Prussia. See Germany
Purishkevich, Vladimir, 151
Pushin, Gavriil, 79, 88, 109, 110
Putna, Vitovt, 97, 110, 111
Pyatakov, Yuri (Georgi), 12, 15-17, 19, 24, 27, 34, 35, 41, 46-49, 76, 77, 79, 81-83, 85, 87-95, 97, 99-101, 103, 105, 114, 116n

Radek, Karl, 12, 15-17, 19, 24, 34, 38, 42, 46, 49-51, 79-84, 87, 90, 93-98, 98n, 110, 111, 114, 116
Radio Moscow, 211
Railroads, U.S.S.R., 26, 88, 100, 106-108
Rakovsky, Christian, 13, 17, 46
Ramzin, Leonid, 87
Ramzin trial. See Industrial Party, trial of
Rapallo Treaty, 36
Rataichak, Stanislav, 100, 108, 109
Red Army. See Soviet Army
Rehabilitation, U.S.S.R., 116n, 172
Reichstag, German, 230
Reims, France, 70, 71
Reingold, Isak, 14, 15
Reiss, Ignace, 70, 71
Renaissance, 181
Renner, Karl, 120-127, 130, 132-134

Reparations, 130, 131, 131n, 136, 164
"Reserve Trotskyite Center." See "Parallel or Reserve Trotskyite Center"
Revolution, French. See France (French), Revolution
Revolution, Russian. See Russian Revolution
Revolutionary Committee, Kiev, 48
Revolutionary Military Council, U.S.S.R., 51
Rhine, Germany, 154, 177, 194, 220
Ribbentrop, Joachim, 78
Rockets, 201, 209, 210, 225, 234
Rodionov, a Soviet guerilla, 29n
Rodos, NKVD official, 64
Roginsky, G. K., 74, 76, 77n
Romm, Vladimir, 83, 98, 98n
Roosevelt, Franklin D., 173, 215, 231
Rostov, Don, U.S.S.R., 43
Ruhr, Germany, 220, 237
Rukhimovich, M. L., 106
Rumania, 118, 141, 173
Russia (Russian), 39, 40, 49, 147–154, 157, 158, 161–163, 165–172, 174, 177–182, 184, 187, 189, 191, 192, 194, 211, 216, 217, 220–222, 228. See also Soviet Union
Russian Army (tsarist), 51, 106, 158, 161, 163, 165–167
Russian emigrés, 6, 61, 71
Russian Revolution: 1905, 51; of March, 1917, 47, 152, 161, 174; November, 1917, 50, 52, 69, 147, 149, 151, 152, 161–174, 177, 178, 185, 189–193, 214
Russian Social-Democratic Labor Party, 54, 183
Ryazanov, David, 122
Rychkov, N. M., 87, 107
Rykov, Alexei, 13, 15, 16, 18, 19, 90, 94, 116, 187

Saar, Germany, 220
"Sabotage," charged at Moscow trials, 11, 24, 43, 63, 100, 107
St. Petersburg, 47, 50, 150, 161, 165, 183
Sakhalin, 36, 164
Salzburg, Austria, 125
Samara (later Kyiubyshev), U.S.S.R., 51
Satellites, 45, 119, 126, 127, 133, 134, 193, 222, 223, 233, 234
Sazonov, Sergei, 151
Scandinavia, 47, 180, 235
Schärf, Adolf, 121, 121n, 125n
Scheidemann, Philipp, 120
Scorched earth policy, 28
Secret agents of the NKVD, 8, 59–62, 66–72
Secret police, U.S.S.R., 13, 20, 22, 44, 56, 58, 60, 63, 66, 67, 69, 83, 165, 174. See also Cheka, GPU, NKVD, MVD, MGB, KGB
Security Commission. See Communist Party of the Soviet Union, Politburo-Presidium, Security Commission
Sedov, Jeanne, 67
Sedov, Lev, 35, 41, 62, 65–72, 89, 90, 92n, 93n, 98, 103
Sedov, Natalia, 46, 47, 93n
Sedov, Sergei, 93n
Seksots. See Secret agents of the NKVD
Semionov, Nikolai, 112n
Senate. See United States of America, Senate
Senin, A. See Soble, Jack
Serbia, 180
Serebryakov, Leonid, 15, 16, 19, 46, 51, 52, 79, 82, 87, 88, 90, 95, 99, 100, 114
Shakhta trial, 24, 74, 87
Shaposhnikov, Boris, 12
Shatskin, Lazar, 15
Shestov, Alexei, 42, 60, 61, 74, 76, 77n, 88, 90, 103, 104, 106
Shkiryatov, Matvei, 18
Shlyapnikov, Alexander, 15

Index

Shpigelglas, Mikhail, 68, 69
Shubin, Feodor, 74–76
Siberia (Siberian), 25, 31, 42, 43, 45, 47, 62, 74, 101, 103, 104, 148, 152, 158
Sieyes, Emmanuel-Joseph, Abbé, 186
Skrypnik, Nikolai, 172
Slavophilism, 158
Slavs, 221
Slovenia, 128
Small [Inner] Council of People's Commissars, 54
Smilga, Ivar, 15, 46
Smirnov, Ivan N., 46, 68, 93n, 94, 103
Soble, Jack, 72, 72n
Soblen, Dr. Robert, 72, 72n
Sobolevizius brothers. See Soble, Jack and Soblen, Dr. Robert
Sochi, U.S.S.R., 20, 43
Social-Democrats, Russian. See Mensheviks
Socialism (Socialists), 49, 51, 65, 147, 147n, 149, 169, 175–178, 180, 184, 200, 235; German, 176, 177, 182; French, 175–177
Socialist camp, 141, 232, 236. See also Soviet bloc and Soviet sphere.
Socialist International (Second International), 50
Socialist Party of Austria, 118–121, 123, 124, 126, 134, 135, 139
Socialist-Revolutionaries, 48, 183; Leftist, 107; trial of, 48
Socialists (Western), 48–50
Society of Equals, 175
Sokolnikov, Grigori, 12, 15, 16, 19, 34, 41, 42, 52, 53, 58, 78, 79, 82, 87, 90, 95, 98, 99, 114
Sotsialisticheskii Vestnik (The Socialist Courier), Berlin, Paris, New York, 80n
Southeast Asia, 193
South-Urals Railway, 26, 88, 107
Soviet army, 7, 9, 12, 12n, 28, 32, 48, 51, 108, 113, 117, 119–125, 125n, 126, 130, 132, 134, 136, 137, 139–141, 148, 150, 151, 158, 165–167, 171, 173, 202, 207, 218, 219, 233
Soviet bloc, 213, 214. See also Soviet sphere and People's democracies
Soviet empire, 222, 232
Soviet-French Treaty of Alliance (1935), 37
Soviet-German mixed companies. See Mixed companies
Soviet guerillas. See Guerillas, Soviet
Soviet-Japanese mixed companies. See Mixed companies
Soviet Military Intelligence. See Intelligence, Soviet
Soviet navy, 7
Soviet satellites. See Satellites, Soviet bloc, and Soviet sphere.
Soviet sphere, 118, 232, 233. See also Satellites, Soviet bloc and People's democracies.
Soviet Trade Organization, 39
Soviet trade unions. See Trade unions, Russian
Soviet Union, 4, 9, 12, 28, 31, 32, 34–36, 44, 61, 84, 87, 91, 95–97, 104, 112, 165, 169, 170, 173, 178, 179, 186–188, 191, 192, 215, 221, 226–231; foreign policy of, 37, 38, 71, 73, 78, 117–122, 124–143, 164, 171, 195–212, 219, 220, 222–224, 232–237
Soviet-Yugoslav Treaty (1945), 128
Soviets, 159, 160
Sovnarkom (*Sovet Narodnykh Komissarov*). See Council of People's Commissars.
Sozial-Demokraten, Copenhagen, 92n
Spain, 194, 216, 230, 235
Spanish Civil War, 119
Spartakus Bund, Germany, 49, 154
Special Commission on Security.

See Communist Party of the Soviet Union, Politburo-Presidium, Security Commission
Sputniks, 186
Staatsvertrag, Austria. *See* Austria (Austrian), Peace Treaty (1955)
Stakhanov movement, 101
Stalin, Joseph, 4, 5, 9, 16, 18, 19, 39, 46–55, 59, 66, 69, 70, 72, 94, 169, 171–173, 178, 185, 186, 191, 193, 214, 227, 228; alleged attempts on, 43, 77 101, 107, 116; death of, 143, 227; de-Stalinization, 172, 173 —foreign policy of, 164, 200, 211, 212, 215, 232, 236; on Austria, 117, 118, 121–125, 127–130, 130n, 131n, 132, 134, 135, 142; on Germany, 36–38, 219, 220, 236, 237; Kirov's assassination, role in, 6, 44, 45; Moscow trials, role in, 17–19, 22–25, 27, 28, 30–33, 55, 73, 80–82, 84–86, 89–91, 97, 110, 113, 114; terrorism of, 5, 8–11, 13, 14, 18–22, 40, 55, 62–64, 112, 113
Stalin-Hitler Pact, 38
Stalinism (Stalinists), 17, 23, 30, 39, 59, 60, 94, 112, 142, 187, 212, 230
State Department. *See* United States of America, Department of State
State Treaty, Austrian. *See* Austria (Austrian), Peace Treaty (1955)
Stein, German engineer, 83
Sten, Yan, 15
Stepanov-Skvortsov, I. I., 183
Stettin, Germany (now Poland), 232
Stickling, Emil, 74, 75, 77, 78, 105
Stirner, Gustav, 91
Stockholm, Sweden, 50, 122
Stockholm Socialist Peace Conference, 122, 122n
Stroilov, Mikhail, 73n, 74, 76, 88, 103–105, 114
Subasich, Ivan, 128
Suez, 197
Sukhomlinov, Vladimir, 47
Summit meetings, 193, 198
Supreme Council of National Economy, U.S.S.R., 48
Supreme Court of the U.S.S.R.: Military Collegium, 7, 13, 15n, 27n, 87, 89, 91, 95–97, 101, 103, 107–115; Special Session, 12
Supreme Soviet, 114, 143, 193; Fourth Session (1939), 204, 204n
Sverdlovsk, U.S.S.R., 26
Sweden, 50, 170, 216
Switzerland (Swiss), 47, 49, 70, 118, 122n, 123, 177

Tabriz, Iran, 45
Taganrog, U.S.S.R., 51
Tamm, Leonid, 109
TASS, 197
Teheran, Iran, 191
Teheran Conference, 191
Temps, Le, Paris, 37
"Terrorism," charged at Moscow trials, 6, 7, 11–14, 16, 39–44, 72, 76, 77, 83–85, 87–89, 94, 95, 97, 98, 101, 103, 104, 106, 108
"Terrorist Center," 11
"Terrorist groups," U.S.S.R., 43
Three International Conference. *See* Conference of Three Internationals
Tiegerson, Tieger, 60
Tito, Josip Broz, 127–129, 130, 142
Togliatti, Palmiro, 232
Tokyo, Japan, 231
Tolbukhin, Feodor, 120, 123
Tolstoy, Alexei, 86
Tomsk, U.S.S.R., 43
Tomsky, Mikhail, 12, 15, 16, 18, 57, 90

Index

Torture, U.S.S.R., 10, 62–64, 79
Trade unions, Russian, 12, 54, 57, 158, 159
Transcaucasia, 43
"Treason," accusation of at Moscow trials, 12, 13, 17, 53, 56, 57
Trianon Treaty (1920), 221
Tribunal. *See* Supreme Court of the U.S.S.R.
Trieste, Italy, 128, 129, 142, 232
Trotsky, Leon, 4, 6, 46, 47, 93n, 122, 171, 187; "accusations" at the Pyatakov-Radek trial, 17, 19, 33–35, 41, 48–52, 54, 56, 62, 64, 75, 84, 87, 89, 91–93, 97, 98, 98n, 109–111, 114; alleged "letters" from, 38, 80–83, 90–96, 99, 104; archives of, 65, 66, 68–72; as creator of Red Army, 166; NKVD agents around, 60, 65, 66, 68–72
—views on: annexations, 163; foreign policy, 190, 193, 211; indemnities, 164
Trotskyism (Trotskyites), 13–15, 18, 19, 27, 35, 39, 43, 44, 46, 49–51, 53, 54, 57, 59–61, 64–68, 70, 72, 74, 75, 80, 81, 84, 85, 89, 91–93, 93n, 101, 103–105, 107–111, 114, 116, 212. *See also* Communist Party of the Soviet Union, Opposition, Left; French Trotskites, 65, 67, 68; Russian Group in Paris, 65, 66, 68, 69
"Trotskyite-Zinovievite bloc," 20, 34, 95, 96, 99. *See also* "Trotskyite-Zinovievite Terorist Center
"Trotskyite-Zinovievite Terrorist Center," 15n, 16, 19. *See also* "Trotskyite-Zinovievite Bloc"
Truman, Harry, 129, 130, 206
Tsar (tsarism), 22, 122, 149, 158, 161, 171, 191
Tsentral'naya Pit, U.S.S.R., 25, 74, 101

Tukhachevsky, Mikhail, 12, 81, 97, 98
Tukhachevsky trial, 12, 97
Tula, U.S.S.R., 43
Turkestan, U.S.S.R., 171
Turkey (Turks), 71, 93n, 202, 221
Turok, Yosif, 27, 35, 88, 107, 108
Tyszka, Jan (Jogiches, Leo), 49

U-2 incident (May, 1960), 202
Uborevich, Ieronim, 12
Uglanov, Nikolai, 16, 94
Ukraine (Ukrainian), 34, 43, 48, 54, 96, 100, 170–172
Ukrainian Rada, 54
Ulrikh, Vasili, 27, 87, 100, 112, 114
Umansky, Konstantin, 98n
Union of Returnees to the Fatherland, 67
United Nations, 196, 197, 200, 214, 215, 224, 226; General Assembly, 193, 214; Security Council, 215, 224
United States of America, 32, 43, 71, 86, 98, 106, 115, 138n, 162, 173, 179, 180, 193, 206, 207, 215, 226, 228, 233; army, 106, 117, 125, 128, 129, 132, 201, 205, 208 (n.29), 233, 234; Democratic Party of, 206; Department of State, 115, 197, 206; foreign policy of, 45, 121, 125, 126, 129, 131, 136–138, 153, 161, 187, 197, 198, 200, 201, 206, 208n, 209, 218–220, 222, 223, 229–231, 233–236; military bases of, 202–205, 210, 234, 235; Republican Party of, 206, 207; Senate, 67n, 71n. *See also* America (American)
Ural, U.S.S.R., 26, 43, 107
Ushakov, NKVD official, 64
U.S.S.R. *See* Soviet Union
Utopian Socialism, 175

Vaillant-Couturier, Paul, 86
Versailles Treaty (1919), 221

Vienna, Austria, 119, 122–126, 130, 132, 134, 136–141, 143, 193

Vilno (Vilnius), U.S.S.R., 183

Voina i Rabochii Klass, Moscow, 118, 120

Volksdeutsche, 137

Volkspartei, Austria. *See* Christian Social People's Party of Austria

Volksstimme, Die, Vienna, 138

Voroshilov, Kliment, 18, 42, 43, 203

Vyshinsky, Andrei, 11, 16, 18, 19, 22, 23, 26, 29, 30, 32, 33, 35, 39, 41, 42, 55, 59, 61, 62, 70, 74, 80–83, 85, 87, 88, 92–94, 97, 101–103, 105, 106, 108–110, 115

War and the Working Class. *See Voina i Rabochii Klass*, Moscow

War Commissariat, U.S.S.R. *See* Ministry of Defense, U.S.S.R.

Warsaw, Poland, 49, 194

Warski, Adolf, 49

Washington, D.C., 98n, 126, 211, 231, 233

Weksal, Norway, 65

Wel', Roman. *See* Soblen, Dr. Robert

West Germany. *See* Germany (German), West

West, Western powers. *See* Western Alliance

Western Alliance, 37, 38, 118, 119, 124, 125, 127, 130–132, 134, 136, 137, 141, 143, 148, 162, 163, 203, 208, 211, 212, 217–220, 222, 223, 234

Western armies, 118, 129–131

Western *Entente*. *See* Western Alliance

Western Hemisphere, 231

Westphalia, Germany, 194

White armies, 54, 167

Wiener Neustadt. *See* Vienna, Austria

Wilhelm II, 162

Wilson, Woodrow, 190, 200

Windfeld-Hansen, 60

Winterer, Franz, 126

Wolf, Erwin, 71

Women's University in Yenan, China, 184

Workers' Party of Norway, 202

World revolution, 177, 191

World War I, 31, 51, 120, 130, 150, 152, 161, 217, 236

World War II, 117, 164, 168, 191, 192, 207, 212, 215, 218, 219, 230, 236

"Wrecking" accusation of at the Moscow trials, 12–14, 23–30, 53, 59, 61, 64, 72–74, 76, 77, 80, 83–85, 87–91, 97–99, 101–109, 187

Wüster, German Intelligence agent, 105

X., Mr. *See* Hiroshima, S.,

Yagoda, Genrikh, 8, 11, 13, 14, 20–22, 30

Yakir, Iona, 12

Yenan, China, 184

Yenukidze, Avel, 12

Yenukidze-Karakhan trial, 12, 13

Yevdokimov, Grigori, 7, 11

Yezhov, Nikolai, 8, 11, 13–15, 18, 20–22, 42, 59, 62, 63, 65, 70, 72, 79, 82, 86, 112, 113

Yezhovshchina, 8

Young Communist League. *See Komsomol*

Yugoslavia, 118, 119, 125, 127–129, 130n, 131, 136, 142, 229, 237

Zborowski, Mark (Etienne), 66–71

Zemlya i Volya, 39

Zhdanov, Andrei, 18, 20, 42

Zheltov, Alexei, 120, 122

Zimmerwald Conference, 50

Zinoviev, Grigori, 6, 7, 11, 14–16,

45–47, 49, 50, 56, 68, 78, 81, 86, 91, 95, 187
Zinoviev-Kamenev group, 7, 14, 53, 111
Zinoviev-Kamenev trial: First (1935), 7, 11; Second (1936), 11, 12, 14, 18, 33, 42, 58, 60, 81, 87, 92n, 94, 114
"Zinovievite Center," 19
Zinovievites, 16, 19, 95
Zistendorf Oil Fields, Austria, 133